Raphaelle Peale, *Corn and Cantaloupe,* 1813. Oil on wood panel. Courtesy of Crystal Bridges Museum of American Art, Bentonville, Arkansas. Photography by Dwight Primiano.

A Taste of Power

The publisher gratefully acknowledges the generous support of Michelle Ciccarelli Lerach and William Lerach, Mrs. James McClatchy, and Marjorie Randolph as members of the Publisher's Circle of the University of California Press Foundation.

A Taste of Power

FOOD AND AMERICAN IDENTITIES

Katharina Vester

UNIVERSITY OF CALIFORNIA PRESS

University of California Press, one of the most distinguished university presses in the United States, enriches lives around the world by advancing scholarship in the humanities, social sciences, and natural sciences. Its activities are supported by the UC Press Foundation and by philanthropic contributions from individuals and institutions. For more information, visit www.ucpress.edu.

University of California Press
Oakland, California

Library of Congress Cataloging-in-Publication Data
Vester, Katharina, author.
    A taste of power : food and American identities / Katharina Vester. — First edition.
        pages   cm.—(California studies in food and culture ; 59)
    Food and American identities
    Includes bibliographical references and index.
    ISBN 978–0–520–28497–5 (cloth : alk. paper)—ISBN 0–520–28497–6 (cloth : alk. paper)—ISBN 978–0–520–28498–2 (pbk. : alk. paper)— ISBN 0–520–28498–4 (pbk. : alk. paper)—ISBN 978–0–520–96060–2 (ebook)—ISBN 0–520–96060–2 (ebook)
    1. Food—Social aspects—United States.   2. Cooking, American— History.   3. Food habits—United States—History.   4. Cookbooks— Social aspects—United States.   I. Title.   II. Title: Food and American identities.   III. Series: California studies in food and culture ; 59.
    GT2853.U5V47 2015
    394.1′20973—dc23
                                                          2015009594

Manufactured in the United States of America

24   23   22   21   20   19   18   17   16   15
10   9   8   7   6   5   4   3   2   1

sine te nihil

CONTENTS

ACKNOWLEDGMENTS

I would like to thank the American Association of University Women and their members for generously supporting my research with a yearlong American Fellowship that allowed me to write this book. The German Academic Exchange Service provided me with funding for six months of research in the United States that enabled me to expand the scope of my project to what it is now while I was still a doctoral candidate at the Ruhr-Universität Bochum. The Schlesinger Library, with its excellent collection of cookbooks, has been a never-ending treasure trove, and the research librarians I worked with proved to be another immensely valuable resource. My special thanks go to research librarian Sarah Hutcheon for her assistance. My work at the Schlesinger Library was partly made possible by a Research Support Grant through the Carl and Lily Pforzheimer Foundation, to which I am grateful.

Some of my analysis of Gertrude Stein and lesbian cookbooks presented in the third part of the book, "'The Difference Is Spreading': Recipes for Lesbian Living," appeared in earlier versions in "Tender Mutton: Recipes, Sexual Identity and Spinster Resistance in Gertrude Stein," in *Another Language: Poetic Experiments in Britain and North America*, eds. Kornelia Freitag and Katharina Vester (Berlin: LIT Verlag, 2008), 289–300; and "Queer Appetites, Butch Cooking: Recipes for Lesbian Subjectivities," in *Queers in American Popular Culture*, ed. Jim Elledge (Santa Barbara, CA: Praeger, 2010), 11–21.

Kornelia Freitag, initially my dissertation adviser and now a friend, has supported me and my work over the years tirelessly and unconditionally. It is an invaluable experience to have her in one's corner. She and her husband, Jürgen Heiß, to whom I owe my appreciation for nineteenth-century

American literature, gave me my first academic job as a research assistant. Without their encouragement I would not have considered a university career. Walter Grünzweig, my co-adviser and now a friend, too, helped me to think of my dissertation as a future book, which meant to delete most of it and start over again. No doubt an invaluable service not only to me, but also to the reader.

I received an excellent graduate and undergraduate education at the University of Potsdam and the Freie Universität Berlin. Thanks to the German taxpayers, it was free of tuition. I owe much to the excellent instructors I encountered there in the English and Philosophy Departments and at the Latin American Institute. I am especially indebted to Hans-Peter Krüger, who made me read Norbert Elias and Michel Foucault, which, against my initial youthful suspicions, turned out to be a life-changing experience. "But what is philosophy *good* for?" I asked him once. "To think differently," he replied.

I would like to warmly thank my father-in-law, Martin Friedman, who edited my dissertation and made it beautiful, all along gently teaching me the intricacies of English punctuation and syntax. Some of his edits made it into this text, too: these are the good sentences. Many discussions with him and my mother-in-law, the beautiful Elena Burgess, always over some good food, helped me sharpen my argument and inspired me to go out and do more research. My thanks go also to another Berkeleyan, Sandra Gilbert, who became my mentor shortly after I moved to the United States in 2007. Her faith in my book helped me through the times when I was no longer sure. While it was possible that I was wrong, it was impossible that she was. Similarly important to me was the friendly encouragement of my wonderful chairs, the late Bob Griffith as well as Pam Nadell, who supported me and my research with her typical kindness and generosity. They are only one example for the support I found at American University's College of Arts and Sciences. I am thankful to my always supportive dean, Peter Starr, and all my colleagues in the History Department for being so welcoming. I would like especially to thank Lisa Leff, Alan Kraut, and Eileen Findlay, whom I have found to be generous mentors over the past few years, volunteering their time and giving me good advice whenever I asked for it.

I appreciate all the thoughtful comments from the three readers who reviewed the manuscript for the University of California Press, as well as the support of Darra Goldstein and my editor, Kate Marshall, and the thorough and gentle work of my copy editor, Lindsey Westbrook.

I am most grateful to the many people who have helped me to make this a better manuscript: Warren Belasco and colleagues from the Chesapeake food studies group read an early draft on my thoughts on republican cuisine and provided invaluable advice. My writing group, Monique Laney and Anita Kondoyanidi, read lovingly through many drafts of chapters and always asked the right questions. Celine-Marie Pascale was so kind as to help me think through the theoretical implications of my work any time I needed it.

I am grateful to my family. My parents, Ilka-Maria and Klaus Vester, filled my childhood with books and good food. They, and my Oma, the late Gertrud Wisniewski, set me on the right path and supported me in every way they could. Besides the families we are born into and that we marry, there is also the family we pick up along the way. Gerd and Ines Kaiser supprted me with their warmth and infinite hospitality. Having Marion Hirte, Elke Sandtner, Oda Henckel, and Petra Krimphove in Berlin and Cathy Schaeff in Silver Spring on speed dial helped me keep my sanity during the writing process.

And finally, I would like to thank my love Max Paul Friedman, who has, since I met him seventeen years ago, changed my life every single day. I know what spouses of authors birthing monographs go through. I have done it twice. But Max, unlike me, never lost his patience, gentleness, or humor in the process. His resourcefulness for dealing with and eventually solving any possible crisis never ceases to astonish me. A lucky dog—me, that is.

Introduction

IT SEEMS ONLY RIGHT TO BEGIN a book on food by feasting on Jean Anthelme Brillat-Savarin's ubiquitous aphorism. The phrase often has been simplified to "You are what you eat." But M. F. K. Fisher's translation, "Tell me what you eat, and I shall tell you what you are," is truer to the 1825 French original (3). The difference between the two renditions is of no small importance: following Brillat-Savarin, identity is not simply created in the process of eating—you are what you eat—but within the discursive structures surrounding it: *tell me* what you eat, and I shall *tell you* what you are.[1] Physiologically viewed, there is little difference between eating corn, caviar, or cockroaches; all three are potential suppliers of protein and calories. The differences between the edible and the inedible, the prestigious and the profane, and even the desirable and the disgusting are constructed by culturally contingent discourses. If eating were only about nutrition, we could have ourselves "fed and watered," as the philosopher Elizabeth Telfer ironically proposes, intravenously, while asleep (1). This would save us time and trouble and would probably be healthier, too. But, as the philosopher Deane Curtin states, "Food consumption habits are not simply tied to biological needs but serve to mark boundaries between social classes, geographical regions, nations, cultures, genders, life-cycle stages, religions and occupations, to distinguish rituals, traditions, festivals, seasons and times of day. Food structures what counts as a person in our culture" (4). Elspeth Probyn, more succinctly, writes: "We consume and ingest our identities" (17). How food and identity interact is determined by cultural narratives and the specific

I

historical moment: eating quinoa in 1965 versus 2015 has different meanings, and marks different subjectivities, although the food is the same. Food is given significance by how it is narratively framed, and by the significance we digest along with the calories.

Food instructions, discussions of meals in literature and media, images of dishes in films and paintings, and the many other narratives in which food figures prominently generate knowledge in which power relations are inscribed and produced. They are embedded in and play a part in the production of gendered and racialized subjects, as well as class, ethnic, regional, national, and religious ones. Brillat-Savarin's maxim rightfully does not claim that food choices reveal "who you are," but "*what* you are." Beyond mere personal tastes and preferences, food choices disclose an individual's station in society, making and marking his or her subject position. As food helps to nourish the individual, food discourses aid in producing the subject. They tell us how to properly perform as heterosexual men or women, members of middle-class culture, and Americans. They also offer the opportunity to resist being molded into the categories society prescribes.

Discourses produce experts, people invested with the power to decide what is right or not—the "I" in Brillat-Savarin's quote. Knowledge, privilege, and power intersect in food discourses, pronouncing who belongs by performing appropriately, and marginalizing and excluding those who do not from equal access to cultural, political, and financial resources. Conversely, food discourses have (albeit limited) democratizing potential: being raised in a culinary culture leaves everyone with a vast treasury of knowledge about the gender, race, and class implications of foodways[2] as well as table manners (of some kind), preparation procedures, regional and national food habits, and diverse clusters of information that may include botanical, zoological, nutritional, chemical, and historical fragments. When we talk about what we eat, we talk about what we are, and sometimes what we want to be. It is in our power to change our eating habits to fit them to what we aspire to become. Since all of us engage in eating and many of us in cooking, the power relations within food discourses are complex and notoriously volatile. As the ever-growing number of food blogs and restaurant review websites demonstrates, expertise can be more easily claimed here than in some other realms. But food blogs on the quest for the latest kick, the authentic hole in the wall, the newest ethnic cuisine to explore, can also contribute to cultural appropriation, the exoticization of cuisines, and the othering of immigrant foods.[3] Examining how food advice interacts with gender, class, national, and ethnic identity allows a glimpse into how knowledge creates privilege, tastes can marginalize, and how we endorse what we are, or are expected to be, in the act of eating and talking about food.

A TASTE OF POWER

Today we are immersed in food blogs and food memoirs, an increasingly fragmented cookbook market, an exploding number of cooking shows, food films, and food magazines, and an abundant accompanying scholarship. This makes it easy to forget that thirty years ago, food and its discourses were mostly neglected by academe (with a few famous exceptions, such as Mary Douglas, Claude Lévi-Strauss, and Sidney Mintz), since food was considered something biological, nonnegotiable, intake for the physical body rather than a pursuit of the mind. Food belonged to the private sphere and therefore was not of obvious scholarly interest; it was a topic slightly too mundane, too feminine, and (within the context of affluent societies) insufficiently political. But recent scholarship has enthusiastically endorsed the importance of food as a lens for approaching the past, or a gateway to studying culture. Building on and indebted to this scholarship, *A Taste of Power* thinks about how American culture has employed representations of food to create subject positions. Food advice in cookbooks and magazines has traditionally told readers not only how to eat well, but how to be Americans, how to be members of the middle class, and how to perform as heterosexual men and women. Dominant ideas of food have been reflected, and also often negotiated, in literature, film, TV shows, and art, helping to manifest and circulate the connection between food and identity. Analyzing a wide range of materials discussing food, *A Taste of Power* explores how these materials have engaged with the identity categories a historical moment produces. Expert discourses on food before World War I were mainly concerned with producing white, heterosexual, middle-class bodies, unmarked by debts to minority cultural heritages, and fully invested in the American project. What this actually entailed frequently changed and was by no means a stable ideological concept. While experts such as cookbook authors, home economists, and nutritional scientists commonly legitimized their own privileges when talking about food, the narrative strategies to do so, as well as the ideals pronounced, shifted in accordance with dominant ideas of gender, sexuality, and nationality. While pronouncing a right way to eat, it was always implicitly or explicitly implied that there were wrong ways to eat, which were deemed irrational, unhealthy, or unvirtuous, and therefore made the noncompliant eater suspect. Men could be feminized by a yearning for food too fluffy, too light, or too colorful, or by the simple act of preparing food in a kitchen. White Southerners could put their racial privilege at risk by eating foods once considered part of their regional culture but later identified with African American food traditions, such as collard greens and chitterlings. Schoolchildren from immigrant families saw their Americanness called into question when they brought tortillas or dumplings for lunch.[4] In this way, food discourses are not only normative but also exclusive, and, as they accompany the quotidian practices of eating and cooking, often seem innocuous and are invisible in their violence, but they are effective and enduring, as they are literally incorporated into the subject.

Rejecting the rules of polite, genteel, or scientific dining could serve as an act of resistance, as when Italian immigrants, despite the pressure of Progressive reformers and home economists to Americanize their culinary habits, continued to eat as Italian as was possible in their adopted country.[5] But as Michel Foucault has argued, a simple view of oppression and resistance is inadequate. The power relations implicated in discourses that he defined as paradigmatic for modern, democratic, Western societies are not stable but constantly changing. They are volatile and comprehensible only within their unique historical and local context, since hegemonic discourses are constantly challenged by marginalized ones struggling for access or counter-hegemony (*History*, 95–97). Any power constellation is a fragile balance of these competing discourses, making complete oppression (or complete liberation) an impossibility. The notion of a clear-cut binary of dominance and resistance, or of a resistance that will not produce its own power effects, is in this model futile. Women authors of domestic advice have endorsed an ideology of separate spheres, but they used their publications for successful careers outside the home. They promoted women's education and defended women's intellectual capacity, but commonly thought of their female servants as stupid and incompetent. Male cooks, after losing authority over domestic cooking in the nineteenth century, rewrote themselves into the home kitchens of the twentieth, asserting their natural superiority over female cooks by claiming to be born gourmets. Health reformers arguing that individuals could improve their lives by choosing the right foods excluded ethnic cuisines from their menus and contributed to the imperial claims of American expansion by promoting exotic ingredients. These and many other examples in this book illustrate that resistance and power are intimately intertwined, and that resistance is not always liberating, nor power necessarily oppressive.

This understanding of the connection between food and power opens up new fields of investigation for cultural studies. Kitchens and tables are now understood as prominent sites in the production of subjects through processes that are guided, reflected, and contested by a variety of food discourses ranging across cookbooks, household manuals, popular fiction, cooking shows, food blogs, and still-life paintings. Investigating these discourses emerging around food allows insights into the modes in which specific cultural contexts attempt to control the formation of national, gendered, and sexual subjectivities. *A Taste of Power* explores how food discourses, and especially expert advice, have helped to produce national identity in the early republic, masculine identities from the late 1800s to the 1970s, and lesbian subjectivities in the twentieth and early twenty-first centuries. Thus it sheds new light on how we are told what to be when we are told what to eat.

This book owes its underlying understanding of how American culture employed food discourses in the production of subjectivities to the theoretical frameworks of Norbert Elias, Pierre Bourdieu, and, most prominently, Michel Foucault. Foucault defines power relations as the struggle of competing discourses that create forms of knowledge that discipline individuals into subjectivities. The complex relations of empowerment and disempowerment cannot be described as simply repressive, for simplistic concepts of power are not sufficient when analyzing cultural phenomena such as the complicated and contradictory texture of modern foodways. To understand the interplay of disciplining and resistance in modern democratic Western societies, Foucault suggests the concept of productive power, which he conceptualizes as complex and effective arrangements of power relations that are produced and administered by knowledge—the discursively regulated and institutionalized production of truth. He breaks with Enlightenment concepts that render power as institutional, negative, and merely oppressive, and the production of knowledge as opposed to it. In contrast, he defines power as

> the multiplicity of force relations immanent in the sphere in which they operate and which constitute their own organization; as the process which, through ceaseless struggles and confrontations, transforms, strengthens, or reverses them; as the support which these force relations find in one another, thus forming a chain or system, or on the contrary, the disjunctions and contradictions which isolate them from one another; and lastly, as the strategies in which they take effect, whose general design or institutional crystallization

is embodied in the state apparatus, in the formulation of the law, in the various social hegemonies. (*History,* 92–93)

This power is not stable but constantly challenged and administered by a continuously increasing number of discourses and practices contesting for hegemony. Some of them may crystallize as dominant and oppressive, and all of them are necessarily restrictive (since they govern what can and cannot be said and done), but they are also productive: they produce reality, since they control what is true, and they produce their subjects. Discourses determine what counts as a subject in certain contexts and which position the subject will hold. Individuals go through disciplining and normalizing practices regulated by discourses that allow them to recognize themselves and be recognized as subjects, but instead of being forced by outside repression, they adjust themselves by internalized disciplining mechanisms to perform what is expected of them.

In *The History of Sexuality,* Foucault argues that the concept of "sexuality" emerged with the rise of the bourgeoisie and served the stabilization of a status quo that privileged the middle class (superseding the concept of "blood" that served aristocratic rule). He explores how the discourses emerging around sexuality in the nineteenth century created categories such as homosexuals, perverts, and hysterics, and normalized in the abjection of these categories the (white) middle-class body. This, he claims, is only one example of how productive power works ("Subject," 126). Another, I argue, is food. Food and the discourses around it are another decisive *dispositif* or apparatus coordinating disciplinary mechanisms in ways that normalize or marginalize subjects and steer social processes as well as individuals. Thinking about and engaging in sex are central aspects of ordinary people's daily lives, with powerful constituting potential, since sex is tied to deep-seated biological drives yet highly regulated by law and custom. Thinking about, obtaining, and consuming food, even more basic and frequent concerns, are where the mental world of the individual meets the regulation of basic drives and functions by an elaborate apparatus of control. In the nineteenth century, scientific discourses began to regulate and govern the food intake of the American population, implementing ideas of eating "right"—which meant according to context, in conformity with etiquette, properly American, or to promote individual and national health. Other discourses around gender, race, and sex established who should and who should not engage in cooking in order to stabilize or avoid putting at risk socially recognized identity categories. The twentieth century witnessed an explosion of food discourses that competed with one another but nonetheless ensured that eating today, too, marks one's class, race, and gender, and defines who belongs and who is excluded.

In Foucault's concept, nobody—neither an individual nor a group—"has" power. Power rather is understood as a network of discourses that has no center. All individuals are subjected to discourses, although some are privileged by them and some are not. Power relations organize themselves into effective strategies and eventually may crystallize into institutions, such as those that produce experts: schools, universities, medical establishments, psychiatric and legal associations, culinary institutes, or a genre such as cookbook writing. These experts are disciplined into administering the mechanisms that produce the subject. They have the authority to establish, maintain, and even—within limits—change the rules of the discourse, that is, of what can be said and what cannot be said, or what statements are considered to be reasonable or unreasonable, true or false. But the position of the experts, too, is unstable and subject to constant negotiation and change. Questioning the experts' authority challenges the power relations that are based on the knowledge they administer, and eventually might alter them.

Feminist scholars have produced a substantial body of work that criticizes Foucault's gender blindness.[6] The discourses Foucault examined in his own work privileged white, male experts. Some have pointed out that Foucault's ideas meet feminist thought on crucial points such as the suspicion of transcendental truth. Foucault's focus on historical, specific, and local knowledge, they argue, allows a valuable alternative. Scholars such as Susan Bordo have successfully found ways in which to complement Foucault's theories by investigating discourses producing gender and using his analytical instruments for feminist interpretations. Analyzing food discourses unveils how identity categories are implemented while opening up new perspectives on the categories themselves, as Elspeth Probyn argues: "As eating reactivates the force of identities, it also may enable modes of cultural analysis that are attentive to the categories with which we are now perhaps overly familiar: sex, ethnicity, wealth, poverty, geopolitical location, class and gender. Eating . . . makes these categories matter again: it roots actual bodies within these relations" (9).

Bordo, and, to a lesser degree, Probyn, have introduced Foucault's power concept to studies of food while critically reformulating the subject as a gendered and racialized one. But so far, the disciplining mechanisms in food discourses and practices as an important step in the construction of subjectivity have not been thoroughly investigated. Nor has the potential of resistance within foodways been systematically and critically examined. Throughout most of his work, Foucault identifies scholarly discourses as the locus of the specific form of modern power that uses truth to gain authority and govern its subjects. Discourses, bodies of knowledge that are organized around the concept of universal truth, serve the legitimization of power relations in an increasingly secular age, when the divine is no longer deemed satisfactory as a mode to explain the world. Discourses implement and authorize disciplinary mechanisms that minimize the deployment of force but allow a greater control of the individual, since they transfer the task of control onto the individuals themselves. The examples Foucault focused on in his work are prime sites of the exercise of discipline principally in the eighteenth and nineteenth centuries: the prison, the military, the factory, the school. But clearly these institutions did not reach all individuals equally. Most women, for example, were excluded from these places in this period, or, if admitted—as in the case of factories—only in subordinate positions. These exclusions and subordinations were not arbitrary but based on ideas of femininity that claimed that women were weaker, less effective, less rational, and less intelligent, but possessed greater moral capacities. Their exclusion from these institutions helped to ensure that such clichés were perpetuated. Foucault focused on institutions that disciplined mainly men; disciplinary institutions and practices that regulated gender outside the immediate space of paid labor and the state need to be investigated. Looking for the production of subjects marked as male or female before the twentieth century, one can usefully turn the gaze to focus on other sites and other discourses, namely kitchens and cookbooks, that constituted and regulated the "women's sphere" as a space in which femininity was produced—and then required new discursive strategies to manage men's involvement in cooking in historically contingent contexts.

Food discourses present a body of knowledge based on the concept of truth. They govern practices and human behavior. Like the scholarly discourses Foucault analyzes, they, too, are authoritative, normalizing, and disciplining. Cooking advice traditionally not only spread ideas about how to prepare dishes properly and healthfully (with reference to medical authority), but also circulated instructions on how to set tables, how to organize a household, how to treat servants, how to raise a family, and how to contribute to one's community and nation. They therefore served the normalization and legitimization of proper white and middle-class womanhood and manhood, American citizenship, heterosexual marriage, and the nuclear family. Recipes told readers from the late nineteenth century onward exactly how to handle food. Written in the imperative, giving their orders in detailed steps, they remind the reader of the military manuals Foucault quotes in *Discipline and Punish* (on how to handle a rifle properly [153]). Yet these instructions were not mere commands. The word "recipe" is derived from the Latin *recipere,* to receive. (Indeed, until the mid-nineteenth century, recipes were called "receipts" in the United States.) The recipe becomes a recipe not through the act of being given, but through the act of being taken, executed, and eventually embodied. While the reader conventionally is not overtly acknowledged in, say, a novel (aside from fleeting references to the "dear reader" in Victorian fiction), he or she is always directly and repeatedly addressed by the recipe and called into action.[7] The imperative structure explicitly invites readers to engage with the text instead of passively consuming it. Sometimes the authority of the author is implicitly questioned: since recipes are derived from oral tradition, they imply a concept of authorship distinct from written tradition. In cookbooks and other texts featuring recipes, recipes are often named after their "authors" (a person, a country, a region, or an ethnic group) to identify their (often mythical) "origin." This can transform the writer of a cookbook into a compiler or archivist, and the cookbook into a communal project. The identity-constructing qualities of food can be encapsulated within the recipe. As the reader is invited to participate, the recipe becomes a textual conversation over the metaphorical and actual breaking of bread. Recipes can pass on traditions, overcoming distances of time and space as well as differences between groups, taking part in the invention of traditions that can help to establish the story of the nation, the boundaries of the masculine community, the sisterhood of non-hegemonic sexualities. Food discourses are an important site of power relations and a site of dominance and resistance within the establishment and performance of identities in daily life.

Considering culinary discourses as sites that produced power-knowledge while granting disenfranchised groups access to expertise amends Foucault's representation of power relations in important ways. At the same time, Foucault's framework allows an understanding of nationality, sexuality, and masculinity as contested fields of knowledge and power that are not static but constantly changing, and not solely produced by political, medical, or scientific discourses, but from below and in the everyday. Equally important for my work is Foucault's critical understanding of resistance as discourses that compete with hegemonic ones without necessarily offering more just, or more liberating, alternatives.

Norbert Elias was important for this work, as he explored how instructions around food and eating intend to have social impact. This paved the way to look at representations of food as discourses. In his examination of the evolution of etiquette in early modern times, Elias demonstrated in *The Civilizing Process* (1939) that table manners can produce social order, whether on a small scale, when "civilizing" a member of court, or on a large scale, by structuring the distribution of political power within the nation-state. Based on his readings of courtly etiquette guides, Elias lays bare the political agendas in advice literature and their impact on the subject as well as on society. The advent of courtly culture brought about the implementation of stricter rules of behavior at the table, since self-restraint increasingly became the mark of social distinction and a sign of commitment to the royal family and the centralized nation-state. Refined manners signified the individual's closeness to the center of power, the royal court. Constantly changing rules of etiquette demanded continuous self-improvement and distinguished those in the know from recent arrivals or occasional visitors. Elias outlines an increasing individualization and implementation of hierarchy in the process of refining disciplinary mechanisms. Here, too, it is a previously unsuspected space—the space of the dinner table—where power relations are negotiated and incorporated.

Like Foucault, Elias does not consider gender or race in his analysis. *A Taste of Power* expands on his work by looking at food advice in a democratic society, where it becomes a biopolitical tool that can have many, often conflicting, agendas. "Biopolitics" is a Foucauldian term to describe the regulation of populations not only through government policy but also through the more intangible, yet deeply powerful, development of cultural practices and media representations in everyday life. As newly independent Americans made the transition from being subjects of the British empire to citizens of a young republic, food discourses were a key way that the cross-cutting debates in the public sphere became intangibly linked to private everyday practices, which allowed limited participation by educated white women—and in some rare cases African Americans, and, later, immigrants and residents of initially disfavored regions—to join in the construction of a new nation. Writers and artists who took up culinary themes promoted what they hoped would be the right ingredients to constitute good citizens embracing the right national values. If Elias found political power in aristocratic table manners, I find political disputes in the development of a republican cuisine pitting New England's claim to hegemonic representation of the national culture against counternarratives from the South; a democratic agrarian ideal concealing the defense of white middle-class privilege; and proponents of imperial expansion voting with their choice of recipes and ingredients against advocates of isolationism who patrolled the boundaries of acceptably "American" foods. They all have in common the idea that self-discipline and the regulation of bodily functions are crucial to citizenship and building a successful nation.

Similarly important to my understanding of food's significance to the social order is Pierre Bourdieu, according to whom the location of individuals in social space is not determined by their economic capital alone but also by their "cultural capital" (symbolic capital that is based on knowledge in a field that is socially widely valued). Like economic capital, cultural capital produces its own inequalities, as it is unevenly distributed and expressed through "habitus" (values, beliefs, and lifestyles held in common by certain social groups and realized in the individual as mindset and embodiment). Cultural capital can translate into social and economic profit. It can also make up for a lack of financial resources in terms of social recognition. Bourdieu's understanding of social space yields insight into why individuals willingly subject themselves to biopolitical regimes and regulate their appetites through learned behavior: because they expect to derive social advantages. Culinary instructions provide their readers with cultural competence, or what Bourdieu in *Distinction: A Social Critique of the Judgment of Taste* (1979) calls a "cultural code" that presents a frame of knowledge through which individuals can read and understand works of art and the full significance of food (3). Food instructions provide the knowledge or the code that allows individuals to accumulate culinary cultural capital (or "taste"). They educate their readers in the ability to transform raw ingredients into cooked foods for sustenance, with the promise of improving their social status. Because food choices demand some financial resources, but not nearly as much as transatlantic travel, real estate, or expensive jewelry, I argue that food has been a favored vehicle to acquire middle-class cultural capital and habitus in American history. While many social groups have developed a specific food habitus, food instructions since the early nineteenth century specifically targeted members of social groups that had some freedom in their food choices but insufficient resources to leave their kitchen to a highly trained chef, or have their tastes educated by frequent overseas travel and visits to fine restaurants. Together with recipes that befit the financial resources, studied taste, and knowledge base of a wide range of middle-class readers, texts provided values and instructions on proper embodiments (for instance in the form of table etiquette) that went far beyond nutritional advice.

As cultural codes constantly shift and change—not only because different social groups struggle for hegemony but also because members within social groups compete for political and cultural leadership—cultural capital needs to evolve whenever it has been acquired by too many. A taste widely shared quickly becomes the epitome of tastelessness. New instructions, reacting to the changed ideological context, are constantly in demand.

Bourdieu developed his concepts within the social context of France in the 1960s and 1970s, so his work should not be seamlessly translated to any particular historical moment within the United States. In Bourdieu's view, the tastemaking culture is always upper-class, and elite tastes are the most desirable to members of all classes, although limited resources or solidarity with one's own class does not allow everyone to act on that desire. But historical examples show that elite culture did not always dictate American tastes. As Mark McWilliams has demonstrated, and I will argue later in this work, in early America, middle-class authors moved strategically away from elite tastes, which were linked to European decadence and British imperialism, and embraced simplicity as a marker of genuine American taste (7). As the simplicity of republican cuisine was connoted with virtue, the endorsement of simple tastes became an argument for claiming cultural hegemony for middle-class tastes. Similar strategic movements away from elite culture can be seen in other moments of American food culture: In the early twentieth century, middle-class authors borrowed from nostalgic imagery of the ways of life of the cowboy and the soldier to embrace campfire cooking and the simplest meals as especially manly, after middle-class masculinity came under fire for being too soft and sedentary. In the 1960s, an African American middle class employed soul food, an idealized version of poor Southern foodways, as a political instrument. In these examples, taste is still used as a marker of distinction, but in ways that transgress class hierarchies and the idea of upper-class ways as unquestionably the most desirable.

Inspired scholars of food studies have discussed the history and production of American food and its excluded or appropriated other (food marked as ethnic, foreign, or exotic), generating a comprehensive body of scholarship on what it has meant to "eat American" at different moments in time. Their work has greatly influenced mine.[8] *A Taste of Power* begins by examining popular ways of thinking about an American cuisine from the Revolution to the early 1840s, a time in which nation building and the question of national character were at the forefront of public discussions. It was also a time in which only a few American cookbooks had yet been published, domestic magazines were not so prevalent (they started to appear in the 1830s), and fine dining remained largely a private pleasure, as restaurant culture began to develop only slowly in the 1820s. Exploring key texts, including letters, song lyrics, poetry, cookbooks, and still-life paintings, the first part of *A Taste of Power*, "'For All Grades of Life': The Making of a Republican Cuisine," explores early attempts by American authors to define a genuine national cuisine that would help set the new nation apart from the British identity many Americans took for granted before 1776, and would help integrate its many parts into a coherent whole. Early on, at the time of the Revolution, corn became a political instrument for self-definition and resistance, and laid the foundation for a republican cuisine. In the first cookbooks published after independence, women, who were excluded from most political decision making, wielded the genre to claim citizenship and a political voice in the young republic.

But the notion of a republican cuisine is not static, and it evolved within changing cultural contexts and public debates. In the early nineteenth century, a rising middle class evoked an imaginary settler cuisine to define themselves as makers of American taste and harbingers of American virtue, distancing themselves from European decadence and corruption. Middle-class female authors used cookbooks to inscribe themselves into the nation-building project. They used their culinary authority to publish political commentary, speak in favor of the education of women, and shape national character. They simultaneously promoted middle-class lifestyles over upper-class lifestyles as truly American, and erased ethnic and regional differences to create the image of a homogenous national culture. Health advocates in the 1830s not only promoted whole grains, but also presented new ideas of what constituted citizenship by connecting the individual body with the nation's well-being. Casting white, middle-class women as gatekeepers of the family's health, they also created a politically meaningful (if limited and contested) place for them in the fabric of the nation. As "'For All Grades of Life'" shows, these different approaches to defining American cooking supported existing power relations as they promoted Anglo-Saxon cooking and Northern foodways to assert the preeminence of New England culture in the

United States, presenting a self-image of the nation as a democratic society and eliding any concerns regarding social stratification, a franchise limited by wealth and gender, or slavery. In the pursuit of creating a homogenous nation, ethnic difference was recognized only in the most limited ways and only if thoroughly neutralized and appropriated. But in the late 1820s and 1830s, texts began to appear that contested the hegemonic representation of U. S. culinary culture by promoting regional or cosmopolitan cooking. Far from being simply liberating acts of resistance, some of these texts produced their own normative narratives, for instance by normalizing slavery. Conversely, the (northern and free) African American author Robert Roberts argued that servants could make their professional skills a source of pride and independence, undermining the idea of a classless society so frequently put forward in cookbooks of his time. What emerges is a fresh portrait of the richly complex national debates and simmering sectional conflicts that were carried out not only in the halls of Congress and the editorial pages of leading newspapers, but in cookbooks, short stories, and artworks of this period.

Many valuable scholarly works of the past few decades have thought about the intersection of food and gender in interesting and innovative ways.[9] But traditionally, gender analyses in the wider realm of food studies have concentrated on femininity alone; rarely have works explored how masculinity is defined by food discourses.[10] The second part of *A Taste of Power*, "'Wolf in Chef's Clothing': Manly Cooking and Negotiations of Ideal Masculinity," goes further by examining formations of normative masculinities from the 1890s to the 1970s in cooking instructions and literature.

Over the course of the nineteenth century, women gained authority over domestic cooking and publications that advised the domestic cook. At the turn to the twentieth century, images of manly cooking emerged, not only in cookbooks directed at men, but also in literature and popular culture. In the image of the solitary hero frying flapjacks over the campfire, or the hard-boiled detective subsisting on liverwurst sandwiches, authors expressed an ideal masculinity centered on radical independence from women. But not all food advice directed at men promoted simplicity. In the 1940s and 1950s the "gourmet" became another prominent image to represent men in the kitchen. While at first glance a gender-neutral concept, the gourmet was embraced by men's magazines such as *Esquire* and *Playboy* as the embodiment of a new masculine ideal, the sophisticated cosmopolitan and sexual conqueror.

The misogyny of some of these texts is striking. Male cookery often shielded itself from the effeminizing potential of entering the feminine sphere of the kitchen by proclaiming that women lacked artistry in one of the tasks most closely associated with them, or else posited women as quarries of the domesticated hunt—one carried out with cooking utensils and yielding erotic spoils. Cookbooks written by African American men that entered the market in the 1960s worked differently, promoting the concept of soul food. The framing of a politicized, nationalist cuisine made defensive references to sexual conquest and campfire unnecessary to preserve masculine capital in a domestic cooking context, but soul food produced its own moments of gendered power. Beyond offering a detailed analysis of the emergence and varieties of the male amateur cook in American mainstream culture, the discussions in "'Wolf in Chef's Clothing'" provide insights into how to conceptualize masculinity in the twentieth century and how to theorize changes in gender norms from the perspective of instructional discourses regulating the everyday.

Traditionally, cookbooks and other food writing have promoted heteronormative structures, directing readers not only in how to cook, but also in how to conduct their relationships, shape their expectations, and form their families. The final part of *A Taste of Power,* "'The Difference Is Spreading': Recipes for Lesbian Living," takes up the highly commodified connection between food and sexuality, investigating how authors excluded from the heteronormative economy, promoted by cooking instructions, reinscribed themselves into culinary discourses.

Implicitly, much of the work on food and gender has discussed the heteronormativity of cooking advice. A few scholars working on food and sexuality have gone beyond looking at sexuality as a by-product of gender; Julia Ehrhardt has called for a queering of food studies.[11] This section explores strategies in which texts have disturbed the implicit and explicit sexual norms cooking instructions traditionally served, and discusses how literature, memoirs, and cookbooks have tried to construct alternative sexual subjectivities.

Since the late nineteenth century, cooking discourses have played a role in normalizing the notion of the nuclear family and promoted the idea that cooking is a woman's way to express love for her husband and children. Women who loved women and wrote about it appropriated this image for their own goals. Gertrude Stein's *Tender Buttons* (1914), a text firmly established in the modernist canon, worked with echoes of, and grammatical references to, household manuals, simultaneously undermining their authoritative quality and using the evoked images to create another economy of desire, a "household with a difference." *The Alice B. Toklas Cook Book* (1954) in a number of different ways corresponded with Stein's work. Toklas mixed recipes with autobiographical writing, creating a text narrating her life together with Stein that did not follow the mandatory heterosexual economy of desire traditionally ascribed to women by cookbooks.

A generation later, authors of memoirs, short stories, and cookbooks focusing on same-sex relationships began to use food imagery to describe relationships, heartbreak, and the experience of being marginalized or rejected. Working with a practically unexamined body of texts—cookbooks and cooking blogs directed at a lesbian audience—the final section of "'The Difference Is Spreading'" shows how the texts reappropriate the trope of cooking as an expression of a woman's love and attempt to avoid stereotypical depictions of lesbians by employing a number of different strategies. In the process, the texts create new normative expectations for their readership. Thus the analysis shows the challenge of renegotiating subjectivities in nonexclusionary terms.

A Taste of Power investigates constellations of historical food discourses in the nineteenth, twentieth, and twenty-first centuries, examining a broad corpus of texts, among them newspaper and magazine articles, novels, cookbooks, autobiographies, short stories, domestic manuals, poems, paintings, and blogs, all of them dealing explicitly with food. These varied ingredients from two centuries of American culinary culture yield an argument that food practices and discourses are decisively implicated when it comes to the production of national, regional, racial, sexual, gender, and class identities, as well as the limits they enforce. Power relations are at work when we eat and cook and when we talk, read, or hear about eating and cooking. We emerge through this process and can resist against it. Analyzing representations of food within their specific cultural contexts therefore helps us understand how we become what we are, who is telling us how to be, and where we stand in the food chain.

ONE

———

"For All Grades of Life"

THE MAKING OF A REPUBLICAN CUISINE

The destiny of nations depends on how they nourish themselves.

—JEAN ANTHELME BRILLAT-SAVARIN,
The Physiology of Taste (1825)

IN SEARCH OF AN AMERICAN CUISINE: NATIONAL IDENTITY AND FOOD

THERE IS NO AMERICAN CUISINE, argues Sidney Mintz provocatively in "Eating American" (106). Many Americans and non-Americans will agree, some of the former ruefully, some of the latter with a smirk, since a national cuisine is often associated with cultivation. But having a cuisine may say nothing about the quality of a culture or the refinement of a society, writes Mintz. He believes it may even be quintessentially American *not* to have produced a national cuisine, as the concept reflects an old-fashioned idea of a nation-state that represents a seemingly homogeneous people and its unitary culture—a model unable to encompass American diversity.

Mintz may be right that to have or not to have a national cuisine is not a measure of refinement, but he is mistaken if he believes that Americans have not tried to come up with one. Since the American Revolution, authors of cookbooks, newspaper articles, and nutritional advice as well as poets and painters have attempted to create practices, dishes, and rituals expressing a specific American character, thus acknowledging that inventing a national cuisine is indeed an important part of imagining a community, history, and tradition.

National cuisines consist of iconic dishes, methods of preparation, and culinary rules for holidays and everyday eating that claim to represent the history, ambitions, and *terroir* (and thereby the territorial claims) of a unified nation. As Arjun Appadurai has shown for India and Jeffrey Pilcher for

Mexico, ideas of sharing the same food and symbolically breaking bread with one another hold strong social signification and invoke images of unity—be it among community, kin, or family—that serve as powerful tools in nation building when translated into a nationwide scope (Appadurai 3–10, Pilcher 1–6). And as Kyla Wazana Tompkins has pointed out, since food advice regulates embodiment, "Nationalist foodways—and the objects fetishized therein . . . become allegories through which the nation and its attendant anxieties play out" (4). The notion of a homogeneous cuisine, shared by an entire people, projects order on chaotic transnational and regional foodscapes and simulates stability and tradition, while manifesting the cultural dominance of certain populations. Print and other forms of mass distribution make possible the nationwide standardization of certain dishes and their canonization into a cuisine with the main aim to create a national community (Pilcher 2). The dishes featured often reflect desired national virtues such as patriotism, gentility, or frugality, depending on what the specific cultural moment requires, thus urging citizens literally to incorporate them.

Reviewing postrevolutionary and antebellum American culinary culture, the following chapters will show that in the United States, ideas of a national cuisine emerged along the fault lines of race, ethnicity, religion, region, class, and gender. The choice of dishes canonized in any cuisine reflects hegemonic tastes and beliefs. In early America, these were for the most part British-inspired dishes preserved in New England traditions that adopted indigenous ingredients and those from other cultures, sometimes strategically, in order to distinguish their own culture from their British heritage, attempting to open a space to constitute American identity.[1] Typically they promoted puritan self-denial as well as middle-class virtues such as self-control, restraint, and rational lifestyle choices as genuinely republican and therefore American. By selecting which traditions and ingredients to include, authors of advice literature determined who was participating in the national project. The question of what is considered typical and traditional, or deemed inedible, served to legitimize privilege as it normalized the tastes and beliefs of one or a few groups while marginalizing others.[2]

Exploring the architecture of a national cuisine exposes the underlying assumptions a society makes about its citizens. Within the American context, self-governance through the most elementary—alimentary—regulation of the body is crucial for participating in governing the country, culturally as well as politically.[3] The management of one's body as in table manners or diet is believed to be an indicator of character and rational ability, and thus a sign not only of physical fitness but of fitness for citizenship. In their early culinary texts, Americans reflected their awareness that their status was changing from subjects to citizens. Instead of being bound to the rule of a monarch, as in the examples Norbert Elias cites in *The Civilizing Process* (1939), Americans after the Revolution began to conceptualize themselves as a free people that must govern themselves, in a republic whose sole political legitimation was the well-being of its citizens. To make a civil society work, its members had to agree on regulations and responsibilities. Unlike in European nations, as Kyla Wazana Tompkins has posited in a modification of Foucault's concept of biopolitics, the concerted effort to keep the population healthy was not led by state intervention but driven by reform movements she describes as a "series of uneven, asynchronous, and local campaigns, each of them reworking republicanism to construe the ideal citizen as self-policing, temperate, and moral" (5–6). Citizenship, understood as individuals' commitment to public life and the common good, encompassed not only political activity but also a new concern with quotidian behavior. Living frugally, remaining temperate, and being committed to one's work and nation were crucial to the success of the republic.[4] Eating, cooking, and providing certain foods became part of a citizen's commitment to the nation, as they were associated with the moral fiber and material well-being of the country. But despite the narrative inclusiveness of the texts, which took pride in transcending class boundaries, they addressed only certain populations and excluded others when it came to race and ethnicity. They thus reveal quite literally who was invited to sit at the American table, and who was not.

Discussions of citizenship implicitly describe an individual's protected access (ensured by state, society, or culture) to national resources and civil rights that can include education, health, political representation, marriage, and individual expression. Traditionally, access to such resources has been unequally distributed in the United States—a legally or socially sanctioned injustice in a society striving for democracy that was frequently legitimized by attributing a lack of self-control, reason, ethics, or refinement to those excluded. The alleged inherent inferiority of marginalized groups is thought to be displayed by modes of speaking, eating, consumption, or other arbitrary markers. In early America, prescriptive food discourses such as nutritional advice, recipes in magazines, or manuals on table manners attempted to discipline individuals into desired national subjects by linking individual behavior to national identity. Those who did or could not comply served as cautionary models for the rest. In this way, prescriptive food discourses serve as testimony not only to the prevailing notions of health and nutrition, but also to contemporary definitions of citizenship.

Often, scholarly discussions of early examples of American cuisine begin with Sarah Josepha Hale's *The Good Housekeeper* (1841) or Catherine Beecher's *American Woman's Home* (1869). But other authors before them had already struggled to define what American cuisine meant and how it constituted American nationalism, a heritage to which Hale and Beecher refer in their writings. During the Revolution and the constituting decades that followed, food rhetoric played a significant role in political discourse. Europeans ridiculed Americans for their boorish table manners and unsophisticated cooking, whereas Americans celebrated the abundance of their natural food resources as part of their identity.[5] As Mark McWilliams has noted, these attacks on national foodways were usually thinly veiled disparagements of what was perceived as national character.[6] British writers such as Charles Dickens caricatured American table manners (Americans "suck their knives and forks meditatively until they have decided what to take next" [*American Notes*, 158]). Prominent Americans such as Nathaniel Hawthorne retaliated by making fun of the English ("a nation of beastly eaters and beastly drinkers" [*The English Notebooks*, 404]). British travelers often reported in detail on the unspeakable meals they claimed to have suffered through at American tables, shorthand for conveying Americans' provincialism and lack of refinement.[7]

With a topic so politically charged, it is no surprise that American authors tried to take control of defining an American cuisine worthy of their values and aspirations and defying European prejudice against the New World. Since the late eighteenth century, writers and artists had discussed the characteristics of American cooking and eating, and came up with recipes that would produce the right kind of citizens and embody superior national values. The earliest version of an American cuisine was thought to reflect the lifestyle of an agrarian society, just and equal access to nutritional resources, and a rejection of the European aristocratic decadence and waste that was associated with British imperialism. It is best described as a republican cuisine that embraced democracy, simplicity, and health.[8] Different interpretations of what a republican cuisine entailed emerged from the 1790s to the 1830s—a time determined by the search for American national identity and character—reflecting different modes of thinking about citizenship and heavily influenced by contemporary political debates over territorial expansion, the role of women in the new republic, and the impact of industrialization. The texts discussed in these chapters—Joel Barlow's mock epic "The Hasty Pudding" (1793), Amelia Simmons's *American Cookery* (1796), Raphaelle Peale's food still lifes (1813–22), Lydia Maria Child's *The American Frugal Housewife* (1829), and Sylvester Graham's *A Treatise on Bread, and Bread-Making* (1837)—were formative in the first fifty years of debate on how to eat like an American and present key issues in the formulation of a national cuisine. The texts reflect changes in the conceptualization of the nation, identity, and national values, showing that the idea of a republican cuisine, a cuisine devoted to "public and private virtue, internal unity, social solidarity, and vigilance against the corruption of power," as Robert Shalhope has defined the core values of republicanism, was not static but a flexible and nuanced concept reacting to the political debates of the day.[9]

All incarnations of republican cooking had in common that they associated recipes with notions of liberty, equality, and democracy, and promoted these values as truly American. But, as I will show, they simultaneously reinscribed into American society the unequal distribution of labor and resources based on class, gender, and race via the acts of cooking and eating. Concepts of republican cuisine typically promoted New England cooking as quintessentially American, thus making a claim for its regional hegemony. Similarly, in its desire to establish a clear demarcation from European cuisines, much cooking advice implicitly propagated anti-cosmopolitan and isolationist politics that translated into the dismissal of spices and other imported goods as well as a mistrust of exotic foods. Finally, while directed to a middle-class audience, cooking advice celebrated the classlessness and allegedly inherent social equality of American cooking, ignoring the existing stratification of society. But as a reaction to the contradictions and conceptual difficulties republican cuisine presented, authors from the 1820s onward produced cooking advice that, inadvertently or not, challenged its parameters. Mary Randolph's *The Virginia House-wife* (1824) contested New England's hegemony in American cooking. Eliza Leslie's French-inspired cookbooks (1832–44) advanced the concept of a transnational American cuisine, emerging together with the idea of the United States as a plausible global player able to compete with European empires. Robert Roberts's *The House Servant's Directory* (1827) explicitly discussed class differences in American society. Thus, republican cuisine was a concept that was contested from early on, reflecting the struggles for cultural hegemony and inclusion happening on a greater scale in American society.

"ALL MY BONES WERE MADE OF INDIAN CORN":
MAIZE, REVOLUTION, AND DEMOCRACY

The earliest attempts to formulate a politically meaningful American cuisine centered on the reappropriation of corn. Maize was a New World starch European writers generally dismissed as animal fodder. Initially, corn was also unloved in the colonies: European settlers coveted wheat and other European grains for their social cachet, but had to make do with corn, as it could be reliably raised in the new environment. Only in the revolutionary period did American authors begin to embrace corn, as an emancipatory movement slowly gained momentum.[10]

In January 1766, Benjamin Franklin wrote to a London newspaper in response to a letter whose author had claimed that Americans were dependent on English imports of tea, as their breakfast of cornmeal was indigestible without it. In his rebuke (tellingly published under the pseudonym "Homespun"), Franklin wrote:

> Pray let me, an American, inform the gentleman, who seems ignorant of the matter, that Indian corn, take it for all in all, is one of the most agreeable and wholesome grains in the world; that its green leaves roasted are a delicacy beyond expression; that samp, hominy, succatash [*sic*], and nokehock [*sic*], made of it, are so pleasing varieties; and that johny [*sic*] or hoecake, hot from the fire is better than a Yorkshire muffin. (395–96)

Here he introduces the mantra of a decade of nutritional writing to come: simple equals healthy equals American (in contrast, the question of deliciousness will soon decline in importance). But obviously Franklin in this passage is not engaging in a discussion of the nutritional merits of muffins or hoecakes. By citing the signature corn dishes of different regions in the British North American empire, he evokes the specter of the colonies unifying and rising up against the policies of the English crown. Even if "Indian corn were as disagreeable and indigestible as the Stamp Act," he writes, Americans could easily replace it with other produce their abundant lands provide, attesting to the colonies' economic independence (396). Using the Native American names of corn dishes, Franklin invokes the colonies' cultural difference from the mother country, perhaps menacingly, with the allusion to its "savage" heritage, the way protestors would soon masquerade as Native Americans to dump English tea into Boston harbor. Instead of a lack of refinement, he casts Americans' reliance on corn as a sign of health and strength. The letter culminates in a thinly veiled and prophetic threat to boycott English imports ("the expensive, flimsey [*sic*], rotten, black stuffs and cloths you used to send us"), presenting the colonies as just as unified in their determination to defy English taxation as in their appreciation for corn (396). Indeed, when the Townshend Act passed in 1767, the colonies staged a boycott that reduced British imports by 50 percent.

Despite Franklin's encomium, American colonists had a troubled and ambivalent relationship with corn. The first inhabitants of Jamestown would not eat corn even when faced with the prospect of starving, since they associated it with savagery and feared for their humanity.[11] Settlers in Plymouth started cultivating corn only after all their European crops failed, making it the most easily available but hardly the most prized grain in New England. Throughout most of the history of the colonies, corn was thought to be inferior to wheat or rye. Since the starches a culture eats play an important role in its self-definition and the stratification of its society (the poor usually eat more and different starches than the rich, who have access to more nutritious and prestigious foods), this was of no small consequence. In Europe, grains were a marker of class: wheat was a sign of gentility.[12] Those who could not afford wheat bread tried at least to mix some wheat with other flours into their darker, less desirable breads. The lack of wheat bread in parts of the colonies was therefore perceived as a lack of sophistication.[13]

Europeans had grown corn—imported from the New World—since the late sixteenth century, but it was consumed mostly in rural areas and by the poor.[14] Cornmeal was dismissed by many British authors as too coarse for fine dining, and fit only for feeding animals.[15] When American authors such as Franklin embraced corn and its products in the revolutionary era, they were engaging in a political act. Corn as an image for the determination of the colonies trickled into popular culture, as in the revolutionary anthem "Yankee Doodle." The song, probably originating with British soldiers in the French and Indian War to mock American troops for their poor dress and training, devoted a few lines to the inferior food they consumed, as in this version printed in late-eighteenth-century London:

> Sheep's Head and Vinegar,
> ButterMilk and Tansy,
> Boston is a Yankee town,
> Sing Hey Doodle Dandy.
> First we'll take a Pinch of Snuff,
> And then a drink of Water,

And then we'll say, How do you do,
And that's a Yanky's Supper.[16]

While the rhymers here deride the provincialism and lack of sophistication
in the colonies, they go further in other stanzas where the "Yanky" is accused
of cowardice and a lack of masculinity—which made this the perfect tune for
British troops to sing during the Revolutionary War.[17] But by then the
Continental troops had appropriated it, and in their adaptations food
appeared, too, as in this version published in 1787:

> Father and I went up to camp
> Along with Captain Goodwin;
> And there we saw the men and boys
> As thick as hasty pudding.[18]

Hasty pudding, or corn mush, here becomes a metaphor to describe not only
the numerousness but also the unity and determination of the American
troops. In a later stanza, the text claims that the American military had plentiful supplies of molasses, a derisive reference to the Sugar Act of 1764, which
helped trigger the American Revolution by limiting the importation of
molasses to the colonies (and therefore threatened the production of liquor,
an important export).[19] In these examples, Americans inverted the disdainful
tone and content of the British versions of "Yankee Doodle" and used food
imagery to underline patriotic and defiant messages. In the process, the humble hasty pudding became a symbol for the glue that kept the colonies
together. (This nationalist spirit may have been behind the 1770 founding of
Harvard's Hasty Pudding Club, an institution that still endures and counts
among its members five U.S. presidents: John Adams, John Quincy Adams,
Theodore Roosevelt, Franklin Delano Roosevelt, and John F. Kennedy.)[20]

After the Revolution, Joel Barlow used corn as a quintessential American
food to describe the values the nation hoped to uphold. In his famous mock-
epic "The Hasty Pudding" from 1793, corn is an icon of democracy and liberty,
not only in the United States but worldwide.[21] In three "cantos" Barlow sings
the praises of hasty pudding with a sacral timbre ("the purest frenzy of poetic
fire" [3]), creating a humorous effect in the discrepancy between the quotidian
content and the hyperbolic diction. As Theodore Grieder and others have
argued, mock poetry of the eighteenth century not only served the purpose of
entertainment but provided critical interventions in contemporary debates,
mostly on the aesthetic, but also on the political.[22] Barlow, a not-so-successful

author of monumental poetry, spent the years between 1788 and 1795 in Paris and London.[23] He was politically engaged with pro-revolutionary thinkers, among them Thomas Jefferson and Thomas Paine. His support of the French Revolution earned him honorary French citizenship in 1792, the year before he wrote "The Hasty Pudding," the work for which he is best remembered today. After his radical political views made him unwelcome in England, he ran in Savoy for a seat in the French National Convention, but without success. Leo Lemay, who describes Barlow as an "avant-garde radical," writes that "The Hasty Pudding," like Paine's *Rights of Man,* responded to Edmund Burke's attack on the French Revolution, published in 1791 as *Reflections on the Revolution in France* (3–23).[24] Barlow wrote "The Hasty Pudding" while crafting his formal rebuke to Burke, *Advice to the Privileged Orders,* and some of his pro-revolutionary thought informs the heroic couplets.

In January 1793, the month Louis XVI was tried, sentenced to death, and beheaded, Barlow was inspired to write this poem by a bowl of cornmeal mush served to him in the French countryside, or so the legend goes. The text opens with a disclaimer distancing itself from the history-making events happening around it: "Ye Gallic flags, that o'er heights unfurled, / Bear death to kings, and freedom to the world / I sing not to you . . . " (3). But, of course, these are exactly the topics upon which Barlow elaborates.

"The Hasty Pudding" tells the story of a proudly self-identified Yankee traveler who experiences a bout of homesickness and nostalgia while eating a cornmeal dish at a Savoy hostelry.[25] In a Proustian moment, the dish serves as a mnemonic overture to a humorous discussion of the speaker's childhood memories of the cultivation of corn, the preparation of cornmeal mush, and its "proper" consumption. Barlow imbues hasty pudding with republican values, connected to a utopian agrarian society that centers on the production of maize. As the cultivation of corn, the speaker avers, provides everyone with enough to eat, corn itself becomes the symbol of a democratic and just society in which everybody contributes equally to the common good, and in which everybody is equally entitled to enjoy the proceeds: Mother Earth "gives her bounties to the sons of toil" (8). A family's breakfast, a "Yankee . . . abundant feast," becomes the moment in which democracy is reflected in the fictitious experience of the meal:

> With simples furnished, and with plainness dressed,
> A numerous offspring gathers round the board,
> And cheers alike the servant and the lord;

Whose well-bought hunger prompts the joyous taste,
And health attends them from the short repast.
While the full pail rewards the milkmaid's toil,
The mother sees the morning cauldron boil;
To stir the pudding next demands their care,
To spread the table and the bowls prepare;
To feed the children, as their portions cool,
And comb their heads, and send them off to school. (7)

The United States is depicted as an idyllic place where people of all classes eat together peacefully to take a break from the process of building a nation together. Everyone works; nobody lives off another person's labor, and all are rewarded by having their needs satisfied. In this passage the exaggerated heroic tone that dominates other parts of the text is noticeably absent, replaced by earnestness.

Obviously this is a romanticized version of equality that does not account for gender or racial difference. In this passage, in which everyone is supposed to get a break to enjoy the fruits of their labors, the mother still works and serves the others. Her labor is cast within a different economy of care and love that is supposed to be its own reward. The idyllic description of rural living, with a mother working in the home rather than in the fields, and children sent off to school, represents a middle-class ideal of an agricultural society rather than the tougher reality then predominant among smallholders. The question of racial inequality is circumvented by placing this agrarian idyll in an ostensibly slave-free New England, neatly eliding slavery's challenge to the new American narrative of equality and justice.

In omitting modes of unequal access to resources in the United States, Barlow idealizes the nation's commitment to equality, and allows an unchallenged rendering of the United States as democratic torchbearer. In Barlow's epic, sun deities (about whom, as the text argues, myths and legends exist all over the world) bestow corn upon a hardworking population in a democratic mode. This universalist interlacing of sun and corn implies humanist, cosmopolitan ideals and the concept of natural and unalienable rights, as the sun shines on everyone regardless of status or creed.[26] Barlow defines cooking with corn in great detail as a genuinely American practice, thus suggesting that Americans received corn and democracy first, but not exclusively, and now are helping the gods in their mission to spread both.

For this he locates the origin of hasty pudding in the mythic, distant past when he credits a "lovely squaw" who invented the dish long before Columbus brought it back to Europe. Creating a pre-European ancient history has the purpose of equaling, and perhaps rivaling, the European heritage, as the "lovely squaw" becomes the (racially marked) Roman goddess of grain when described as "tawny Ceres" (4).[27] The New World's indigenous populations share their cornmeal dishes willingly, first with the European settlers and then with the world, a benign narrative that obliterates the violence of conquest. With its origins in prehistory, hasty pudding, in method a traditional English dish, becomes in Barlow's hands a New World invention, bequeathed by the unknown indigenous woman directly to the American revolutionaries, as the speaker jumps from pre-Columbian to prerevolutionary times by picking up the thread of tradition with his father's consumption of corn and then his own (". . . all my bones were made of Indian corn" [6]). Thus the text creates an imagined line of tradition from the now conveniently vanished indigenous cultures to European settler society and its "pure hereditary taste," with the intention of giving evidence of the newcomers' legitimacy.[28] In relating them to the indigenous populations, Barlow depicts the settlers as the legitimate heirs to the land rather than as colonizers, a role now projected upon the defeated British. Barlow further exaggerates the idea of an unbroken tradition passed down from Native Americans to immigrants when the speaker exclaims (addressing the hasty pudding): " . . . I know thee by that yellow face, / That strong complexion of true Indian race, / which time can never change nor soil impair" (5). Here the eating of the mush becomes an act of incorporation of the racial other to create American identity. As Rafia Zafar quips, "Tell me whom you eat, and I will tell you who you are."[29]

Barlow's idealized New World will free the Old from injustice and oppression, thus inverting notions of origins and historic development in such a fashion that the United States is cast as the beginning of a new world order. In this process the young nation triumphs over older, established ones, and the United States becomes the bearer of democratic promise and religious freedom for all humankind. It exports not only corn mush but democratic thought to France. Here the speaker not only encounters revolutionary determination but also hasty pudding under the name of "Polente" (5), a dish to be found in the French countryside (and other rural European regions) but in neither Paris nor London, as they appear in the poem only as doomed places of decay and decadence. The countryside and the working populations are cast as the bearers of hope for societies that have outlived their relevance.

Barlow's closing lines are critical of European mores, as he dismisses etiquette and table manners as representative of an outmoded social hierarchy:

"Fear not to slaver ... / Like the free Frenchman, from your joyous chin / Suspend the ready napkin; or, like me, / Poise with one hand your bowl upon your knee" (12). The free Frenchman and the American are connected not only in their appreciation for corn mush and democracy, but also in their liberation from decorum, which is closely associated with the dominance of elite culture.[30] Thus Barlow suggests that traditional rules of conduct are adverse to the democratic project, and instead proposes informality and pragmatism—snubbing the many European writers who had made fun of American casualness at the table.

Like Franklin, Barlow lists different regional signature corn dishes—including succotash, hoecakes ("fair Virginia's pride" [5]), charlottes, and corn bread—to create the image of a heterogeneous but united nation. While he recognizes regional difference in the local specialties, the universal appreciation of corn (and the symbolism for which it stands) keeps the former colonies together as a society that shares cultural traits that go beyond their European heritage. At the same time, Barlow asserts New England's cultural and culinary leadership by praising the hasty pudding as superior to all other corn dishes and taking its name as his epic's title (5).

Barlow's poem received wide-ranging media attention in its time.[31] Today the text is widely anthologized as an example of mock poetry and/or neoclassical American literature. Literary critics recognize the political dimensions of the text (as did contemporary editors, who praised "The Hasty Pudding" for its republican values and its "freedom and boldness").[32] But it generally has been overlooked that Barlow thought his mock epic had more than poetic value. He advertised it as advice to his audience on how to "eat right," as a guideline for nourishing oneself as an American: "A simplicity in diet, whether it be considered with reference to the happiness of individuals or the prosperity of a nation, is of more consequence than we are apt to imagine" (iv), he wrote in the preface to the early editions. As unlikely as it may seem today, there is evidence that his contemporaries, too, understood Barlow's homage to corn pudding as a contribution to an emerging scientific discussion of food's intrinsic value. In contemporary sources, Barlow is mentioned in the same breath as nutrition experts of his time such as Benjamin Thompson Count Rumford, an American-born, British, self-taught nutrition expert who researched the most effective diet for prison inmates in the late eighteenth century.[33] Not only was the cuisine Barlow outlined as genuinely republican based on the use of corn, but he explicitly stated that a "SIMPLICITY OF DIET" [capitals his] should be counted among the virtues of the new nation. In line with this call, he advised Americans not to engage in "sumptuous entertainments" (iv). Instead of mimicking European elite table manners, Barlow wanted the new republic to create a culture around agricultural practices, thus guaranteeing the nation's and its citizens' health and welfare. In this signature piece of early American literature, corn is cast not just symbolically as American food, and the dishes Barlow lists are an early example of what a genuine American cuisine could look like. Together with the political claims in his culinary manifesto, "The Hasty Pudding" served as a blueprint for ideas of American cooking in the late eighteenth century, defining it through its use of corn, the infusion of dishes with political values, and a focus on simplicity as a truly republican cuisine.

All of these features can also be found in a text that is widely recognized as the first American cookbook, Amelia Simmons's *American Cookery*. The author, of whom little is known besides what she revealed about herself in the book's introduction, published the text in 1796 in Hartford, Connecticut, promising her readers recipes "Adapted to this country" (cover). Until then, Americans who used cookbooks had to content themselves with books imported from Europe that often did not acknowledge the conditions of colonial life.

Simmons's text did not present an entirely new cuisine responding to colonial realities. Instead, as promised in the title, she adapted mostly British dishes to the United States. Most recipes in *American Cookery* were copied from English texts, notably from Susannah Carter's *The Frugal Housewife,* an indication that Simmons saw American cooking as firmly rooted in British culinary traditions and did not intend to break with them.[34] But the cookbook promoted domestic American ingredients and notably included five recipes that made use of cornmeal (referred to as "Indian meal"), such as "Johny Cake [*sic*]" or "A Nice Indian Pudding" (34, 26). Recipes using cornmeal were rarely found in English cookbooks of that time because of the food's low status. By including the recipes, Simmons embraced corn as a grain Americans had learned to rely on, and by putting lowly corn dishes in print, helped to liberate them from their stigma. But the inclusion of corn dishes was only one of the strategies that Simmons used to stake a claim to authoring an American cuisine. She also included other American ingredients. She recommended the use of potash for leavening, offered a recipe for a pumpkin pie, and accompanied turkey with cranberry sauce, thus putting recipes in print that reflected the culinary exchange with indigenous cultures and are now considered iconic in American cooking.[35] Simmons transformed classic English recipes so that Americans could enjoy them, and gave culinary testimony to a newly emerging national identity that no longer was to follow British culinary instructions unconditionally. But the British heritage still dominated her vision of an American cuisine. Despite its emancipatory impetus, by promoting amended British recipes, the text perpetuated the colonial notion that British cooking equaled civilization and refinement, and was in general superior to indigenous cooking or what other colonial cultures may have had to offer. As Kariann Yokota argues, postrevolutionary Americans struggled to define themselves culturally. The new Americans confronted widely circulating theories that held that even the most civilized people would regress into a state of savagery if exposed to insalubrious conditions of nature, climate, and food (12–18). Anglo-Americans strived to demonstrate that they were not corrupted by living in an untamed landscape and in proximity to indigenous peoples. The endorsement of a cultural heritage that was associated with the powerful British empire helped to legitimize a perceived superiority over indigenous and other cultures present on the continent. Only a few recipes in *American Cookery* directly acknowledge cross-cultural references, such as the recipe for "Cookies," which came from the Dutch tradition, as the name indicates (it means "little cake" in Dutch), and is one of the rare pieces of evidence in an early cookbook for the multilayered processes of culinary hybridization the colonial condition encouraged.

While still firmly rooted in British culinary traditions, Simmons's announcement of an *American Cookery* implied an understanding of a national identity that exceeded the individual states, and the insight that nations are not only political units but lived entities that are reflected in the most mundane activities. While essentially declaring its dependence on British cuisine, *American Cookery* still attempted to imbue familiar dishes with republican values. Simmons promised that the text would satisfy the needs of "all grades of life" (cover), a ploy to maximize her potential readership, but also an implicit argument that American families have more in common than separates them by class. In her introduction dedicated to American women, she claims that even the most unfortunate have the right to opportunity and the responsibility to make themselves "useful members of society," formulating an early version of the American dream, but one that included women, too (3).

The text promoted Northeastern fare as truly American, in the process metonymously taking the culture of the region for the whole of the nation.[36] The cookbook thereby claimed New England's hegemony over other regions, a strategy that Barlow also employed, and excluded other emerging regional traditions from this early version of an American cuisine.[37]

Beyond the recipes, the text offered commentary on education and other issues reaching far beyond the kitchen. In the second edition of *American Cookery,* Simmons claimed that most of the commentary in the earlier text was not authored by her, but by an unnamed transcriber who prepared the text for the press.[38] It is not possible to substantiate or refute that claim. But regardless of authorship, the cookbook was the first in a long series of recipe collections published in the United States that used the cookbook as a vehicle to provide political opinion together with the dishes it promoted. Unlike in Europe, cookbooks in the United States were from the beginning mostly published by women catering to an emerging middle class that defined cooking as women's work. Women used the authority the cookbook lent them to opine on a wide range of domestic issues that went far beyond the household, from economics to citizenship. Cooking advice served as social commentary, and, as in the case of Simmons's text, a forum for proposing unusual solutions to the nation's problems. The planting of apple trees, *American Cookery* suggests, not only keeps families living in cities healthy, but also serves the common good:

> There is not a single family but might set a tree in some otherwise useless spot, which might serve the two fold use of shade and fruit; . . . and essentially preserve the orchard from the intrusions of boys, &c. which is too common in America. If the boy who thus planted a tree, and guarded and protected it in a useless corner, and carefully engrafted different fruits, was to be indulged free access into orchards, whilst the neglectful boy was prohibited—how many millions of fruit trees would spring into growth—and what a saving to the union. The net saving would in time extinguish the public debt, and enrich our cookery. (17)

Menial tasks such as tending an apple tree are connected to a wider economic and political context, redefining and upgrading domestic work to make it part of building a healthy nation with a responsible and engaged citizenry. The realm of food had traditionally given women a space to engage politically without overstepping the boundaries of propriety. In prerevolutionary times, the boycott of tea and other British imports saw women organize politically into what Nancy Siegel has called "culinary activists," and express their patriotism (54, 58).

Despite Simmons's appeal that women should be able to attain their own livelihood, the text is aware that labor is gender differentiated. When discussing the advantages of growing potatoes, the author concedes that this "would better suit a treatise on agriculture and gardening than this—and be inserted in a book which would be read by the farmer, instead of his amiable daughter" (11). But despite the concession that cultivating potatoes may not be a topic of interest to a female readership, the paragraph ends with the announcement: "If no one treats on the subject [the profitable raising of potatoes], it may appear in the next edition" (11). Here the author establishes the cookbook as contributing to a wider political dialogue. Even if the author did not think of women as farmers or the ones to raise potatoes on a grand scale, they were fit to engage in economic and agricultural discussions, and participants in public debates who could expect to be taken seriously. In another place, the author encourages readers to start rabbit farms for their own benefit but also for the good of the nation, and includes a quick calculation on the capital one would need to start such a farm (9). *American Cookery* is notable not only because of its attempt to define a national cuisine, but also for claiming that women actively engage on many levels, thanks to their work and their expertise, in building the nation.

The second edition, lacking the first seventeen pages of commentary that made the first edition so remarkable, was more frequently reprinted and plagiarized over the next few decades, relieving the text of some of its political potential. But the second edition had its own political moments. Simmons added recipes such as "Election Cake," "Independence Cake," and "Federal Pan Cake" (while also retaining the traditional "Queens Cake" and "Royal Paste," perhaps covering all her bases), thus giving her dishes political resonance by tying them explicitly to themes of national governance.[39]

Not only were her titles explicitly patriotic, but some of the ingredients Simmons called for in her recipes were politically charged, for instance Madeira wine. The British began to tax the popular Madeira wine with the Revenue Act (or Sugar Act) of 1764, part of the chain of events that eventually launched the Revolution. Simmons's use of Madeira wine in the text must have resonated for her readers with the benefits of a post-mercantilist market structure and newly gained economic independence. Similarly politically loaded were sugar and molasses, imported articles that had become luxury items after the Sugar Act, and were now liberally used in Simmons's dishes (more than half of the recipes in *American Cookery* are sweet). It is not without irony that recipes that celebrated American independence by using sugar, Madeira, and other items such as curry supported via consumption colonialism in other parts of the world, and slavery in the Caribbean.[40]

While Simmons's cookbook remained the only known cookbook published by an American author for the next two decades, the many reprints and plagiarized versions of the text attest to its success. Although Americans commonly formulated their own culinary identity in competition with English cooking, English cookbooks still dominated the market, but bowed to the new sense of culinary independence and included recipes geared to an American audience.[41] Authors added appendices for American readers at the turn of the century that reflected the sentiments described above by displaying an accentuated simplicity and featuring corn (but without the republican rhetoric). The 1805 edition of Hannah Glasse's *The Art of Cookery Made Plain and Easy*, a best-seller for almost half a century in the English and American markets, included an appendix on "the American Mode of Cooking" that opened with three recipes using cornmeal (among them one for hasty pudding, or "Mush" [137]). Also included were recipes for "Pumpkin-Pie," "Dough Nuts" and "Cranberry Tarts," and advice on how to make "Maple Sugar" (188, 136, 138, 140). Other recipes listed in this section were markedly simplified versions of English recipes, apparently thought to accommodate the republican taste of the American audience (137–43). But with increasing urbanization under way, the onset of industrialization, and a changing global political and economic structure in which the United States had to position itself, American society underwent dramatic changes, and so did the notion of what an American cuisine should be. A fascination with the new culinary possibilities urban markets offered, as well as nostalgia for an imagined colonial simplicity and romanticized country life, started to dominate concepts of republican cuisine in the early nineteenth century.

AN AMERICAN PAINTER'S PALATE: RAPHAELLE PEALE'S FOOD STILL LIFES

Cookbooks, political discourse, and poetry were not alone in shaping ideas of American cooking and American identity. In the course of the nineteenth century, food still lifes became an important medium for conveying ideas about what the American table should look like. After the Revolution, American professional painters sought to redefine art as a democratic endeavor and detach it from its association with European luxury, decadence, and sensuality as well as aristocratic patronage. Monumental depictions of revolutionary events became a vogue; they traveled through the States and could be viewed by the public for an entrance fee. In method, American painters were inspired by ancient Greek and Roman art and Enlightenment theory, expressed through classical simplicity, austerity, and geometric forms. In the search for an American interpretation of the European tradition that would interest a non-aristocratic audience, American painters moved to genres they regarded as more democratic and hoped would appeal to a new class of sponsors, such as merchants and tradesmen, as aristocratic patrons were no longer readily available.[42] Landscapes and representations of American nature became an important point of definition for American artists and symbols of national pride. Content that required no further explanation or knowledge of classical literature and ancient history was believed more appropriate for a democratic society, and complicated allegories fell out of fashion. Portraiture, from which most professional artists lived, became more realistic, distancing itself from the flattery that was common in court paintings.

The first professional painter to explore the political and economic possibilities of food still lifes was Raphaelle Peale, son of Charles Willson Peale, an important artist in the revolutionary and federal period, known not only for his portraiture but also for his devotion to natural history and Enlightenment science. The older Peale closely linked education and art within democratic culture to enable Americans to participate in the intellectual discussions of their time, and was one of the American thinkers to conceptualize the role of art in nation building. He founded the first public museum in the United States. A good example of how republican thought and economic concerns changed portraiture is his rendering of a Baltimore merchant, *William Smith and His Grandson* (1788), showing Smith in front of an architectural structure with classical details and a landscape of orchards, in a moment of tender engagement with his grandchild (fig. 1). The agricultural landscape and classicist facade symbolically merge democratic thought with an agrarian society. The child holding a quill and a piece of fruit fuses the cultivation of land with the cultivation of the mind. An open book, from which Smith may have been reading to the boy, invokes the education and intellectual engagement of the American elite. As it seems that the grandfather has cut the fruit from a branch and given it to the youth, this may indicate that the following generation is raised within the spirit of the founding fathers and will be able to enjoy the fruits of what they sowed. Thanks to a few props and the specific setting, the painting becomes a narrative of republican citizenship and virtue. The absences are telling, too. The image is a

FIGURE 1. Charles Willson Peale, *William Smith and His Grandson,* 1788. Oil on canvas. Reproduced by permission of the Virginia Museum of Fine Arts, Robert G. Cabell and Maude Morgan Cabell Foundation and the Arthur and Margaret Glasgow Fund. Photo: Katherine Wetzel, © Virginia Museum of Fine Arts.

patriarchal idyll in which power is effortlessly maintained and handed down from fathers to sons; those who work the fields, build the house, and sew the clothes remain invisible, echoing their absence from the political franchise.

In the 1810s the younger Peale started to exhibit still lifes, mostly of food, and eventually became the first professional American painter specializing in the genre. His oeuvre of still lifes spanning from the early 1800s to the 1820s reflects the changes that were taking place in the conceptualization of food as an expression of nationalism caused by a rising middle class, technological and scientific advancement, and urbanization.

Peale made food still-life paintings fashionable, partly by understanding and utilizing the symbolic value food carried at this time.[43] As in Europe, in the early republic, still lifes initially ranked low in the hierarchy of artistic appreciation.[44] They were thought to be decorative, mere imitations of nature, more reproduction than interpretation, a mechanical rather than an artistic pursuit. Peale infused the genre with new significance. His paintings were thoroughly composed in soft colors, the light focused on the apples and nuts, giving the quotidian new importance. Transposing the ordinary into the artistic, he challenged assumptions of what constituted high and low art. His still lifes depicting simple repasts in modest settings participated in shaping notions of what constituted a republican lifestyle and an American cuisine. They reflect the change these concepts underwent when the United States slowly began to move from an agrarian to an increasingly industrialized and urban society: hanging in the dining rooms of the urban middle class, who had stopped making their livings directly from the fruit of the land, they served as reminders of the country's agrarian roots and admonitions of republican virtue.

Peale had a wide range of European still-life traditions to draw upon, whether French, Dutch, Flemish, or Spanish (tellingly, British painters had not produced their own school of still-life paintings).[45] Most prominently, Dutch painters had created an authoritative corpus of still lifes in the seventeenth century that was mostly sponsored by a wealthy class of merchants. This, as Nicolai Cikovsky writes in "Democratic Illusions," must have held some attraction for an American painter "at a time of high national consciousness and democratic feeling—because of the political and social pertinence of its associations with republican government and middle-class culture" (47). Dutch still lifes by iconic painters such as Jan Davidszoon de Heem were problematic models, however. They favored tables and shelves bowing under the weight of piles of food and glittering dinnerware, unabashedly displaying their owner's wealth and praising their patron's success as well as celebrating the abundance of the nation and God's creation in general (Cikovsky 46–47). Peale's still lifes, while borrowing from Dutch tradition, were also influenced by Spanish still-life paintings that were austere in composition and color, and engaged a harsh, almost otherworldly contrast between light and dark.

While copying the simplicity of this *bodegón* tradition, Peale did not feature the religious contemplation and mystic quality of the Spaniards. Instead, he concentrated on the secular. Peale's view of the wonders of nature was refracted through a scientific rather than religious lens. In his austerity, he created an almost modern aesthetic, and a new way of painting that drew on European models but did not copy them. His carefully rendered objects, depicted with flaws, spots, and bruises, attempt to trick viewers into believing that what they see is real. By tempting them to reach out to touch the scene in front of them, the images draw the viewer into the painting.[46] These *trompe l'oeil* still lifes do not exhibit wealth and abundance, nor do they seem to contemplate the fleetingness of time or life as memento mori, another established purpose of the genre. The few objects are carefully composed, often in a loose symmetry. The background is dark and the objects brightly illuminated so as to put their texture and condition under a scientific light. Peale's images are reminiscent of botanical drawings. His symmetrical compositions reflect not only the architectural and aesthetic ideals of the time but also a nation-state concerned with checks and balances, as a National Gallery of Art curator suggests, thus executing the rational paradigms of Enlightenment philosophy on a visual level.[47] In this way Peale created a decisively American version of the food still life that reflected republican values, as his arrangements featured a conscious simplicity, modest pleasures that are earned by one's labor and can be shared by many. They emphasized reasoning and the control of appetites, and cherished the society's agricultural roots. Peale's deliberately humble arrangements seemed to forgo markers of social distinction, and valued self-sufficiency and self-control. The small format he painted in was not aimed at public spaces such as galleries or courthouses, but at private and domestic spaces where art could give pleasure during everyday activities. The beginning of the nineteenth century saw the assignment of special spaces for eating in middle-class homes. Food still lifes gained popularity at the same time, and became the preferred decoration for dining rooms.[48] Besides their decorative effect, they reflected their owners' desire to display their commitment to republican thought.

Alexander Nemerov argues that Peale's work bridged the period of transition from a Jeffersonian view of republican virtue grounded in agricultural self-sufficiency to the Madisonian acceptance of market forces and the rapid continental expansion that followed.[49] Peale's early still lifes typically evoked the spirit of pride in the homespun that informed Franklin, Barlow, and Simmons's work. In *Corn and Cantaloupe* (1813; see cover illustration), Peale also echoes their reverence for maize by having an ear of corn dominate the painting, husked just enough to reveal a small strip of fresh and perfectly aligned yellow kernels, thus placing corn at the center of the American table. Behind the corn gleams domestic stoneware rather than imported porcelain—like the corn, a sign of independence from British tastes and imports.[50] The rough setting idealizes simplicity and frugality, and invites the viewer to enjoy an American harvest.

An increasing urbanization and industrialization brought porcelain into Peale's later paintings, along with fruit raised in hothouses and sold at urban markets such as in his *Strawberries, Nuts, &c* (1822) (fig. 2). In these still lifes, Peale celebrated new American wealth and expanding trade. But even here, his pictures show bruised fruit and fruit with stems and leaves, indicating that it was raised, not bought, and not grown for the market, but to be eaten by those who grew it. This was a nostalgic reflection at a time when the emerging urban middle class increasingly started to purchase foods that previously had been raised and produced in the home, such as breads, fruits, and meat—all of which appear on Peale's carefully staged tables. Pleasingly arranged, ready to be consumed, the food presents a moment of peace earned through hard work—even if those for whose consumption the still lifes were meant no longer had to directly engage in agricultural labor to eat. The feasts Peale serves are modest affairs, framed within the mode of their production, making them fundamentally different from European still lifes depicting opulence. Peale's works represented republicanism in muted colors, reminiscent of the pleasure Barlow took in a plate of corn mush. A sprig of blackberries casually draped over a plate becomes an impromptu dessert, a chunk of cheese with three crackers or a roughly cut watermelon decorated with a morning glory a repast.[51] The stems and leaves reference freshness—suggesting that the fruits were just picked from the garden—thus establishing intermediacy between the harvest and the eater (see fig. 3). The stems and leaves bear witness to the labor that went into the produce, reminding the viewer that this food was raised, cared for, and picked by someone. Like Barlow's poem and the first edition of Simmons's cookbook, both describing not only the preparation but

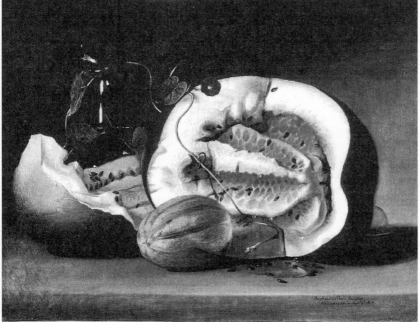

FIGURE 2. Raphaelle Peale, *Strawberries, Nuts, &c,* 1822. Oil on wood panel. Reproduced by permission of the Art Institute of Chicago, gift of Jamee J. and Marshall Field.

FIGURE 3. Raphaelle Peale, *Melons and Morning Glories,* 1813. Oil on canvas. Reproduced by permission of the Smithsonian American Art Museum, gift of Paul Mellon.

FIGURE 4. Raphaelle Peale, *Still Life with Dried Fish (A Herring)*, 1815. Oil on wood panel. Private collection. Photo: © Christie's Images / Bridgeman Images.

also the raising and marketing of produce, the close relation between food and work attests that this is the fruit of a household's own labor and therefore duly earned, not granted or seized from the exploitation of other people's labor, thus expounding a republican ideal that ignored the actual conditions of agriculture in early America.

Later still lifes, such as *Still Life with Dried Fish (A Herring)* (1815) or *Still Life with Steak* (1817), also depict the work that went into the preparation of food; they are set not at the dining table, but at the kitchen table (figs. 4, 5). Instead of an inviting meal, the viewer beholds a few ingredients that, the pictures seem to suggest, are ready to be prepared. A piece of meat, a cabbage, some carrots, and a turnip may become a stew; a fish, an onion, and herbs are about to be pickled, thus creating what one could call recipe still lifes, paintings that show a dish disassembled into its ingredients. As in "The Hasty Pudding" and Simmons's text, kitchen work is of political and social importance in Peale's paintings and equal to the act of eating (thus veiling the existing class differences in U. S. society). The acts of farming, cooking, and eating become one.

Like the authors discussed above, Peale depicted the American table as a preindustrial, agricultural idyll, even after the redware was replaced by silver

FIGURE 5. Raphaelle Peale, *Still Life with Steak*, 1817. Oil on wood panel. Courtesy Munson-Williams-Proctor Arts Institute / Art Resource, NY.

bowls, porcelain, and crystal; fruit was replaced by more elaborate cakes as dessert; and sugar began appearing in some of the images, as in *Lemons and Sugar* (1822), which are ready to become lemonade (fig. 6). Fruits with stems and leaves still reminded the viewer of America's rural roots, but Peale's images increasingly recorded urban middle-class life, referencing gardens rather than farms. Like Barlow's agrarian utopia, or Simmons's civic apple orchards, farming in Peale's still lifes is a romantic reference to republican origins in an urban context rather than a reflection of life on a real farm. In spite of the agricultural self-sufficiency celebrated in them, most of Peale's later arrangements showed the benefits of living in modern metropolitan centers and the pleasures of consumption by increasingly including objects that were no longer produced in the home.

These later paintings often include books, European dinnerware, and fruit that was imported or raised in modern greenhouses. Farming and agriculture now appear as genteel, mostly metaphorical occupations anchoring American middle-class citizens symbolically to their soil.[52] Peale's oeuvre thus reflected changes the United States underwent in the first decades of the nineteenth

FIGURE 6. Raphaelle Peale, *Lemons and Sugar*, 1822. Oil on canvas. Courtesy of the Reading Public Museum, Reading, Pennsylvania.

century, culinarily as well culturally. Improvements in transportation technology, especially the introduction of steamboats and the construction of canals that connected agricultural areas to urban centers, changed the diet of Americans who had disposable income. Regional imports were now widely available throughout the country in produce markets and a growing number of shops such as butcheries, bakeries, and groceries.[53] The increasing urban population could rely on food items that grew in other parts of the country for their daily meals. Scientific advances allowed the raising of fruit and vegetables independent of climatic limitations, which enabled wealthy citizens to expand their diets. The growth of cities and the middle class also changed early notions of an American identity based on agricultural labor and equality, and reformulated earlier versions of republican cuisines by focusing instead on self-control and the discipline of appetites.

From the citizen who incorporated democratic ideals by eating corn dishes to the simplicity of Simmons's table to the quiet elegance of Peale's still lifes, the table was prepared by the 1820s for the first best-selling cookbooks and nutritional experts such as Sylvester Graham and Lydia Maria Child. Both Graham and Child took up the idea of simplicity as the guideline for an American cuisine that was both unassuming and healthy. The resulting republican cuisine presented a nostalgic image of an idealized agrarian settler nation that historically never existed, propagating a past that was imagined as without social injustice and with perfect equality. As these were considered times when the nation was healthy, free of corruption and vice, the food these early celebrities promoted was considered healthy for the individual body as well as the nation. While in Barlow's time everyone who ate corn could become free and an American by proxy, Child and Graham promoted citizenship as a daily duty in which constant self-control was the foundation of full citizen rights. Peale's depictions of the middle-class table had introduced the notion that even in the presence of a cornucopia, true republican pleasure consists in self-restraint.

DOMESTIC VIRTUE AND CITIZENSHIP IN THE WORK OF LYDIA MARIA CHILD

In the 1820s, American society underwent major changes: it started to move from an agricultural to a market economy, with a declining number of Americans directly involved in farming. More Americans than ever before lived in cities.[54] Technological developments encouraged westward expansion and travel. Westward expansion also provided a greater variety and greater quantities of food to Americans.[55] Many joined social movements such as abolitionism and temperance to campaign for social reform. The traditional organization of class, gender, and race came under scrutiny. In reaction to the dramatic changes, nostalgia for an ideal prerevolutionary America—simpler, purer, and safer than the contemporary one—became popular, but often framed and presented within the new amenities that urban and middle-class life had to offer. In the gradually increasing number of American cookbooks that found publishers, a new ideal of an American cuisine emerged that celebrated imagined ancestral frontier cooking as the epitome of the nation's culinary achievement, while concurrently defending rigid class or gender relations. It also advanced a middle-class citizenship ideal based on rationality, orderliness, frugality, and self-restraint, and understood middle-class lifestyles as the expression of genuine Americanness. One of the most popular examples of this version of republican cuisine was Lydia

Maria Child's *The Frugal Housewife* (1829), "dedicated to those not ashamed of economy," as the cover announced, a manifesto of thriftiness and republican virtue.[56] Cookbooks and household manuals in the early nineteenth century, mostly still imported from England, commonly catered to the affluent and/or socially ambitious who would be likely to invest in such a book. Child's American household advice was directed at (and enthusiastically endorsed by) a broader demographic, as it consisted emphatically of down-to-earth and money-saving recipes.[57] By 1842 the text had gone through twenty-eight editions.[58] Framing quotations from Benjamin Franklin's *Poor Richard's Almanack* defined frugality for her intended middle-class audience not as an unavoidable necessity but a conscious choice and a prudent way to live.[59] "True economy," Child claimed, "is a careful treasurer in the service of benevolence; and where they are united, respectability, prosperity, and peace will follow" (8).

At the time of the book's publication, Child was already an established writer of historical fiction (most famously her novel *Hobomok: A Tale of Early Times* [1824]) and children's literature, and was known as a promoter of rights for Native Americans. Later in her career she became an outspoken abolitionist and women's rights advocate, which eventually stalled her career. Child wrote advice literature, such as *The Frugal Housewife,* to support herself and her husband. The book addresses families who live on a budget but at least occasionally employ one or more servants, families in which the women are literate and able to spend money on a cookbook. Child's own reference to her readers as "poor" may therefore be slightly misleading (7).

The text is critical of any kind of waste, be it of time or money, and of social ambitions. As the historian Susan Williams observes, Child attempted to counter "European aristocratic culinary decadence with American republican virtue" (63). Like Barlow and Simmons, she claimed that the consumption of food was crucial to building national character. But where Barlow stressed the pleasure in virtuous eating, and where Simmons tried with herbs and skill to substitute what was not available or difficult to obtain, Child promoted cooking that was deliberately bland and eating ruled by health concerns and economy rather than good taste. Her version of republican virtue consisted in the conscious choice to do without the growing number of goods easily available to Americans, because, she thought, such consumption would create either debt or decadence. Child, who in her political writing was critical of expansionist policies, promoted in her manual frontier-style cooking (making do with what is available) for it was, she argued, in the best interests of the individual as well as of the country.[60] Virtue becomes the leading maxim for eating and cooking, the pursuit of good health and avoidance of any kind of temptation the duty of American citizens. Child's catalog of advice for maintaining one's health seems an arbitrary mix of physical and moral issues. "Rise early," she writes, "Eat simple foods.... Wash very often, and rub the skin thoroughly with a hard brush," or "Do not make children cross-eyed, by having their hair hang about their foreheads, where they see it continually" (87–88). Her advice focuses on discipline, avoiding indulgence, and eschewing vanity as much as on health issues.

The authorial voice is often moralizing, teaching its audience "how money can be *saved*, not how it can be *enjoyed*" (her italics) (7). Among other money-savvy tips, she recommends putting children to work, as much in order that they not be idle as to earn income:

> In this country, we are apt to let children romp away their existence.... [A] child of six can be made useful.... They can knit garters, suspenders, and stockings; they can make patchwork and braid straw; they can make mats for the table, and mats for the floor; they can weed the garden, and pick cranberries from the meadow, to be carried to market. (4)

Child's manual becomes a jeremiad at times, criticizing the laxness and "extravagance of all classes" she perceives around her (6). She warns darkly that laziness will be the downfall of the republic:

> Nations do not plunge at once into ruin.... [T]he causes which bring about the final blow, are scarcely perceptible in the beginning; but they increase in numbers, and in power; they press harder and harder upon the energies and virtue of a people.... A republic without industry, economy, and integrity, is Samson shorn of his locks. A luxurious and idle *republic!* Look at the phrase!—The words were never made to be married together; every body sees it would be death to one of them. And are not we becoming luxurious and idle? Look at our steamboats, arid stages, and taverns! (99)

With her domestic version of the wisdom of *Poor Richard's Almanack,* she envisioned a nation free of vanity, indulgence, and luxury, governed by "honesty and prudence" (6). Like Barlow, she envisioned the ideal United States as morally centered on agriculture, "for we look to that class of people, as the strongest hold of republican simplicity, industry, and virtue" (102). Those not practicing a trade and not producing goods ("adventurers, swindlers, broken down traders,—all that rapidly increasing class of idlers, too genteel to work, and too proud to beg" [102]) do not fare too well in Child's estimation, and are a threat to the nation.

Domestic practices are tightly intertwined with domestic policies, and one of the most dreaded threats to domestic economies is debt, be it public or individual. Spending money beyond one's income, Child argues, "is wrong—morally wrong, so far as the individual is concerned; and injurious beyond calculation to the interests of our country. To what are the increasing beggary, and discouraged exertions of the present period owing?" (6) Frugality is therefore not simply caused by individual necessity but programmatic for the good of the country. Engaging in it honors the republican spirit in which the nation was born. The constant control over and rejection of pleasure Americans are asked to demonstrate in the act of eating disciplines them into ideal citizens, mindful of the nation's resources and embracing of their social status. Avoiding aristocratic waste and debt preserves society from injustice and hubris.

Child warns especially against any form of entertainment and travel, as class boundaries may deteriorate when people engage in activities that used to be reserved for the upper classes. In an association of spatial with social mobility, Child tells of farmers and servants who leave "their place" to enjoy the theater or travel and are ruined in the process. Giving in to the desire of wanting more than what has been allotted to one is severely punished in Child's universe. Her vision of a local, self-sufficient lifestyle, reminiscent of Barlow's New England agrarian idyll, is a call for the maintenance of the social order:

> Self-denial, in proportion to the narrowness of your income, will eventually be the happiest and most respectable course for you and yours. If you are prosperous, perseverance and industry will not fail to place you in such a situation as your ambition covets; and if you are not prosperous, it will be well for your children that they have not been educated to higher hopes than they will ever realize. (5)

Here Child presents a static model of social development, conservative in outlook and rather anti-utopian in scope, but simultaneously sees pride in middle-class status, redefining the middle class as America's true backbone. By giving advice to city dwellers as well as people in the countryside, she creates the idea of class spanning the newly emerging rural-urban divide. Under headlines such as "Soap," she advises making the best use of the resources available, be it in the countryside or the city. But she also recommends cooperation: "If practicable, get a friend in the country to procure you a quantity of lard, butter, and eggs, at the time they are cheapest" (16), emphasizing the merit of alternative private economies beyond the urban markets that developed in the 1820s.

Surprisingly, given Child's political engagement for women's rights, her text advances a fairly conservative stance on the role of women in society. Child admonishes parents to educate girls according to their future station in life, and not to nourish hopes or expectations of overcoming the conditions in which they were raised. An illustrative anecdote tells the story of a low-income family that raises a daughter with music and dance lessons and sends her to school instead of having her mend clothes or contribute in other ways to the family's fortune. The mother, proud to give her child such a genteel education, defends her decision: "*Now* is her time to enjoy herself, you know. Let her take all the comfort she can, while she is single! . . . I am determined that she should enjoy herself while she is young" (95). The narrator is scandalized by such irresponsible and potentially gender-subversive conduct:

> What a lesson is taught a girl in that sentence, "Let her enjoy herself all she can, while she is single!" Instead of representing domestic life as the gathering place of the deepest and purest affections; as the sphere of woman's enjoyments as well as of her duties; as, indeed, the whole world to her; that one pernicious sentence teaches a girl to consider matrimony desirable because "a good match" is a triumph of vanity, and it is deemed respectable to be "well settled in the world" but that it is a necessary sacrifice of her freedom and her gayety. (95)

Failing to prepare girls for their roles as wives and mothers, Child concludes, leads to disappointment, unhappy marriages, and women evading what should be their "whole world." Women's unpaid labor, strictly confined within the home, is not only central to individual fulfillment, but of the greatest importance for the stability of the republic. As Carolyn Karcher argues, this needs to be read within the context of an emerging ideology of separate spheres and "true womanhood," an ideology that established class privilege, racist sentiments legitimizing an imagined inherent superiority of whiteness, and a hegemonic view of proper conduct for white middle-class women.[61] All of this, household advice in the nineteenth century helped to promote and circulate. Under the ideology of "true womanhood," women were removed as far as possible from the accounts and budgets of their families, as handling money began to be considered insufficiently genteel for women.[62] Child's women, however, were actively engaged in their households and building their fortunes—at the expense of their self-realization.[63]

Child's parsimony extends to the recipes. The food is mostly bland and artless (despite the liberal use of alcohol, brown sugar, and molasses), sticking firmly to the less-inspired dishes of British heritage. The recipe for asparagus reads: "Asparagus should be boiled fifteen or twenty minutes; half an hour if old" (32), making no suggestions for the use of herbs or spices as Simmons's cookbook did. Taste becomes here a marker of distinction, but in contrast to what Bourdieu envisions, it is the deliberate absence of taste that marks class superiority. The voluntary renunciation of taking pleasure in eating serves as sign of self-control and a commitment to a stable social order. In keeping with her austere vision of a national cuisine, Child's recipes promote national products over imports, and locally grown produce over fruits that need to be transported from other parts of the country. While a decade earlier, Raphaelle Peale had in his paintings of republican repasts included generous quantities of lemons and oranges raised in hothouses or transported up north, Child's version of American cuisine uses citrus sparingly and only as a spice.[64] Instead of encouraging the use of ingredients that were the fruit of imperialist ambitions, such as the removal of Native Americans in Georgia and other states, Child offers ample advice on how to substitute non-local ingredients with what is available locally.[65] Both Child and Peale advocate a simple republican cuisine, but by painting lemons, oranges, sugar, imported china, and silverware, Peale implicitly endorsed territorial expansion and the role of the United States in a global market. Child's cuisine is explicitly anti-expansionist, and advocates an isolationist vision in its promotion of local ingredients and economies. Occasionally, Child refers to Old World cookery, but in a way that clearly demonstrates her resentment: "French coffee is so celebrated, that it may be worth while to tell how it is made; though no prudent housekeeper will make it" (83). Instead of coffee and tea, she recommends beer, "a good family drink" that can be brewed at home and from locally grown crops. How the British do things she declares entirely useless for the American family. She added the "American" in *The American Frugal Housewife* to distinguish her book from the British *The Frugal Housewife* by Susannah Carter, the text Simmons quoted from so freely. Distancing herself from Carter emphasizes the outspokenly nationalist character of the work: "[I]t was the intention of the author of the *American Frugal Housewife*, to have given an Appendix from the *English Frugal Housewife;* but upon examination, she found the book so little fitted to the wants of this country, that she has been able to extract but little" (121). Child's declaration that there is nothing the English could teach Americans is an assertion that appears repeatedly in the book (2, 122). While the dishes Child promotes are firmly based in the British tradition, they reappear here purged of any suspicion of decadence, and thus fit for the American table.

Most consequential for the nineteenth century is Child's claim that eating in the simple and frugal manner she describes is not only patriotic but healthy, too. Her concept of health was still firmly based in the notion of the Galen model, in which four humors regulate the body: blood, phlegm, and yellow and black bile, and they need to be in balance to permit a long and productive life.[66] Individual health is not only a personal choice: all the citizens of a republic owe it commitment and service, just as it is obligated to protect its citizens. The pursuit of health is framed within a discourse of self-control and accountability. She thus introduces the idea of healthy living as a citizenship right as well as a duty, as it is the foundation for a healthy society.[67] These ideas opened the way for health reformers later in the century, such as Sylvester Graham, who emerged from the movement for evangelical renewal.

"BREAD OF OUR MOTHERS": SYLVESTER GRAHAM AND THE HEALTH OF THE NATION

Sylvester Graham, who was engaged in the temperance movement in the 1820s, started in the 1830s to promote vegetarianism and homemade bread as a way to maintain virtue, health, and the social order. He became the first prominent health reformer of the nineteenth century, basing his nutritional advice mostly on scripture. His appeals for healthy living were always accompanied by political concerns and the promotion of patriotism. Especially in his campaign for home-baked bread, he reappropriated the idea of republican cooking as the foundation for a sound nation. Industrialization and urbanization in the 1820s had led to the commercialization of bread consumption. In the 1830s, when Graham launched his health campaigns, bread could be bought ready-made from bakeries and groceries in many parts of the country, marking the modernization of everyday life.

Like Barlow, who had endowed cornmeal with almost magical properties, including health, vitality, democracy, and patriotism, Graham transferred corn's republican virtues to unbolted wheat. Nationwide access to wheat had become possible through westward expansion, aggressive territorial policies, and the opening of the Erie Canal in 1825, permitting the economical transport of wheat back to the East Coast. Wheat widely replaced traditional corn in many dishes. By embracing wheat as the stuff Americans were made of, Graham, unlike Child, implicitly endorsed expansion and the fruits of empire.

The concept of health became an important vehicle for many nineteenth-century reformers to legitimize a moral imperative. Graham in *A Treatise on Bread* projected the "invention" of bread making onto a vague, ancient past of humankind, anchored by references to the five books of Moses and the Roman Empire, thus creating an illustrious ancestry for the American nation. Conceding that processed food such as baked bread is a hallmark of civilization and humanity in general, he argued with reference to Genesis that food is best when left in as natural a state as possible (26). Unbolted wheat bread, unleavened and produced in the home, Graham claimed, is healthiest and therefore best for "our country" and "our nature" (26). Graham connected individual well-being with the well-being of the nation, both of which were to be produced in the home kitchen. Kyla Wazana Tompkins calls this kind of rhetorical link the "imperial metonymy between body, home, and nation" (81).[68] Any disobedience of his rules, Graham proposed, would have severe consequences by violating natural, historical, and religious law: "A very large proportion of all the diseases and ailments in civic life, are originated by causes which are introduced into the alimentary canal as articles of diet; and disturbance and derangement of function—obstructions, debility and irritations, are among the most important elements of those diseases" (52). Poor eating habits cause the "disturbance and derangement of function" and sabotage civic life. Eating healthily becomes an act of public duty, and in a Foucauldian sense serves as a measure of biopolitical intervention to keep a population productive and discipline its citizens, as they were now asked to eat with self-control—a visible sign of their willingness to sacrifice their own pleasure for the greater good.

Graham's contribution was central. When he began his crusade, processed bread made from fine white meal had become a marker of social status and urban living. In *A Treatise on Bread,* it is described not only as unhealthy, but as standing for the decline of republican values. Like many health reformers in the nineteenth century, Graham believed that rich foods led to disease, madness, and social decline. Republican food was simple, wholesome, and avoided any kind of overstimulation. Graham seemingly promoted an anti-elitist standpoint, but his call for moderate consumption came at a time when a broader slice of the American population had access to items that before were reserved for the rich—not only white bread, but sugar, tea, sweets, and meat—all of which were prohibited under Graham's regime. Even more than Child, who assumed that her readers would not have sufficient means to procure what were formerly luxury goods, Graham called upon the middle class to voluntarily renounce these foods in the interest of republican virtue and thus to maintain the moral fiber of the nation. Implicitly, Graham's stance protected class interests, as the alleged moral superiority of the middle class, demonstrated through their controlled eating habits, implicitly legitimized newly earned political and economic privileges. Health food, framed as true republican food, identified the middle-class eater as the bearer of patriotic commitment, as Graham associated simple lifestyles (and whole-grain bread) with the virtues of an agricultural republic that he located a generation earlier:

> Who that can look back thirty or forty years to those blessed days of New England's prosperity and happiness, when our good mothers used to make the family bread, but can well remember how long and how patiently those excellent matrons stood over their bread troughs, kneading and moulding their dough and who with such recollections cannot also well remember the delicious bread that these mothers used invariably to set before them? There was a natural sweetness and richness in it which made it always desirable; and which we cannot now vividly recollect, without feeling a strong desire to partake again of such bread as our mothers made for us in the days of our childhood. (92–93)

Such nostalgia for the individual's and the nation's childhood recalls Barlow's nostalgia in his idyllic description of the rural New England of his youth. This peaceful vision stands in stark contrast to Graham's depiction of the practices of contemporary professional bakers, striving to produce the white, fluffy bread that their customers misguidedly craved. To gain the desired lightness, bread was leavened with chemical accelerators, which Graham despised as modern inventions, instead of yeast. Since the price for fine meal fluctuated, commercial bakers mixed in fillers such as beans, peas, or chalk, making processed bread, he claimed, not only unhealthy but dishonest, too (42–48). Graham's concerns about commercially produced bread reflected social fears about the erosion of a republican economy based on sustenance, familial production, and neighborly help, and its replacement by capitalist structures without a developed ethical code of behavior. This could lead,

Graham feared, to the dissolution of society, and eventually anarchy. The remedy for a heartless modern economy he found in the symbolic return to a mother's labor of love and a domestic economy based on skilled but unpaid labor:

> [I]t is the wife, the mother only—she who loves her husband and her children as woman ought to love, and who rightly perceives the relations between the dietetic habits and physical and moral condition of her loved ones, and justly appreciates the importance of good bread to their physical and moral welfare—she alone it is, who will be ever inspired by that cordial and unremitting affection and solicitude which will excite the vigilance, secure the attention, and prompt the action requisite to success, and essential to the attainment of that maturity of judgment and skilfulness [*sic*] of operation, which are the indispensable attributes of a perfect bread-maker. (105–6)

Home-baked bread was therefore an antidote not only to dyspepsia but also to the erosion of republican values, now promulgated by women in the domestic space. Graham's vision gave women a central role within the republic without challenging the political inequality that denied them full participation.

In contrast to Child's, Graham's nutritional advice embraced the idea of an American empire.[69] New lands seized offered the opportunity for individual and national renewal: "They who have never eaten bread made of wheat, recently produced by a pure, virgin soil have but a very imperfect notion of the deliciousness of good bread; such as is often to be met with in the comfortable log houses in our western country" (34). He not only expunges in a single sentence the sacrifices that accompanied the European settlement of the West, but also extinguishes all traces of indigenous cultures. The West presented here is empty, free for farmers of European origin to take. The soil is pure and virgin, perpetuating the assertion of the earliest colonists that indigenous peoples had no right to the land because they did not cultivate it. Those living off the produce of the exhausted soil of the East Coast and the South are invited to partake in the expansion of the nation by enjoying the fruits of conquest in the form of whole-wheat bread. Eating coarse bread (and supporting territorial expansion) becomes an act of citizenship: it "is most certain, that until the agriculture of our country is conducted in strict accordance with physiological truth, it is not possible for us to realize those physical, and intellectual, and moral, and social, and civil blessings for which the human constitution and our soil and climate are naturally capacitated," he writes (36). Taking the land and eating the bread are mandatory for Americans who want to live up to their full potential as individuals and as a people.

Graham's contribution to an American empire becomes even more pronounced when he argues that eating coarse wheat bread makes a nation strong and virile, as in the following passage that praises unbolted wheat bread as the food of champions:

> It was a fact well understood by the ancients, that this bread was much more conducive to the general health and vigor of their bodies, and in every way better adapted to nourish and sustain them than that made of the fine flour. And accordingly, their wrestlers and others who were trained for great bodily power, "ate only the coarse wheaten bread, to preserve them in their strength of limbs." The Spartans were famous for this kind of bread; and we learn from Pliny that the Romans, as a nation, at that period of their history when they were the most remarkable for bodily vigor and personal prowess and achievement, knew no other bread for three hundred years. The warlike and powerful nations which overran the Roman Empire, and finally spread over the greater part of Europe, used no other kind of bread than that which was made of the whole substance of the grain. (60)

In Graham's take on history, those who ate coarse wheat bread won the contest for empire. And now it was the Americans' turn.

In Graham's world, all foreign foods were associated with decadence and moral decay. This corresponded not only with Americans' disdain for European aristocracy but also with their distrust of increasing waves of immigration. From 1814 to 1860, the American population quadrupled, and cities grew denser with immigrants searching for employment. As Gilbert Seldes and others have pointed out, Graham's nutritional advice firmly rejected spices and imported stimulants such as coffee and tea, as they led to moral decline that, it was believed, would manifest itself in masturbation and "excessive" forms of sexual desire.[70] Dismissing imported goods as unhealthy encouraged economic independence as well as the consumption of nationally produced merchandise. This culinary self-sufficiency was reminiscent of the homespun rhetoric of the early republic.

Graham's regime may have given some Americans a sense of control over their bodies and fates in a time of dramatic transition. His nutritional advice helped to integrate ideas of territorial expansion and an American Empire into the rhetoric of republican value and simplicity, and therefore to legitimize expansionist policies.

COOKING CONTEST: REGIONAL, TRANSNATIONAL, AND CLASS-BASED CUISINES IN THE ANTEBELLUM UNITED STATES

While the new iterations of republican cuisine were successful and popular, alternative models did emerge. Republican cuisine promoted middle-class lifestyles and Northeastern recipes as truly American, often featuring a pronouncedly anti-European and isolationist stance, and turning a blind eye to class difference within the United States. Cookbooks such as those by Mary Randolph, Eliza Leslie, and Robert Roberts, who saw American cooking differently, implicitly challenged the republican paradigm.

In featuring Northeastern recipes as truly American, the authors discussed above complied with the region's claim to cultural hegemony. Mary Randolph's *The Virginia House-wife* from 1824 presented a different perspective. It is often referred to as the first Southern cookbook, and it does break with the promotion of Northern fare. Still, Karen Hess has called it "the earliest full-blown American cookbook," arguing that instead of stoically following British culinary traditions, it was eclectic in its selection of methods and dishes, recognizing, among others, the French and Spanish culinary inheritance of the United States.[71] Randolph's text differed in a number of crucial ways from the texts discussed above, and offered an alternative way to conceptualize an American cuisine by including different regions and broadening the scope of what a national cuisine entailed.

Randolph was raised on a plantation, in a family that belonged to the Virginian political and economic elite. Initially able to maintain her upper-class lifestyle in her marriage to her cousin David Randolph, the family fell on hard times after David lost his position as U.S. marshal due to his political views. Mary opened a boarding house in Richmond in 1819 to support her family. After giving up the business and moving to Washington to live with her son, she wrote the cookbook, presumably to earn money.[72] Despite its title's regional specificity, *The Virginia House-wife* included recipes from other parts of the country, most notably some from New England that had by then been canonized as all-American, such as pumpkin pudding. But unlike Simmons and the American appendices that were now commonly added to English cookbooks to appeal to the American market, her recipes also included traditionally Southern ingredients such as sweet potatoes, okra, and catfish, and many ingredients that were considered exotic and rare in *The Frugal Housewife* such as lemons, tomatoes, and oranges. Some well-established recipes she presented with a twist. Her Johnny cakes were made with rice, not cornmeal (113). Besides her awareness of regional diversity, her cuisine also featured broader ethnic inclusion. She incorporated recipes she marked as Spanish and West Indian, and she also made unapologetic use of Italian and French ingredients—all under the rubric of Virginian cooking— thus depicting an American regional cuisine open to the world and (if only mildly) interested in cultural multiplicity. Where she included a cornmeal recipe, she made it "Polenta," giving the humble dish some cosmopolitan flair.[73] As explicitly as these non-British traditions were referenced, African American and Native American contributions went unmentioned.

Economic household management, one of the pillars of republican cooking, appears in *The Virginia House-wife* in the form of "methodical nicety" (xviii). Giving accurate measurements helps by saving resources, Randolph promises, and it also guarantees the success of the end result (and therefore helps to eliminate waste through failed attempts to reproduce a vaguely written recipe). While sharing with republican cooking a commitment to rational and reliable cooking practices, however, Randolph is not interested in simplicity. Her text addresses hostesses of elegant affairs. Often using affordable ingredients, such as the produce one's own garden could provide, she manages to come up with impressive displays. To this end, most of her recipes are accompanied by instructions for how the dish should be served: "serve . . . with lemon cut in thin slices," "serve it up garnished with green pickle and sprigs of parsley," or "serve it up in your sauce boat" (34, 31, 62). Thus the text adds to cooking a visual component that Simmons and Child do not have, as if they were not cooking with an audience in mind. Randolph's dishes are meant for meals that can be shared with non–family members one wishes to impress. She aims to amaze the people for whom she cooks, a notion foreign to texts such as Child's, which warned its readers not to entertain in an elaborate manner. But for Randolph, elegance is an important characteristic of the American table. Dinners are social events rather than meals shared only within the family. That the splendid dinner is a common rather than an exceptional event, Randolph indicates by assuming that her readers have special tools in their possession that are geared to serve fancy dinners, such as sauce boats. While engaging in upper-class decorum, Randolph's advice also allows for shortcuts: a squirrel can stand in for a rabbit, and she gives recipes for the pedestrian catfish, one of which is for an elegant curry (18, 19, 30).

Randolph's text diverges from Simmons and Child's cookbooks in its expectations of class performance. Unlike Barlow, Randolph does not suggest that servants and family members share meals together. In contrast to the communal spirit that often informed the texts of republican cooking, Randolph introduces a household that is strictly organized in hierarchical terms. Servants and slaves (the latter mentioned only once) run the household and make the elegant dinners Randolph describes possible, but cannot be fully trusted. Anticipating a trope from later in the century, servants (who after the Civil War are usually marked as immigrants) are depicted as a necessary liability (xvii). The mistress of the house needs to pay constant attention and maintain control over her household by instilling discipline and serving as a model:

> The Virginia ladies, who are proverbially good managers, employ themselves, while their servants are eating, in washing the cups, glasses, &c.; arranging the cruets, the mustard, salt-sellers, pickle vases, and all the apparatus for the dinner table. This occupies but a short time, and the lady has the satisfaction of knowing that they are in much better order than they would be if left to the servants. (xviii)

While the mistress herself is not expected to cook in Randolph's text, she is expected to exert firm control over the kitchen. Every morning, in Randolph's Virginia, the mistress enters the kitchen to give the cook instructions. After that she devotes her time to preparing the dinner table that always needs to be in such an order that the husband can bring home unexpected dinner guests. The work of the "Virginia ladies" consists of decorating and making finishing touches, matters of taste that cannot be left to people who lack their class background. Taste serves in this context as a marker of genteel birth that cannot be taught or acquired by those who were not so lucky. While servants can be trained and cooks educated, the social hierarchy of the household is unquestionable, as taste is beyond their reach.

The housewife's work, and a family structure that allows women to devote themselves to the finer points of life, are crucial to the well-being of the family and subsequent generations: "The sons bred in such a family will be moral men, of steady habits; and the daughters . . . will each be a treasure to her husband" (xviii). The work of the "Virginia ladies" here becomes the moral fiber of American society.

Unlike the egalitarians Simmons and Child, Randolph writes for an audience that is expected to have dominion over many hands and does not care for equality within the home. Managing these small entities successfully Randolph likens to running a country: "The government of a family, bears a

Lilliputian resemblance to the government of a nation" (ix). Randolph seems to believe that this is enough responsibility for white middle- and upper-class women, and, unlike the authors of republican cuisines, she refrains from any more explicit political and economic commentary, thus relegating educated and well-off women to the home. She thus helped to construct and circulate an ideal of white middle-class femininity that institutionalized itself within the idealized gender organization of the nineteenth century as separate spheres, in which men went out into the marketplace and the political arena while women stayed at home, gaining an increased but firmly confined authority.

Randolph's version, unlike the Northern variations, has little use for piety and endorses social ambition and class performance. Stressing gentility as one of the main characteristics of white, middle-class womanhood, she asserts racial superiority and legitimizes class privilege. In her text, the work her intended readers do is explicitly juxtaposed with the heavy lifting that is left to servants and slaves, removing the labor of white, middle-class women from the realm of physical work and its side effects. Their role is confined to consumption and reproduction, not production. But, as Nancy Hewitt has claimed, the authors of "true womanhood" cultivated "the seeds of destruction that the cult of womanhood itself had sown."[74] Like Simmons and Child, Randolph wrote the cookbook to earn money when her own life defied the ideal she proclaimed. Domestic advice that relegated women to the home suffered from the internal contradiction that it was written by women who wrote for income. This had become possible because the newly emerging idea of domesticity also created a space for women's expertise and authority, and an opportunity to make a living.

Whereas Randolph's *The Virginia House-wife* complicated standard assumptions of republican cuisine by defining American cookery from a Southern and slave-holding perspective, the Philadelphia-based author Eliza Leslie, who wrote a number of successful cookbooks and advice texts, presented an American cuisine fully engaged with its European heritage. Leslie boldly promoted elegance and richness in her meals, which led Child to recommend to her readership that if they did not wish to submit to her stern hand, they should buy Leslie's *Seventy-Five Receipts for Pastry, Cakes, and Sweetmeats* (1828): "I have written for the poor! I have said nothing about *rich* cooking; those who can afford to be epicures will find the best information in the 'Seventy-five Receipts'" (7). Clearly, Child had no love for epicures, so her casual reference to Leslie's first cookbook was likely ironic. But she also assumed that the text was known to her readers, thereby acknowledging Leslie's popularity.

Leslie wrote for an emerging audience of social-climbing Americans interested in adding some elite culture to their menu by adapting French dishes to the cooking skills and ingredients available to them.[75] Leslie's cookbooks are, compared to Child's, cosmopolitan, ambitious, and what Child calls "rich" in all the facets the word entails, rejecting all notions of republican thriftiness. *Seventy-Five Receipts for Pastry, Cakes, and Sweetmeats* is an unapologetic butter-and-sugar fest. People who cannot afford all the expensive ingredients are advised to cut "the spice, wine, brandy, rosewater, essence of lemon," but no changes may be made to the substantial amounts of eggs, butter, sugar, and flour the recipes demand (iv). Leslie, too, was explicitly trying to formulate an American cuisine ("The receipts in this little book are, in every sense of the word, American" [iv]). The American cuisine she presents displays refinement and a new national self-confidence. Her recipes, she assures her readers, are in no way inferior "to any of a similar description made in the European manner" (iv). Her definition of what differentiates European and American cooking entails above all greater practicality: "There is frequently much difficulty in following directions in English and French Cookery Books, not only from their want of explicitness, but from the difference in the fuel, fire-places, and cooking utensils, generally used in Europe and America; and many of the European receipts are so complicated and laborious, that our female cooks are afraid to undertake the arduous task of making any thing from them" (iii). Here the American housewife is depicted as more down-to-earth than English and French ones and too busy to investigate the mysterious ways of European cuisine. The recipes Leslie offers cater to this need. However, the families she addresses employ at least one cook. To those living in cities, she promises they will save money by producing sophisticated pastries at home; to those in the countryside, she promises access to the refinement of the cities (iv).

Where Child chides a young nation for its wastefulness, Leslie sees that its national cuisine needs to prove its worthiness in the international realm. In spite of her rejection of European-style recipes, she has no concerns about including occasional European dishes. In her immensely popular *Directions for Cookery* (1840), "a manual of American housewifery," she promises international recipes "particularly adapted to the domestic economy of the country" (7). She lists a few French recipes, others that call for "maccaroni" [*sic*], vermicelli, and Parmesan cheese, or "China turmeric" as in "Mullagatawny

Soup. As made in India," "Chicken Curry," and "Pilau" (210–11, 24, 25, 29, 146, 147). She also offers an American cuisine that is transregional; in spite of her focus on seafood-heavy New England cuisine such as chowder, lobster, and clam soup (55–56, 37, 38), she also lists recipes for "Ochra Soup" (32), "Chitterlings" (102), "Tomata [sic] Catchup" (177), and "Fried Sweet Potatoes" (186), all of which would rarely be found in republican cooking but by the end of the century would be staples of American cookbooks. While aiming for a cuisine that is elegant and sometimes showy, Leslie, who had some cooking school training, confidently placed among the European recipes such American dishes as "Hominy" or "Indian Corn," "Cat-fish Soup," "Preserved Water-Melon Rind," and "Pumpkin Chips" (182, 36, 237–38, 238–39). In doing so, she placed American cooking on an equal footing with European cuisine.

Unlike Child's rejection of the indulgence and decadence associated with European nobility, Leslie encouraged such pleasures. Her asparagus recipe, half a page long, has the vegetable eaten with toasted bread dipped into savory asparagus broth and melted butter (199). The recipes she included reflect the promise of upward mobility. She spends much time suggesting that country folks can live as richly as town folks by baking and cooking expertly in their own homes. The few foreign recipes speak of travel and European style, without overshadowing the author's pride in American culture.

Her taste for a cosmopolitan and transregional cuisine is also transparent in her later cookbooks, perhaps even more pronouncedly so. *New Receipts for Cooking* (1854) includes even more recipes from the South. In her introduction, she claims that they are equal to French recipes, and that together they are best for the "elegant table." The text also shows her pride in the American heritage. Dishes made from cornmeal she calls "most valuable" (8). She offers an entire chapter on cooking and baking with cornmeal, giving it space and importance. The genuinely American corn-based recipes are presented as the United States' contribution to the cuisines of the world. Any reference to their humbleness has disappeared.

The cookbooks also launched Leslie's career as a writer of non-advice literature.[76] In her fiction, Leslie discussed American ideals within a domestic setting. Here, too, food played an important role. Leslie utilized her short stories to share her expertise and give her readers domestic advice. In "Mrs. Washington Potts," for instance, readers meet young Albina Marsden in the midst of preparing a party. Everything is doomed to go wrong, giving Leslie the opportunity to instruct her readers on coping with the upsets that can come with putting together a social event, one the protagonist desperately wants to be a success. Albina has been set up by her father to live after his death in a small town where the cost of living will not exhaust her inheritance. The setting is rather idyllic, described with words such as "innocence," "modesty," "contentment," "peace," and "simple pleasures" (10). Albina's goodness and wholesomeness are marked not only by her surroundings but also by her domestic skill, signified in the opening, where we find her baking cakes. She represents an ideal of white femininity as indicated not only by her name, but also by her juxtaposition to a "black girl named Drusa, who had been brought up in the family" and who serves as a foil of incompetence to Albina's cleverness (10). The servants in the story perpetually fail, and it is only thanks to Albina's supervision that everything does not dissolve in a general meltdown.

Albina and her mother give a party in honor of Mrs. Washington Potts, who, having lived in Paris and London, considers herself, and is considered by others in the small town, part of the American elite. The Marsden women are smitten with her, and her seemingly superior taste. But, as the first pages already indicate, Washington Potts's character is questionable, and she exploits the Marsden women's adoration shamelessly. In mistreating Albina and her mother, Washington Potts is even worse than the English family, the Montagues, who are also expected to the party as revered guests and whose appearance and demeanor are caricatures of British travelers. They are foppishly dressed, fully convinced of their own superiority, and biased against the American society that they view as backward and boorish. Through their observations—rude remarks on the classlessness and casual manners they perceive in American society, both of which they criticize harshly—Leslie makes her strongest case for the moral superiority of the young nation.

Albina's infatuation with Washington Potts and desire to impress her almost cause her to lose the love of the desirable bachelor Bromley Cheston, who has taken an interest in Albina since she was a child. Observing the Marsden women so eager to impress the pretentious Washington Potts, he thinks to himself, "I never can marry into such a family" (26). In the end he saves Albina from public embarrassment and lectures the women to be proud of their middle-class status and American upbringing: "[I]n our country the only acknowledged distinction should be that which is denoted by superiority of mind and manners" (36). In her stories, written with a pedagogical impetus that was common for the time, Leslie mapped the importance of middle-class domesticity for the nation's identity and self-identification.

While insisting on a classless society as a hallmark of American living, she clearly outlined the importance of middle-class ideals for the well-being of the nation.

While the ideal of a classless society dominated early-nineteenth-century cookbooks (simultaneously enforcing a rigid hierarchy within the household among servants, slaves, and the mistress of the house, emphasizing the latter's sophistication and natural superiority), there were rare exceptions. Chief among these was Robert Roberts's *The House Servant's Directory* from 1827. The text addresses servants in private households (and implicitly their employers, too). On the cover it proudly pronounces that it was written "to suit the manners and customs of families in the United States." It was also the first book written by an African American to be published by a commercial press. Roberts, a butler to the governor of Massachusetts, was a member of a small but growing politically active New England African American middle class. The publisher's preface asserts that American servants (unlike recent immigrants) lack "proper gloss and finish" (iii), which it promises the book will provide.

The text, as it details servants' labors and responsibilities, not only gives a different insight into the operations of an early American household, but also constantly undermines the idea of classlessness by showing the restricted realm within which servants had to function. In an address to readers who are servants or who wish to enter service, Roberts admonishes: "[W]hen you hire yourself to a lady or gentleman, your time or your ability is no longer your own, but your employer's" (x). He instructs that from servants, complete submissiveness can be demanded, as well as compliance to any rule the master or lady of the house may see fit to impose (120–21). However, he also encourages his readers to take pride in their work and understand that the skills they learn are their own, and can be taken to another employer if the present one does not suit them. Roberts encourages servants to support one another instead of competing. "The greatest comfort of servants is their behavior and conduct towards each other," he writes (70), and he goes further by calling on them to be "more ready to assist each other in cases of sickness or misfortune" (71). Even more surprisingly, he lists clear rules for the employers' conduct toward their servants: "[L]et them at least be treated as fellow beings and candidates for a future world," he admonishes (155). In this chapter Roberts mostly quotes from the *Cook's Oracle* (1817), a best-selling British cookbook written by the amateur cook William Kitchiner, who wrote from the employer's perspective and therefore spared Roberts the awkward task of educating readers who were above him in the social hierarchy. ("The servant is not greater than his master," Roberts writes humbly, when introducing the *Cook's Oracle* [154]). Invoking Kitchiner's authority, Roberts quotes his remark that "human nature is the same in all stations," lending weight to his own voice (and perhaps going beyond household politics, as Roberts was an abolitionist) (201). By drawing on the credentials of the *Cook's Oracle,* Roberts reminds employers to treat servants with kindness and respect, offering such suggestions as to "impose no commands but what are reasonable," and "if they are sick, remember you are their patron as well as their master; not only remit their labour, but give them all the assistance of food, physic, and every comfort in your power" (157). Here the text endorses a minimalistic bill of rights, but one that can be overthrown at any moment, as Roberts acknowledges, since a master may discard any rule (154). The household manual contains a few recipes, mostly standard fare arranged around a few New England signature dishes. In this regard the text may not be an attempt to present a new definition of an American cuisine, but what makes it significant is the author's decision to address and advise cooks rather than housewives, working people rather than heads of households. Instead of depicting the United States as a classless society, Roberts highlighted social differences and sought to empower the servant class to negotiate them successfully while subtly interjecting his own critiques of the system. Roberts used the proceeds from sales of the book to buy real estate in Philadelphia and open a catering business. Later he became a political activist, thereby overcoming the hierarchies the text described.[77]

A REPUBLICAN CUISINE

Recognizing the importance of a culinary identity, American authors and artists after the Revolution asked what their compatriots in the new nation should eat to become Americans. The question was by no means abstract, as food as well as climate and environment were thought to have a profound influence on a population, and Europeans since the *philosophes* had written critically of those elements in North America.[78] Simplicity, often ridiculed by European travelers as provincialism, served as a central organizing principle in the early conceptualization of a republican cuisine. Simplicity served two aims. First, it helped to distinguish American from European culinary traditions, now publicly scorned as extravagant and dissolute (but privately often still indulged in by the American elite). Second, simplicity stood for what were considered core values of the new republic, equality and democracy, as everyone was imagined to be able to enjoy a simple meal in a country so abundantly blessed with resources. Embracing simplicity, republican cuisine was therefore a culinary expression of the way American authors envisioned their nation: classless and full of promise.

While the idea of simplicity ran through many of the different iterations of republican cuisine, the concept changed considerably in other ways, reacting to economic and social change. Initially, authors praised corn as a genuine American ingredient and it stood as a symbol of what the new Americans hoped to represent: independence from the European heritage, utopianism, and an endorsement of the environment of their homeland. A cuisine based on corn invoked indigenous cultures and was imbued with revolutionary language. In embracing corn, a staple widely despised by European authors, Americans declared both culinary and intellectual independence.

In the early nineteenth century, with greater accessibility to wheat and other more desirable grains, a changed foodscape in urban settings, and growing transportation networks making possible less-localized economies, cookbooks and other texts nurtured a nostalgia for some mythical, simple past in which settlers made do with what was available. Often this was presented as beneficial to the welfare of both the individual and the nation. Health was established as an important motivation for why one should follow advice literature when it came to eating, as healthy eating implied superseding decadent European ways and practicing responsible citizenship and devotion to the republic. As Norbert Elias has shown, a person's behavior at the table has had a long tradition in signifying loyalty and political alliances. The closely controlled world of the court allowed the finely tuned engineering of courtly culture and etiquette by promising social status to those who complied. Cookbooks and nutritional advice taught the American middle class that eating the republican way demonstrated their commitment to the nation. The experts' advice also suggested that the eater was a patriot and morally superior to those who let their appetites reign. Thus the texts staked claims for an emerging middle-class culture as truly American and the moral backbone of the nation. The texts promised that those who complied could expect health and social stability, and also legitimization of their class and racial privilege.

Republican cuisine gave writers and artists a public space to discuss American identity. While firmly restricted to members of the white middle class, the space of alimentary discourse initially offered open access to men and women. As domestic cookery established itself as a realm of female expertise at the beginning of the century, women had a rare opportunity to publish from a position of authority. They used this space to enter the discussion of a national cuisine, to examine the role of women in society, and to intervene in the political debates of the day. Very few authors used the opportunity to advocate for more or equal rights for women, but every cookbook published by a female expert normalized the idea of female authority and expertise.

Republican cuisines were a dominant but not homogenous mode for thinking about national identity and cooking. While they celebrated an agrarian society, they usually catered to an increasingly urban, middle-class audience. Especially from the 1820s onward, other ideas of what constituted an American cuisine emerged, usually critical of some aspect of republican cooking, such as the hegemony of New England, the claim that America was a classless society, or the isolationist tendencies of republican cuisine's proponents. While the texts were critical of some aspects of republican values, they were not necessarily radical in their scope, nor liberating. At the same time that they advanced their critiques of the dominant narrative, they promoted conservative ideas of gender and race.

Still, the concept of a republican cuisine as a patriotic American way of eating had become so prominent in 1840 that it figured in the presidential election. In the midst of an economic recession, the Democratic candidate, President Martin Van Buren, faced a tough reelection campaign against Whig William Henry Harrison. Harrison depicted Van Buren as the rich man's candidate, living a life of luxury, as he had served French food in the White House (like all of his predecessors), whereas Harrison claimed to live off "raw beef without salt."[79] Harrison thus lay claim to the power republican cuisine had gained over the American public. Although eating French food was still common among the American elite, Van Buren had failed to recognize that American society no longer saw elite behavior as a moral guide for the country, and, despite the wealth of both candidates, Harrison's "log cabin campaign" gave him the image of a man of the people in contrast to Van Buren's image as a snobbish gourmet.

Republican cuisine continued to flourish over the course of the nineteenth century, exploiting the multiple traditions mapped out above, and influenced by the state of affairs of the time. Catherine Beecher and Sarah Josepha Hale would canonize republican cooking in their texts of the 1840s.[80] But by then they could no longer count on a monopoly over defining an American cuisine; the question of what constituted American cooking was continuously contested and widely debated.

Despite the claims of republican cuisine to equality and liberty, not everyone got served equally from the imagined national salad bowl, and not everyone got to sit at lunch counters for most of American history. To say it in Arjun Appadurai's words, "In culinary matters, the melting pot is a myth" (22). The process of making a cuisine is often violent and exclusive, as it defines who has access to the limited resources of the nation, be they pecuniary or political, educational or cultural. Native Americans, African Americans, and more recent waves of immigrants were habitually excluded from the American table as set by nineteenth-century cookbooks. But this did not go uncommented upon. Just as Franklin, Barlow, and Simmons used food writing to challenge existing relations of power, other generations of American cookbook authors, nutrition experts, poets, and artists would discover the genre as a means to challenge the status quo. In the process, they, like the authors and artist discussed here, negotiated issues of national identity and citizenship and many more times asked the question: What is American cuisine? The varying replies would all point to the strong link between culinary discourses, identity constructions, and political ideology across multiple genres of writing and representation while reminding us that there is no single or simple recipe for American identity.

TWO

"Wolf in Chef's Clothing"

MANLY COOKING AND NEGOTIATIONS
OF IDEAL MASCULINITY

Men's stomachs have always been their weakness, and it has fairly been said that if women wished to control the lords of creation it was only necessary to ... feed them.

—DESHLER WELCH, *The Bachelor and the Chafing Dish* (1896)

Women are good cooks, but it is axiomatic that men are better.

—ERIC HOWARD, "If I Had It My Way" (1941)

WHY THE WAY TO THE HEART IS
THROUGH THE STOMACH

DOMESTIC COOKING HAS BEEN so firmly associated with women in American culture that for a long time it has been central to the performance of hegemonic femininity. Being able to cook has traditionally stood for a mother's love and a woman's competence to be a wife. Since the late nineteenth century, this logic was trailed by an equally arbitrary but less widely circulated narrative of manly cooking: when men cooked, advice literature suggested, it was oppositional to women's cooking, but an equally powerful performance of gender. The binary division between undomesticated, manly cooking and feminine domestic cooking reflected the ideological context of nineteenth-century gender organization in middle-class family life. Manly cooking advice and depictions of men cooking in literary texts reveal an unusual and stark insight into ideological constructions of gender. "Women cook merely to put supper on the table; men cook for nobler purposes, shrouded in mystery and smoke, high priests of self-sufficiency," wrote David Bowers half-jokingly in his 1999 *Bake It Like a Man: A Real Man's Cookbook* (1). Unwittingly, he summarized the essence of a hundred years of cooking advice for men, which persistently maintained that men cooked differently from women—better, of course, with distinct methods and artistry. When men cooked, they were not less but rather exceptionally masculine.

In the nineteenth century, hegemonic masculinity and femininity were organized around particular skill sets and repertoires of knowledge. These spheres were rigidly gendered and became visible in such quotidian and elemental tasks as cooking, as Jessamyn Neuhaus, among others, has shown. In a process accelerated by industrialization and urbanization, free men spent less time in their homes and entered the marketplace, leaving the less prestigious tasks of homemaking to their wives, mothers, sisters, and daughters.[1] Women used their assigned responsibilities to claim authority outside the home. Amateur women authors and editors became acknowledged experts on interior design, cooking, fashion, and etiquette, suggesting that all women could easily master the skills necessary to run a middle-class household in style. They took advantage of their newly granted domestic authority to stake claims in all kinds of realms, ranging from architecture and art to political activism and higher education. But not without struggle. At the end of the nineteenth century, cooking advice had become not only a genre that promoted a gendered division of labor, but also a domain in which battles were fought over women's expertise, and over gender and class privilege.

Narratives of "manly cooking" were born as a reaction to the erosion of social differences between the sexes and the decline of male privilege in the early twentieth century. They served as a way to cope with and narrate social change. For Bowers and many of his forgotten predecessors, women cooks addressed the biological need to eat, but men's cooking held an added layer of meaning and significance: it conjured adventurous travel, exoticism, war, or the good life. In short, to use a phrase Sherrie Inness coined, "the male cooking mystique" (*Dinner Roles,* 17) held that women's cooking was quotidian and uninspired. Manly cooking was infused with genius.

Early manly cooking advice claimed that women wielded power over the male body by providing the food men eat—a thinly veiled threat of feminization. Women, the texts warned, controlled men by feeding them dainty, complicated, or (more recently) fat-free and healthy food, to be consumed under the confusing and useless regime of table manners. Cooking instructions for men also claimed that when they chose to cook, they easily surpassed women's abilities. Both claims—the need to defend against the emasculating effects of women's cooking, and the congenital superiority of men in the kitchen—served as evidence of a transcendent masculine essence while reiterating the principle of inherent male primacy in any domain, even one dominated by female experts. At the core of men's cooking advice lay a gendered struggle over power not only in the culinary, but also in broader social and cultural realms.

Historically, reclaiming cooking as a manly art was one way to regain one's masculinity and independence not only from women, but also from effeminizing technological and civilizing practices that were thought to soften and domesticate the male body. It also served the abjection of alternative masculinities, since texts dealing with manly cooking commonly dismissed gentleness, affection, and caring as undesirable traits in men, or marginalized men who came from non-dominant cultural or racial backgrounds by stating that there was only one right way to eat and cook to be a real man: the urban, white, middle-class way. The "right way," of course, was in constant flux and always competing with alternative and subaltern visions, and produced complex, conflicted, and oscillating images of the manly ideal.

Looking at cooking advice for men in memoirs, novels, short stories, men's magazines, and TV shows, the following chapters will outline different discursive strategies that empowered the male cook, enhanced his masculinity, and often denigrated women's work. Beginning with the contest for gendered authority over domestic cooking, cooking advice in the nineteenth century became the domain of white middle-class women, and, in a few instances, African American men, until at the end of the century the bachelor cook emerged, and with him the first cooking advice directed exclusively at men. At the turn of the nineteenth to the twentieth century, ideas of masculinity radically changed. Pitted against hegemonic femininity, masculinity appeared in constant struggle against feminization, a threat coming not only from women allegedly running men's daily lives, but also from social changes that presented middle-class men with work that gave only limited room for competition, individualism, and independence. Nature emerged as a realm in which men could still prove themselves, and, as the writings of Theodore Roosevelt and Ernest Hemingway will show, campfire cooking played an important role in this narrative, as it became shorthand for men's independence from women and the feminizing amenities of civilization. Since camping trips and unlimited access to undomesticated nature were out of reach for many men in the 1920s and 1930s, urban versions of campfire cooking developed, as an analysis of hard-boiled detective novels will show. The 1930s also saw new middle-class masculine ideals becoming prominent that were less rugged and emphasized consumption as central to the performance of masculinity, along with refinement and cosmopolitanism. Exploring cooking advice in men's magazines shows the exploitation of immigrant cuisines and an increasing sexualization of manly cooking, which climaxed in the figure of the playboy cook that manifested itself in the cooking column of *Playboy* magazine in the 1950s.

All of these and many more examples in the following demonstrate that the stomach is not only the way to a man's heart, but a path to power.

"MEN, MEET THE KITCHEN": INVENTING MANLY COOKING

In America, domestic cooking was not always associated with feminine authority, nor did it call one's masculinity into question. Thomas Jefferson wrote down the first American recipe for ice cream. Benjamin Franklin collected recipes he copied from cookbooks. Joel Barlow's mock epic "The Hasty Pudding" (1793) has at its core a recipe ("In boiling water stir the yellow flour ... "). Henry David Thoreau, Henry Ward Beecher, and Walt Whitman, among many others, referred to food and cooking in their writings, demonstrating an interest in food as well as familiarity with the kitchen and no reluctance to admit it. In the first half of the nineteenth century, knowledge of food preparation was still part of a well-rounded education; ideally, a man was master of a household that he could guide in all its aspects.[2] But in the course of the century, home cooking became firmly associated with feminine authority. Kitchens came to be understood as gendered spaces producing normative femininity, where devoted wives and mothers nourished their families, and domestic cookbooks were a women's genre, written by female authors for female audiences.

This marked a departure from older norms. In Europe until the eighteenth century, the cookbook genre was mostly in male hands. Chefs working at court and for the nobility (and, after the French Revolution, in restaurants) published their recipes, mostly addressing fellow chefs and caterers. Male aristocrats published advice on how to manage estates, commonly including a few recipes. The seventeenth century marked the appearance of the first books of domestic middle-class cookery, *cuisine bourgeoise*. Middle-class households were increasingly managed by women who were not only literate but also in charge of servants, the menu, and the social representation of the family and the estate. While initially also written by men (for instance, *The English House-Wife* by Gervase Markham, published in 1615), the books targeted a new audience for cooking advice that began to make it possible for middle-class women to claim expertise, too. In England, the first successful cookbook written by a woman appeared in 1670, *The Queen-like Closet, or Rich Cabinet* by Hannah Wolley. Her recipes were short, demanding less equipment than those written for professional kitchens. The sales of her books motivated publishers to print other cookbooks written by women and addressing a lay audience. But female authorship was still rare nearly eighty years later when Hannah Glasse published her best-selling *The Art of Cookery Made Plain and Easy* (1747), which at first revealed only "A Lady" as the author, the anonymity suggesting that publishing was still risky for a woman's reputation.[3] Glasse's text changed that and established women authors as a fixture in the cookbook market.

Cookbooks by British women such as Glasse traveled with the colonists to the New World, and later overland from the East to the West Coast of the United States. The texts not only provided recipes but were compendia of what had become feminine-connoted expertise and knowledge on domestic issues.[4] They also conveyed information on moral subjects, etiquette, family, home, and community building.[5] When Amelia Simmons published the first American cookbook in 1796, she followed in the tradition of these women, but also started one of her own, claiming the genre in the United States for female authorship. Subsequently, male authors of cookbooks proved to be less successful in the American market. In 1814, the first edition of *The Universal Receipt Book* claimed on its title page that the authors were "a society of gentlemen in New York" (it was actually the work of an Englishman, Richard Alsop). The second edition in 1818 was published under an ironic female pseudonym, Priscilla Homespun—presumably because by this time female authorship and authority promised greater profits.[6]

Domestic kitchens became increasingly defined as feminine spaces, too. Ruth Schwartz Cowan argues that men lost their place in the kitchen gradually with the advent of technological improvements: the transition from the open fire to the wood stove to the coal stove released men from their traditional kitchen work of keeping the fire going. Industrialization moved basic food processing from the kitchen to the factory, further eliminating typical male household tasks such as butchering, milling grain, and distilling. An emerging market economy in demand of workers further motivated men to leave the domestic sphere and to look for more prestigious wage labor (64). Products formerly produced by men in the home were now obtained in stores. The money necessary to purchase them was earned by men outside the house (rather than by women's handiwork or surplus grown in gardens). This created a circle accelerating the institutionalization of a gendered division of labor and consumption.

As a result, women were more tightly bound to the kitchen by a complicated mixture of guilt, love, sense of duty, and, later, the promise of self-expression. The beginnings of this effective cultural strategy can be seen in texts such as Sylvester Graham's nostalgic view of mothers' work as described above. By the end of the century, the notion was well established, for instance in *Miss Parloa's Kitchen Companion* (1887), which proclaimed: "Most wives and mothers are anxious to do that which is best for their families. If they could be brought to see the waste of material and—what is more important— the impairment of health, and consequent loss of happiness, which improperly cooked food causes, they would make constant efforts to bring about a better state of things" (232).[7] Cooking thus turned into a practice that was closely connected to ideals of femininity, even if the actual labor in middle-class kitchens was conducted by a hired cook under her supervision.[8] Families demonstrated class privilege by hiring domestic servants such as Irish immigrants, free African Americans, or, on the West Coast, Chinese immigrants as cooks, but it was assumed that the mistress of the house would oversee the cooking and marketing and be responsible for the results.[9] As a consequence of the gendering of the domestic space, white middle-class men were no longer expected to know how to cook. Indeed, this new ignorance became a badge of honor, a way for men to perform their class, gender, and race privilege.[10]

For the most part, white male authors in the United States eventually gave up on domestic advice literature and left the genre mostly to women experts, although a few successfully relocated into specific cookbook market niches, such as (more or less) scientific books on poisons, household encyclopedias, and specialty texts on beer brewing and distilling.[11] While white middle-class men lost their culinary credibility, not only women but also free African American men stepped into the gap, asserting as (former) high-ranking servants a professional authority over domestic matters. Robert Roberts's *The House Servant's Directory,* mentioned earlier, was the first book written by an African American published by a commercial press. Roberts's manual demands submissiveness from servants to the master or lady of the house (120–21), but it also formulates servants' rights. "Do as you would be done by," Roberts admonishes employers.

Roberts opens the book by addressing "young friends Joseph and David, as they are now about entering into gentlemen's service" (55), not an unusual narrative strategy for a nineteenth-century manual. But the dedication is also politically meaningful. The name Joseph, as the text discloses, references the Genesis story of the young man sold into slavery who becomes the vizier of Egypt, the second most powerful man after the pharaoh and husband to the pharaoh's daughter. No elucidation is made for David, but then it would have hardly been necessary for a nineteenth-century readership: everyone knew that against all odds, David overcame the mighty Goliath in a struggle for life or death (1 Samuel 17). All of this makes the text less docile and more subversive than it may appear at first.

The book was released, as Graham Hodges noticed, just at the moment when female servants, often Irish immigrants, started to compete with male servants for work in middle-class urban families.[12] The transition from male to female experts accompanied the move from well-off households arranged in imitation of aristocratic models to more bourgeois settings, which included fewer specialized servants, a decline in formal decorum, and a shift toward women (whether servants or mistresses) managing homes. Roberts assured his readers that men can still find dignity and satisfaction in work well done.[13] Hodges claims that Roberts thereby contributed to "the emergence of new self-perceptions of black manliness."[14] While the male servant now needed to report to the lady of the house, Roberts suggests that a manservant who knows his profession well gains control over his work and time: "There are many young men who live out in families, who, I am sorry to say, do not know how to begin their work in proper order unless being drove by the lady of the family, from one thing to another, which keeps them continually in a bustle and their work is never done" (55). Being competent allows the servant some independence from the lady of the house, and protects him from being replaced by cheap female immigrant labor.

Tunis Campbell's *Hotel Keepers, Head Waiters, and Housekeeper's Guide* from 1848, another early successful manual written by an African American author, tried to define a minimum of servants' rights, such as having one day off per week. While suggesting that the servant should find his fulfillment in service, he admonishes employers to pay their servants well if their work is satisfactory, to give praise where praise is due, and to allow for promotions (7–12). In this way he seeks to foster a workplace that grants dignity to the male servant. Campbell organizes his dining room military-style, recommending daily "drills" in "squads" overseen by a "first lieutenant" (20). The allusion to army living takes the servant out of the realm of domestic work and increases the masculine capital of the position, while simultaneously making it harder for women to enter the masculinized space. With a hierarchy in which one can advance, Campbell's prescriptions envision a path to social standing for men who follow his advice.

This sense of pride and dignity in work also characterizes a third major cookbook published by a male African American author before the First World War, Rufus Estes's *Good Things to Eat* (1911). Born a slave in 1857, he experienced the Civil War as a time of intense labor. After all the adult male slaves in his neighborhood escaped to join the "Yankees," the child Estes worked, and, beginning at age ten, contributed to the family income. From sixteen years old he worked in the restaurant business. In 1883 he entered the Pullman service, and in 1897 was put in charge of a "magnificent $20,000 private car" (x). Estes's voice, proud of working himself out of great poverty into middle-class respectability, resonates through the book, celebrating not only typical American values, but also echoing ideas central to hegemonic masculinity such as endurance, independence, and achievement.

In these and other texts, African American male authors utilized cookbook writing for political causes, linking food preparation to assertions of manliness. This included racial uplift as well as more rebellious approaches. It is notable that Roberts and Campbell, who advocated making the best of one's subservient station in life, quit service after publishing their books and became political activists. Roberts promoted abolitionism and racial equality in his hometown of Boston, while Campbell became a justice of the peace and a state senator in Georgia during Reconstruction.

All three texts (by Roberts, Campbell, and Estes) claimed that they were useful to the private as well as the public kitchen. This is a claim that middle-class female authors could no longer make in the course of the nineteenth century. Boarding houses and eateries in antebellum America often granted white middle-class women a respectable income. After the war they experienced stiff competition from restaurants and street vendors. Although home cooking was constructed as a woman's natural responsibility, restaurant work, with its physical demands and odd hours, increasingly was thought to be unfit for women, despite the many examples to the contrary.[15]

More Americans than ever before had the money to dine in hotels, restaurants, and eateries.[16] Early celebrity cooks, such as James Sanderson of Philadelphia and Pierre Blot, founder of the New York Cooking Academy, entered American culture via newspaper articles, word of mouth, references in literature, and cookbooks in the second half of the nineteenth century. One of the most famous chefs of his time was Charles Ranhofer, who,

French-born like Blot, worked for Delmonico's in New York City at the pinnacle of its fame. He is credited with the invention of iconic dishes such as Lobster Newberg. He also published the cookbook *The Epicurean* (1894), bringing fine dining into private households, thereby carving out a new niche for male authors of cooking advice: celebrity cookery for private homes.[17] The gendering of professional cooking began to establish a narrative of men as chefs and women as cooks in American culture.[18] The differences between the two were starkly emphasized for the sake of gender distinction. Despite women's unchallenged reign over the domestic, popular culture started to acknowledge in the 1890s that there are occasionally situations in which a man needed to cook for himself.

At the end of the nineteenth century, the number of unmarried men increased dramatically, as young men in an industrialized and increasingly service-oriented society were expected to pursue careers before getting married. The average marriage age went up, and the number of marriages per capita went down nationwide. Bachelors accumulated especially in cities. New York, Denver, San Francisco, and other urban centers offered young men jobs as clerks and in sales, and a release from social control by family and tightly knit communities. An urban entertainment industry consisting of dance halls, amusement parks, pool halls, cabarets, sports clubs, and red-light districts developed, which offered bachelors diversions and interactions with women. Closely regulated courting was replaced with unchaperoned dating. Unlike in the decades before, when bachelors were understood as an abnormality, now, in an economy in which fatherhood and community-orientedness were less important characteristics of hegemonic masculinity than individuality and competitiveness, bachelorhood was redefined as desirable for a limited period in life.[19]

While some bachelors lived with relatives, others boarded, lodged, or rented houses or apartments together. In many arrangements some kind of board was included, but not in all. Some rooms came with access to a kitchen, some not. The sheer need to eat motivated bachelors to learn how to cook—a phenomenon that received some attention from the press. Reports on bachelor cooking clearly differentiated it from women's domestic cooking.[20] Articles started to argue not only that it was necessary for a man to know how to cook at certain stages of his life, but also that for male amateur cooks, cooking could serve as a sign of refinement. "Many Young Millionaires Are Expert Chefs" headlined the *Washington Post* in 1895, arguing that "The new man, for there is a new man as well as a new woman, is well up on all the things which used to belong to woman's especial province" ("Swells Who Can Cook," 20). As a reaction to these trends, cookbooks specifically addressing the bachelor appeared. Deshler Welch, the editor of a New York theater magazine, used a number of strategies in his cookbook *The Bachelor and the Chafing Dish* (1896) to redefine the act of cooking as a manly activity. The chafing dish—in many bachelor apartments the only cooking equipment available—became a way to safely remove cooking from the feminine-connoted space of the kitchen into the masculine space of the bachelor apartment. Welch also references cooking in the galley of a yacht, thereby giving bachelor cooking an upper-class connotation, associating it with travel, leisure, and wealth.

Welch not only claims that cooking outside the kitchen is a different activity from cooking inside the kitchen, but also argues that his cookbook is different from other cookbooks (presumably written by women): "I am not a maker of cook-books. I have not a single ambition in that direction, and what I wish to say under the warm glow of conviviality will not partake of cold-blooded prescription, as well indexed, and set up in oil-cloth covering for ready reference by Bridget in her basement kitchen" (12). He dismisses other cookbooks as practical instructions, to be used rather than read, by working-class immigrant women. Conversely, his volume—indexed like a regular cookbook—is prefaced with a "Dissertation on Chums," announcing a more literary approach to cooking instructions, intended for well-to-do men who identify with "bon vivants in clubs, yachting circles, army and navy," as the cover page states.

The male lay-cooks in *The Bachelor and the Chafing Dish* have gained their expertise by eating in renowned restaurants (as the many references to Delmonico's or "Del's," indicating familiarity, suggest) or by being of the same sex as the famous chefs Welch invokes. Often these famous chefs are not only cooks but also artists or soldiers, great men whose creative or martial accomplishments make them immune to suspicion of feminization when they engage in cooking, an immunity Welch's text would transfer to his reader (90, 108, 113). There are some continuities with cooking advice for men today, such as an emphasis on alcohol, the narrative distancing from the kitchen and from cookbook writing as realms of feminine expertise, as well as the insinuation that cooking facilitates sexual conquests. But it diverges in other points, for instance in its praise of dainty dishes as the height of refinement, as when he lovingly describes the table decorations and china, all in violet, used for a "Violet Luncheon": "an exceedingly dainty affair"; or the tender feelings the narrator expresses for his male friends (120). The masculine ideal presented here allows men the expression of affect and love for beautiful decor, features that will be lost in what Eve Kosofsky Sedgwick has called the "homosexual panic" that arrived in American culture at about the same time Welch published his cookbook, triggered when the Oscar Wilde trials in England led to a public discussion about homosexuality. In the process of pathologizing homosexuality, experts described homosexual men as insecure in their gender identity, and claimed that one sign of homosexuality was ambiguous gender performance. This led to a restriction of how much emotional expression was thought to be appropriate in general, and specifically in affection toward other men.[21] It also made it necessary that instructions for male amateur cooks increase their efforts to create a manly style of cooking.

As the reference to "Bridget" (a slur against Irish immigrant servants) in the example above demonstrates, *The Bachelor and the Chafing Dish* sets masculinity against a foil of women, people of the working class, and immigrants. This culminates when the narrator visits a friend whose servants go on a strike for higher wages. Instead of giving in, the two men decide to take over the cooking themselves:

> We couldn't understand why the "women folks" shirked the work we then assumed! . . . We cooked such juicy steaks, and then we smothered them in the crispest of onions or the freshest of mushrooms! . . . Fudge! Why, any woman with half an eye ought to enjoy such occupation! Why should she want higher pay? (38)

Mistresses and servants are conflated in the denigration of the low-prestige, badly paid work of domestic cooking, suggesting that this is also a comment on the women's rights activism of the time. In describing the joys of kitchen work, the text belittles the effort that goes into it. But even in this situation there are clear limits to what can be asked of men: "Of course you couldn't expect us to take time to wash *all* the dishes! We put those aside that we had used and took new ones" (40).

Claiming that cooking can be manly, but cleaning up cannot, reorganizes the domestic sphere into creative and routine tasks, thus allowing the man who cooks to define himself against those who have to do the dishes. Similar reasoning can be found in other articles such as one by Edwin Dwight, who wrote for husbands temporarily abandoned by their wives, encouraging them to eat in restaurants and lunch places if they could afford to, and to cook for themselves only if they could not. The cleaning was to be left to the kitchen help or a "darkey" hired for this purpose (15). Again, white masculinity was kept intact by drawing the line between men's and women's work at the cleaning up, not the cooking itself; the person of color is rendered sexless, their labor cheap and their presence inconsequential.

Another early cookbook targeting a solely male audience, *A Bachelor's Cupboard: Containing Crumbs Culled from the Cupboards of the Great Unwedded* (1906) by A. Lyman Philips, gives testimony to the increasing insecurity these social changes caused:

> Possibly it may be the invasion of woman into all the trades and professions of men that accounts for this dollar less portion of so many young men. Where once they reigned supreme, they are now dethroned and doomed to grow round shouldered over a ledger at twelve dollars a week, while a gay, irresponsible miss of seventeen fresh from the Business College runs everything in the office from the temperature to "The Boss," and draws eighteen or twenty dollars from its coffers every Saturday night. (10)

The "gay, irresponsible miss" is successful not because she has earned a degree from a "Business College" but because she can manipulate "The Boss." These unfair female strategies render the young men "dollarless," and the bachelor "has to forego many pleasures that rightfully belong to him" (10). Among these losses is that he can no longer easily eat and socialize in a club with other bachelors. The author therefore advises his reader to create his own club, not only by cooking for himself, but also by decorating the dining room—in Victorian America often imagined as a masculine space—as invitingly as possible. That men have to cook for themselves here is depicted as a direct consequence of women's reckless behavior and their demand to share in men's privileges. The "invasion of women into all the trades" threatens men with having to enter the potentially emasculating space of the kitchen. But this is celebrated as a conquest, a victory in the battle of the sexes, and a sign of independence from women's rule.

FLESH, BLOOD, AND HEMINGWAY: CAMPFIRE
COOKING AND RUGGED MASCULINITIES

As white middle-class women poured into arenas that were traditionally associated with masculinity, health experts, dime novelists, and politicians alike claimed "nature" as a place in which masculinity could be regained—where middle-class men could take a break from their emasculating white-collar jobs, the demands of their wives, and civilization's mandate of self-control. Men prepared their own food when camping, and ate unrestricted by the complicated regulations of the Victorian dining table. In literature, newspaper articles, and adventure stories, these simple acts became signs of men's independence and the rejection of women's authority over men's needs. Campfire cooking evoked hunting, fishing, and warfare (as a reference to soldiers' camp life) as well as the frontier. Engaging in the same ritual enabled citified men to express more rugged masculinities and hark back to a mythical past in which white male privilege was allegedly unchallenged by women, people of color, and immigrants. Except for the camp and campfire itself, some of the traits of campfire cooking, including its simplicity and heartiness, could be transported back into apartment kitchenettes and later to suburban backyards, as a ritualistic act affirming the cook's masculinity—or so cookbooks and literary texts argued, starting in the 1920s, extolling an old, but actually inventing a new, tradition of manly cooking. Simple recipes for game and fish, or beans and potatoes, or eggs, were now associated with freedom from everyday restrictions. Even men who never slept or cooked outdoors could burnish their masculine attributes by following recipes that conjured up wilderness, homosocial settings, and danger. Campfire cooking and its domestic modifications were not only a way to facilitate men's return into the culinary sphere, they also reflected new ideas of hegemonic masculinity framed against femininity and immigration.

For this to work, however, first the masculine tradition of camp cooking had to be invented. In the early twentieth century, authors of cooking advice for men began to claim that there was a tradition of men cooking over campfires originating in the Stone Age. This narrative about male cooking had been unknown in the nineteenth century, when recipes for campfire cooking usually appeared in regular cookbooks addressing women, right next to advice on how to grill steaks for the family. Campfire cooking (like all cooking) and steak grilling (like all food preparation) were firmly established as women's tasks.[22] Early barbecue recipes, too, such as those in Mary Randolph's *The Virginia House-wife* from 1824, did not suggest that this was a form of cooking that was inherently masculine (51–52).[23] For special situations where women could not tend campfires, advice literature addressing sports hunters and fishermen before the 1890s did offer men instructions on how to prepare meals in the wilderness. Usually, these texts were not enthusiastic about cooking and did not claim that it had transformative powers for one's masculinity. Instead, they advised hiring a cook or bringing one's servant on outdoor trips.[24] Campfire cooking was not an experience to strengthen the spirit, but an onerous chore best left to others. Readers were admonished to ensure that cooking in the wilderness resembled domestic cookery as much as possible to protect the civility of cooks and eaters, since cooking over an open fire was closely linked to indigenous cultures and associated with savagery. Guidebooks recommended that campers bring along teakettles, and even cast-iron stoves.[25]

Early camping manuals directed at the leisure camper, such as Howard Henderson's *Practical Hints on Camping* (1882) or John Mead Gould's *Hints for Camping and Walking* (1877), listed recipes copied from well-known domestic cookbooks and explained that bringing a stove to camp would help mimic the home kitchen (Henderson 57–68). Texts typically assumed that if women were present, they would take over the cooking. Camping in this early period was understood as liberating for men and women alike. *Practical Hints* advised women to wear men's clothes in camp to make themselves comfortable, relieving them of some of the burden that came with Victorian femininity such as hoop skirts and petticoats. Gould suggested some laxity with etiquette and table manners (one could keep one's hat on while eating in camp and use the same knife for butter, meat, and cheese), but sternly admonished the reader not to be "rude, coarse, or uncivil" (97).

Articles in newly founded magazines such as *Forest and Stream: A Journal for Outdoor Life, Travel, Nature Study, Shooting, Fishing, Yachting* depicted nature as benevolent, and cooking scenes (often describing all-male expeditions with a designated cook other than the narrator) offered the opportunity to describe a peaceful moment within a serene landscape. Here, as in many nineteenth-century texts (most famously, perhaps, Mark Twain's *Adventures of Huckleberry Finn* [1884]) nature functions as a temporary relief from some of the disciplinary powers of society, but without denigrating the domestic or doubting its general desirability.

This concept of nature changed at the turn of the century. Fear of what Ann Douglas termed the "feminization" of American Victorian culture led to a reconsideration and reaffirmation of American nature as a genuinely masculine space. Women were responsible for the education and upbringing of children (as mothers, teachers, and Sunday-school teachers) and men, leaving the house for work, were less present in the lives of their sons, which kindled concerns about young men's proper development. This fear was enhanced by a social Darwinist worldview and women's demands for political and economic equality, as well as the immigration of allegedly "less virile races" to American cities.[26]

As a response, popular culture as well as experts of all kinds began to construct "nature" as a space that women were less fit to conquer and as a remedy against softness, nervousness, and over-civilization, especially for boys and young men. Camping and hunting experienced a revival at the turn of the century.[27] Theodore Roosevelt's *Hunting Trips of a Ranchman* (1885) promoted hunting exhibitions as adventures that could be experienced by every man who could afford them. Roosevelt cofounded the Boone and Crockett Club in 1887, firmly connecting hunting with earlier narratives of the American frontier. There was a difference, however. As Richard Slotkin has argued, the cowboy figure popular at the end of the nineteenth century was not the yeoman farmer of Frederick Turner's agrarian version of the frontier, but Roosevelt's "hunter/Indian fighter." Unlike Turner's "democratic collectivity," Roosevelt imagined "successive classes of heroes emerging from the strife of races to earn a neo-aristocratic right to rule" (35). "Hunting big game in the wilderness," the Club's constitution promised, produces "a vigorous and masterful people" engaged in "manly sport with the rifle" (*American Big-Game Hunting,* 10–14). Hunting's virtue was to link apparent danger and the application of violence to a method for securing meat supplies that, paradoxically, was no longer necessary because meat was now widely available through mass production.

Since the end of the Civil War, nutritional experts had begun to emphasize the biopolitical importance of healthy nutrition for the nation. They promised men not only increased vigor from eating meat, but also dominance for the nation in which men did so.[28] The abundant lands seized from Mexico and indigenous peoples in the first half of the nineteenth century led to large-scale ranching that allowed a broader part of the population to consume more meat than did their counterparts in Europe. Meat consumption became a source of national pride and an important element of an imagined American cuisine, commonly cited as proof of America's superiority over other nations. George Miller Beard's influential nutrition handbook from 1871 asserted that "the most powerful nations and the greatest and best men everywhere are flesh eaters" (60). In contrast, grain and fish eaters could be so phlegmatic that they "deliberately prefer starvation to work" and "submit willingly to authority" (65). Grain and fish eaters were therefore easy to control, and colonial exploitation of labor was in their best interest, as it would save them from hunger. An article from 1869, "The Diet of Brain-Workers," stated that grain- and fish-eating nations such as "Hindoos" and Japanese were inherently inferior to meat-eating societies such as the American.[29] In 1871, Winwood Reade wrote in one of the leading magazines of his time: "Tell me what a people eat, and I will tell you what they are," thereby merging two of Brillat-Savarin's famous aphorisms, and continuing: "the inferior style of dinner which prevails on the African Continent would have probably enlisted [Brillat-Savarin's] sympathies on behalf of the slave-owners had he lived in the days when that question was so angrily discussed." Not only does inferior nutrition legitimize enslavement, it also serves to support colonialism: "Cookery and civilization are inseparably connected," he argues (412). Foodways serve to code racial superiority and legitimize the building of Western empires.

Unlike the hunter, the cowboy did not carry associations of European elite practice and was firmly anchored in the American past, making him the icon of a new generation of urban American middle-class men. At the turn of the century, dime novels made cowboys, who until then had often been depicted as outcasts at the margins of society, into the heroes of their exploits. Owen Wister's *The Virginian* defined the newly emerging Western novel in 1902, and gave it its modern shape. The book helped to romanticize the American West (although its demise is foreshadowed in the text by East Coast tourists flooding into the prairies) and to celebrate it as an alternative space far from the ailments of industrialization, from East Coast opulence and decadence. *The Virginian* merges adventure story with elements from nineteenth-century sentimental novels and satire, and its episodic structure is held together by a love story conforming to the literary conventions of the times. The nameless Virginian, a cowboy gentleman with Southern roots, meets schoolteacher Molly Wood, who moved to the West from Vermont. Both will find their character and strength tested by the intensity, lawlessness, and rawness of the West as Wister imagines it. Unlike later cowboy novels, campfire cooking is not yet firmly established as part of the cowboy experience. Wister's cowboys eat in boardinghouses or restaurants if possible, and they travel with a cook (12–13, 95–101). Still, the text insinuates that the men know how to cook a meal if they have to. It is a sign of their nomadic lifestyles and undomesticated characters.

Nature in the text is understood as purifying the human soul and uplifting it in the presence of grace. After a long courtship, the Virginian finally gets to marry Molly Wood. The newlywed couple spends their wedding night in the foothills of the Wyoming mountains. His Southern and her New England background are about to merge, no longer only metaphorically, in the Western wilderness, like the beginnings of a great nation reborn. After making camp, the Virginian, as the last act of his courtship, provides and prepares their wedding dinner over the fire, a trout he has caught from a stream running next to their tent. His ability to survive and to provide food for the two of them is as much a sign of his self-reliant masculinity as a gesture of service for his bride. She, true to her new role of wife, will prepare breakfast the next morning, thereby confirming her marital status, since cooking is firmly coded as an act of love and wifely duty. By preparing breakfast, she ends his bachelorhood.

Like Roosevelt's frontier, Wister's is also white and Anglo-Saxon, as he almost entirely edits out the historical racial and ethnic diversity of the American West. When racial diversity appears in *The Virginian,* it is mostly in order to affirm white superiority. The Virginian's whiteness plays an important role in one of the opening scenes of the book, when he encounters a peddler (over a meal) whose sole function in the text seems to be to provide testimony to the Virginian's racial purity. Claiming to have met the Virginian before and boasting that he never forgets a face, the peddler states, "White men, that is. Can't do nothing with niggers or Chinese. But you're white all right" (18). True to this sentiment, non–Anglo-Saxon characters are mostly faceless in the novel and contribute only to setting, providing not much more than, quite literally, local color (154).

Wister presents the cowboy as the personification of American masculinity: artless, honorable, with inborn nobility, healthy common sense, and, of course, white skin. Wister and Roosevelt reinvented the American West as a place in which white masculinity was tested and proven, mostly in struggles with nature and Native Americans, thereby legitimizing white male entitlement to political and economic hegemony at the turn of the century. In "The Evolution of the Cow-Puncher," Wister explains in great detail that Anglo-Saxon men (aristocrats, if possible) make the best cowboys, contrary to all historical evidence:

> No rod of modern ground is more debased and mongrel with its hordes of encroaching alien vermin, that turn our cities to Babels and our citizenship to a hybrid farce, who degrade our commonwealth from a nation into something half pawn-shop, half broker's office. But to survive in the clean cattle country requires spirit of adventure, courage, and self-sufficiency; you will not find many Poles or Huns or Russian Jews in that district; it stands as

yet untainted by the benevolence of Baron Hirsch.... The Frenchman today is seen at his best inside a house; he can paint and he can play comedy,
but he seldom climbs a new mountain.... Except in Prussia, the Teuton is
too often a tame, slippered animal, with his pedantic mind swaddled in a
dressing-gown. But the Anglo-Saxon is still forever homesick for the out-of-
doors. (605)

The lack of ethnic diversity on Roosevelt's and Wister's frontier is echoed in
the choice of foods they describe. Despite the fact that ethnic dishes strongly
shaped the regional cuisines of the American West, and although Roosevelt
and Wister often stress the racial and ethnic otherness of their cooks (mostly
as Chinese or black), none of this is reflected in the food they prepare, which
is always simple and (New) English: "One evening in every three ... is
employed in baking bread in the Dutch oven; if there is no time for this biscuits are made in the frying pan. The food carried along is very simple, consisting of bacon, flour, coffee, sugar, baking-powder, and salt; for all else we
depend on our gun," writes Roosevelt in *Hunting Trips of a Ranchman* (56).[30]
This cowboy cuisine, as defined by Roosevelt and other East Coasters seeking
adventures in the West, defined what American manly food would consist of
for many decades to come: meat-based, with simple ingredients and simple
methods, allowing little room for ethnic influences, thus manifesting culinarily a race-based hierarchy in manly ideals.

Roosevelt shaped his autobiographical accounts according to the literary
conventions of his time. Masculinity is not given, but earned, through hard
work and a "strenuous life," a formula in which the American frontier,
American imperialism, and American masculinity merge. Roosevelt sought
new frontiers for the nation and new places for young men to prove themselves. With the old West gone, the soldier became the logical heir of
Roosevelt's Indian fighter. Pronounced manliness, represented in Roosevelt's
call for "stern men with empires in their brains," served as evidence that
Americans were ready to compete for dominance in a global market and to
advance civilization, if need be by military intervention ("Strenuous Life,"
9–11, 17–22). In *The Rough Riders* (1899), Roosevelt's memoir of the Spanish-
American War, he defined an interclass American masculinity based on
courage and endurance that, with the West closed, only combat could provide. The nation's first major war since 1865 shifted the crucible of American
masculinity from the frontier to the front line.

In Roosevelt's writing, portrayals of men cooking serve as reflections on
their character. In *The Rough Riders,* Roosevelt depicts acts of cooking in

ways unknown in the nineteenth century—as illustrations of men's humility and commitment to their country and comrades. He describes Dr. Robb Church, "formerly a Princeton foot-ball player," who in his colorful past also worked as a cook in a lumber camp, evidence that his privilege has not spoiled him, nor affected his masculine pursuits in athletics and war (39). Woodbury Kane, a Harvard man, enlisted to serve his country; to make this point Roosevelt shows him cooking and washing dishes for other soldiers. Despite his privileged life, he is ready to do whatever it takes (20). Cooking scenes that in the nineteenth century had functioned to represent economic and social status, or mastery over nature and danger, here gain a new dimension as they are used to reflect on a man's character.

This added new qualities to the representation of men cooking in twentieth-century popular culture. Gender was now seen as expressed through actions rather than by inherent traits. Manliness could be earned and proven in the context of war, but that was a rare scenario; leisure pursuits such as outdoor sports mimicked some of the characteristics of the soldier's life, allowing men and boys who worked and studied in urban, peaceable settings to perform feats of survival and self-sufficiency (without the acute physical danger of combat) in settings now deliberately constructed as free of women.

The Boy Scouts of America was founded in 1910 as a reaction to the perceived "feminization" of boys by the excessive influence of their mothers and female teachers in their childhood. As Jay Mechling writes, the "outdoor-based youth movement" was meant "to toughen up boys made soft by civilization" and it was hoped that it "would do much to revitalize American manhood" (69). Part of the effort to revitalize American manhood was to train boys and men how to cook, a sign of independence from their mothers and future wives. From the beginning, training in cooking techniques was not a minor skill, but a core Boy Scout practice: it was (and is) crucial for the boys' promotion to the higher ranks to have mastered specific cooking techniques. In contrast to publications for girl campers, *Boys' Life,* the Boy Scouts magazine, reported recurrently on camp cooking and its positive effects, and published recipes suitable for the campfire.[31]

In the 1910s and 1920s a growing number of publications surfaced that targeted a male audience, such as hobby hunters and fishermen, romanticizing camp cooking as part of the outdoor adventure package that connected every man to the lives of soldiers and primordial hunters.[32] More camping guides were published than ever before. With suggestions such as using "warm skins of animals and birds to prevent oneself from dying of exposure"), camping guides had come a long way from the genteel camping instructions of a generation before, which usually assumed there was a farm or railroad tracks close by.[33] Now, danger and distance from comfort were crucial elements of the character-building experience. In the new generation of camping manuals, campfire cooking became a realm of male expertise. Instructions such as *Camping Out* (1918) by Warren Hastings Miller no longer suggested bringing along elaborate cooking equipment, and certainly not cast-iron stoves. Unlike early camping guides, which often copied recipes from domestic cookbooks, they now offered specialized outdoor recipes. Campfire cooking was commonly understood as substantially different from domestic cooking in equipment, methods, and results.[34] The narrator of *Camping Out* presents his knowledge about cooking as expert knowledge only a veteran or "master" camper would have (vii). Campfire cooking is thus presented as useful capital for surviving in the wilderness, but presumably also at home, as it suggests experience and hardiness. He makes fun of men who cannot cook their meals in the wilderness, which exposes them as greenhorns (221).

The establishment of campfire cooking as an expression of masculine independence by the 1920s accompanied intensifying anxieties over women invading masculine spaces, as gender relations were renegotiated and women gained the right to vote. A third of all people employed were women, more of them married than ever before, and many of them competing with men for white-collar jobs. About half of all college students were women.[35] Popular culture, too, reflected changing ideals of femininity. Women's fashion stressed straight lines instead of curves, with short hair and breasts bound flat. The 1920s opened up a new era of management of the subject via the body. Expert nutritional advice, home economics, and dieting for weight loss regulated the individual and modernized the body into a consumer-citizen ready to fit into the world of prefabricated clothes, furniture, and public spaces such as buses and subways, while the body was admonished to keep healthy and well-nourished with the "right" choice of products. Home economists and other experts called upon women to feel responsible not only for their family's health and well-being (to feed the family what was "good" for them rather than what they liked), but also to express their creativity, love, and joy via cooking. With technological advances equipping the kitchen with labor-saving appliances, the demands on the home cook and on the dishes she prepared paradoxically increased: meal plans suggested complicated, imaginative, and multiple courses on a daily basis.

In the 1920s, like at other times, cooking could be an instrument for performing social mobility. Those who could not afford to participate in the new tourism and restaurant cultures of the affluent could imitate the experience (and demonstrate sophistication) with the help of a growing body of cooking advice literature. Cooking skills now often focused on the ornamental, as the time saved by processed food was invested in the improvement of aesthetic presentation, shifting the focus from taste to the visual.[36] At the same time, home economists embraced processed and canned food, since it allowed for the standardization of dishes as well as a correct calculation of caloric and nutritional intake. Within a climate of concern for hygiene and cleanliness, cans and processed foods were promoted as purer than fresh food, and suspicion fell upon the foodways of immigrants, who did not as readily adopt processed foods.[37]

Campfire cooking served as a form of resistance to this modernizing discourse on many levels, as it challenged the commodification of food and the subjection of the individual to new modes of nutritional discipline. It undermined the growing nutritional expertise of women and their control over boys' and men's food intake. The fascination with campfire cooking and all of its connotations entered modernist literature in 1925, when Ernest Hemingway published *In Our Time*. Here, as in the previous decade, nature is presented as a masculine space. In nature, men can heal from the horrors of war and escape the corrupting effects of civilization and women. Campfire cooking is no longer an act of courtship and no longer shared with girlfriends, brides, and wives as in *The Virginian,* but instead serves to emphasize male independence and self-reliance. Men's cooking is represented as fundamentally different from women's cooking, and as an act of resistance against the control of the male body by society as well as its subjection to consumerism and modernity. Hemingway depicts the disorienting effects of an increasingly corrupt society and the decline of prewar values such as loyalty and patriotism, and the erosion of belief in progress, technology, and the law. In two stories at the end of the text, protagonist Nick Adams escapes from war trauma, heartbreak, and alienation into a wilderness imagined as intact, a Paradise free of Eves and of evil, the "Big Two-Hearted River."

The shell-shocked Nick embarks on a camping trip, the burdens of war metaphorically weighing him down in the form of a backpack so heavy he can hardly lift it (134). He hikes in a landscape "burned over" and charred, like the protagonist, but he has hope: "It could not all be burned. He knew that" (135). And so Nick embarks on a quest to find the green spaces, the life within the destruction, within the wilderness, and within himself. He expertly demonstrates his veteran camping skills, easily orienting himself, building a camp, and feeding himself, all of which slowly restores his confidence. Hemingway lovingly dwells on the details, describing every move Nick makes. The camp plays an important role, as it is a place he can feel more at home in than the domestic spaces that disturb him deeply after the war. In a Stein-esque sequence, the text reads: "He had made his camp. He was settled. Nothing could touch him. It was a good place to camp. He was there, in the good place. He was in his home where he had made it. Now he was hungry" (139). The home Nick makes is under his control alone.

Like the descriptions of the camp, the descriptions of cooking are significant. While the camp speaks to the amount of control Nick has over his environment, the food scenes indicate how Nick regains control over his body and self by eating simple food from his campfire. The first meal he prepares is too hot to devour right away. He struggles for control over his hunger for the better part of a paragraph in order to wait long enough not to burn his tongue. This silent battle ends with Nick staying in control of his impulses. In a mock blessing, he exclaims happily before the first bite: "'Chrise' . . . Geezus Chrise" (140), and then allows himself to let go. Feeding himself Nick experiences as empowering: "It has been a very fine experience. He had been that hungry before, but had not been able to satisfy it" (140). Satisfying his hunger momentarily restores his personhood and independence, and is part of the long-term healing process.

Stepping into the sun the next morning, Nick enters a verdant, not-burned-over nature of meadow, river, and green swamp. Within this scenery he prepares a breakfast that Hemingway describes with great precision:

> Rapidly he mixed some buckwheat flour with water and stirred it smooth, one cup of flour, one cup of water. He . . . dipped a lump of grease out of the can and slid it sputtering across the hot skillet. On the smoking skillet he poured smoothly the buckwheat batter. It spread like lava, the grease spitting sharply. Around the edges the buckwheat cake began to firm, then brown, then crisp. . . . Nick pushed under the browned under surface with a fresh pine chip. He shook the skillet sideways and the cake was loose on the surface. I won't try and flop it, he thought. He slid the chip of clean wood all the way under the cake, and flopped it over onto its face. It sputtered in the pan.
> When it was cooked Nick regreased the skillet. He used all the batter. It made another big flapjack and one smaller one.
> Nick ate a big flapjack and a smaller one, covered with apple butter. He put apple butter on the third cake, folded it over twice, wrapped it in oiled paper and put it in his shirt pocket. (146)

The concentration on the details evokes authenticity, simplicity, and a focus on essential needs. Nick is one with the moment, at peace with his body, self, and the world. The scene differs from other parts in the text that narrate men's alienation from their souls, bodies, and communities.[38] Cooking in the wilderness helps Hemingway's protagonist to anchor himself, while presenting a challenge that can be overcome through grace under pressure. Hemingway depicts manly cooking as functional, unambitious, and unconcerned with nutritional advice or class status. He "salvages" cooking from its connotation with feminine expertise by making it dirty and dangerous and by taking it out of the kitchen: men's cooking is connected to smoking fire and sputtering fat and slowly rolling lava. It is tied to untamed nature, not only by metaphors, but also by the use of a pine chip as a spatula. The reader is invited to participate in the experience. The passage quoted above offers ingredients, measurements, and information detailed enough to reproduce the dish. The careful instructions explicitly invite the reproduction not only of the flapjacks but also of the independent, uncontaminated masculinity they stand for, promising authenticity and control.[39] White masculinity, one needs to specify: another campfire scene, in the story "A Battler," presents an African American cook, Bugs, who travels cross-country with the former champion prizefighter Ad Francis. Bugs is cooking for Ad, whom he calls "Mr. Francis" (Bugs's last name is never mentioned), and this misleads onlookers, readers, and Nick alike into believing that Ad is in charge. It turns out that Bugs is Ad's caretaker, because Ad is no longer in control of his mental faculties. While Bugs easily overwhelms Ad when he gets into a funk, cooking here is not a sign of his superiority, mastery, or independence. It becomes one of the ways in which Bugs cares for Ad, and is a sign of his commitment and love for him. By cooking for someone else, Bugs does not liberate himself but is cast in a role that women and men of color often shared, as caregivers, their labor a labor of love (57–62).

Cooking as a sign of superior masculinity appears in Hemingway's journalistic writing. In his article "Camping Out" from June 1920 for the *Toronto Star*, Hemingway praises the positive effect camping has on men who know what they are doing: "He ought to be able to sleep comfortably every night, to eat well every day and to return to the city rested and in good condition."[40] The inexperience of men who will struggle in nature is partly expressed in their lack of cooking expertise: "If he goes into the woods with a frying pan, an ignorance of black flies and mosquitos, and a great and abiding lack of knowledge about cookery, the chances are that his return will be very different," he warns. Cooking here becomes the hallmark of the "real" man. Giving ample cooking advice in this essay, Hemingway starts by making fun of the greenhorn, describing in detail all the mistakes he makes "on the pathway to nervous dyspepsia" (not accidentally, this is the Victorians' male equivalent of hysteria). For flapjacks, Hemingway gives the following recipe that closely resembles the instructions he gives in *In Our Time,* although it is less wordy: "You take a cupful of pancake flour and add a cup of water. Mix the water and flour and as soon as the lumps are out it is ready for cooking. Have the skillet hot and keep it well greased. Drop the batter in and as soon as it is done on one side loosen it in the skillet and flip it over. Apple butter, syrup or cinnamon and sugar go well with the cakes."

In the article, authority over cooking discourses is not only arranged between master campers and greenhorns (or manly and domesticated men) but also between men and women. Before giving a camp recipe for making pie, a potentially emasculating dish, Hemingway explains:

> In the baker, mere man comes into his own, for he can make a pie that to his bush appetite will have it all over the product that mother used to make, like a tent. Men have always believed that there was something mysterious and difficult about making a pie. Here is a great secret. There is nothing to it. We've been kidded for years. Any man of average office intelligence can make at least as good a pie as his wife. ("Camping Out," 2)

This claim both undermines women's conceived authority over pie making and asserts that men are pie-making masters. Both strategies are staples in cookbooks for men from the 1920s onward. They divert the reader from the question of whether cooking, or pie making, may be unmanly activities by casting men's cooking as a struggle against women's authority and a form of emancipation from women's influence.

Unlike the other sensual experiences of being in nature that could not be transported easily into the home, camp cooking, or aspects of it, could. It translated the memory of the outdoors into the domestic space, allowing men to relive their adventures at will. Emerson Hough describes how his fond memories of camping trips come back to him when he finds his camping pot:

> The most wholly delectable place in the house, as any outdoor man knows very well, is that certain ... room ... usually by the real head of the house called "the junk closet." Here is where your true outer [i.e., outdoorsman] stores much wealth of ... rifles ... rods ... fishing tackle ... cooking utensils

and all of the general gear which he classifies among his chiefest treasures. . . . It is a place full of interest and instruction and history.

For instance, when just the other day while tugging at a bootlace on the top shelf, you pulled down a blackened and battered kettle on your head—the stew-pot which has accompanied you on many tours—it might to another have seemed empty at the time, but not so to you. On the contrary, there is much that a well-educated stew-pot can preach to any man, savage or civilized, out of doors or in the home. (81)

The junk closet becomes the most delectable place in the house for a man, as it is wholly his, holding the camping equipment that is proof of his rugged manhood. While safely confined within the closet, the contents can spill out into the domestic space of the house at any moment, transporting the owner back to his adventures. But even more than the rifles and rods, it is specifically the stew pot that can preach to any man, not only outdoors but also inside the home, and thereby cross the border between nature and the domestic sphere. Campfire cooking, modified for the kitchen, served as a safe way to relive camping memories and rekindle masculinities at home. A man cooking in his kitchen was safe from feminization as long as his cooking evoked the campfire. Indeed, his ancestral ties to his rough outdoor predecessors gave him an edge over women in their own sphere of special competence.

One of the earliest cookbooks targeting a male audience was the widely reviewed and celebrated *The Stag Cook Book* (1922) by Carroll Mac Sheridan, which presented a number of recipes by famous men (of whom some identified themselves as passionate, occasional, or one-dish cooks, while some confessed that the recipe came from their wives or cooks).[41] While the title still refers to bachelor cooking, the text undermines bachelors' culinary expertise, reflecting the new rugged ideals of hegemonic masculinity: "I beg not to be confused with the type of bachelor club man who is a perfect wizard with the chafing dish. I always have viewed those birds with suspicion," writes one of the contributors (31).

The implied slur against the masculinity (and sexuality) of "those birds" is then delivered piping hot: "Their tricks are few and easy of accomplishment—stunts with mushrooms, or chicken à la king done nonchalantly in a dinner coat. I sing my foremost hymn of hate of those persons" (31). Legitimate manly cooking emerges in the text in the form of campfire cooking, or cooking the bounty from a hunting or fishing trip. One contributor writes: "This is a camp dish to be cooked over an open fire. I guarantee nothing on a stove. I know nothing of stoves, and have a dark suspicion of them"

(69). A recipe for "Fried Trout" begins: "As for my favorite recipe, that requires many conditions, among others a mountain trout stream; the inspiration of the odor of the woods; the vigor of early morning and the pursuit" (90). The recipe for "Oysters Pecheur" gives as ingredients: "One keg of freshly dredged oysters put on the deck of the schooner not later than eight p.m. One hundred pounds of ice put on top of the oysters," and instructs the reader: "Shell and eat at 5 a.m. on the way to the fishing grounds, with salt to taste, and occasional draughts of hot coffee" (51). The instructions suggest solitary eating (supporting the principle that women cook for their families, but men prepare food for themselves) and connotes masculine space and activity.[42] The title and the narrative in the "recipe" help to "de-feminize" food preparation and eating by integrating them into the wider masculine-connoted context of fishing.

Men's cookbooks commonly undermined the rules of the genre by making fun of recipe writing as itself a gendered—feminine—discourse.[43] "It sounds rather . . . ladieshomejournalish," one contributor to *The Stag Cook Book* writes, "but is a perfectly good dessert" (53). The painter Walt Louderback ends his recipe for "Corn Chowder" with: "To make this sound extremely professional I suppose I should add, 'Season to taste' but do not mind if a few ashes get mixed in by mistake" (41). The deviation from women's expert discourse of cookbook writing parodied the conventions while transferring cooking into a domain of masculine expertise.

The idea that men had different tastes than women when it came to food took root in American popular culture in the early 1900s. Experts argued that camp fare—simplified recipes for meat, beans, potatoes, and breakfast foods—represented men's true tastes. Recipes sometimes suggested giving established dishes a male twist by adding seasoning, alcohol, or meat, and thus transforming them. This created a niche for male expertise. Manly cooking no longer referred only to methods but also to the dishes a man would want to cook. Cooking advice now often suggested that women's food could weaken and effeminize the male body and subject and only by cooking for himself could a man protect himself. For *Collier's Weekly,* Ted Shane wrote under the headline "Women Can't Cook": "having subjected my stomach to all manner of feminine cooking for all of my life, I wonder that I am alive today" (16). Manly cooking could save men from slow corruption—if not poisoning—by women's food.

Male experts, who carved out a place for themselves in food writing in the late 1920s and 1930s, now drew a larger readership by providing information on what men allegedly really liked and needed. In 1929, Byron MacFadyen started his column for *Good Housekeeping,* in which he reported from the kitchen from a man's viewpoint.[44] MacFadyen did not always comment on gender difference in his articles, but he exerted authority over female readers in arguing that he, because of his sex, knew more about their husbands' culinary preferences than they did. In March 1933, he advised his readers to prepare more simple dishes for men (81). In October 1935, he suggested "Liver with Pineapple," "a dish he knows men will like" (89). In February 1937 ("Breakfast Dishes Men Like"), he warned wives against their routines. The husband "may have ideas about something different to eat, but trouble to dig them out" (82). The suggestions MacFadyen presented for "lazy Sunday breakfasts" were complicated dishes to be served course by course, making the wife's Sunday morning rather less lazy (83, 132).

Cooking authorities admonished women to cater to men's tastes. Ted Shane, for instance, wrote:

> Tradition has installed woman behind a stove. Here she loves to concoct beautiful-looking arrangements made out of baled hay and topped with little red cherries. She refuses to learn that men like food—simple food looking like food, and not like one of Queen Mary's hats. At placing paper ruffles on cold half-cooked lamb chops, let us admit at once that she is a darb [i.e., a talent]. The point is, a man wants the lamb chops cooked properly, not dressed up for Easter. Few if any women can ever understand this simple masculine craving. (47)

Shane summarizes some of the arguments that have dominated men's cookery advice since the 1920s: the gap between what men want to eat and what women want to cook, the gendering of cooking styles, and the potential danger of feminine food to the male body. In the 1930s, male authors added that women lost their knowledge of cooking because of their obsession with weight loss ("dieting has brought household cooking to an exceedingly low point," writes Montague Glass in 1931 [44]) and were starving their husbands along with themselves. Dieting was only another point in the argument that men needed to know how to cook to escape feminization and dependence on women.

In *Cooking as Men Like It,* George Frederick argues that women prefer dishes in which the natural taste of the ingredients had been altered as much as possible (10). Women cook for the eye, he adds, taste playing a subordinate role, if any (23, 34–35). The "feminine" dishes therefore fake a pleasure that they ultimately do not bring to the eater. Food that has been cooked by women, he says, is "mistreated, ruined, butchered, emasculated, smothered, destroyed and perverted" (26). Obviously such cooking poses a serious threat to the physical and psychological health of the male eater.

Men, in contrast, prefer pure, unadulterated, "natural" dishes, Frederick explains (12, 13). This difference is further escalated where he compares women's cooking to French cooking, whereas male tastes stand for American cuisine and values. One of the problems with French cuisine is its "feminine emphasis on appearance, color, and decoration," which is never "masculine" in appeal; indeed, "American men rather despise" French cooking (22–23). "Feminine" cooking is therefore not only artificial, dishonest, and mere embellishment, but also un-American, which alienates the "true" masculine (American) nature. Any "feminine" food, especially anything with a French name, endangers the masculinity (and sexuality) of the eater, which could be corrupted by this kind of "perverted" food. This works both ways for Frederick: "If food is eaten by women with the same gusto as by men, and in the same quantity and kind, it is very likely to accompany, if not produce, a masculine set of qualities" (10). Not only are food items gendered, but when incorporated, they also gender the subject. Whereas Shane feared for the male digestion when eating women's food, Frederick fears for the masculinity of the male target of women's cooking. Food becomes biological essence, not only to sustain human life, but to determine its gender.

For Men Only (1937) by Achmed Abdullah and John Kenny held that men not only knew what other men like but were naturally superior cooks because of their superior tastes: "It is the individualistic note which gives to the art of cooking its honesty, its decency and probity—indeed, its strictly masculine quality and virtue" (xiii). The authors warn (with a wink, unlike Frederick) of the possible poisoning of the male body by feminine food: "The deathly marshmallow and bloody Maraschino cherry lurk in the hidden corners of too many feminine kitchens, waiting to stick a dirty dagger into the honest masculine palate" (xv). While Frederick, Abdullah, and Kenny deem marshmallows and women's bloody cherries dangerous but avoidable, they are most interested in refuting the notion that women's expertise gives them a commanding role in the kitchen, and urge men not only to defend themselves but to go on the offensive to retake a sphere where they should rightfully be in charge.

Thus the struggle over taste was also a struggle over women's authority in the kitchen. Montague Glass suggested in his 1931 article for *Good*

Housekeeping, "Amateur Cooking for Husbands," how his wife and daughter react when he proposes to cook a spaghetti sauce with garlic for them:

> *Important Member of the Family* (formerly president of three suffrage organizations, *count* them, and a charming lady at that, when she wants to be, but now she doesn't *want* to be): "Now, listen, I'm not going to have you smell this entire house up with onions and garlic."
> *Her Daughter* (pleadingly): "Don't *let* him, Mummy!" (44)

The "important member of the family," who, in her capacity as a former suffragist leader has successfully challenged men's political and social privileges, needs to accept defeat in the kitchen even as her daughter's newly empowered generation protests fruitlessly. In a sense, while breaking with gendered assumptions of the appropriate division of labor, in the end a more traditional order is restored that confirms the husband as head of the household. Since, as all these articles stress, men's tastes and preferences are more important than those of wives and daughters, the father gets to make the spaghetti his way in the end, and informs his readership what is at stake: "The onions must be chopped fine, and the chopper must have firmness of character and determination to be master in his own house or he will be chased out of the kitchen" (44). By successfully taking over the kitchen, he not only gets the last word in an ongoing struggle for power, he also demonstrates that he can take on any woman, anytime, even on her own turf.

That the dispute over gendered taste was a contest for power became evident when H. L. Mencken took on Fannie Farmer's *The Boston Cooking-School Cook-Book.* In December 1930, he personally reviewed one of the countless reprints of the best-selling text:

> The weaknesses of the work lie in two directions. First, it is written by a woman and addressed to women, and hence a certain tea-table preciosity gets into some of its recipes. What male with a normal respect for his pylorus, even in America, would actually eat a rasher of celery fritters? Or one of cherry fritters? Clam fritters, yes, and apple and banana fritters perhaps, but who could imagine peach, apricot, pear or orange fritters? . . . Such preposterous rubbish, plainly enough, is not to be taken seriously. It can never form part of a decent Christian meal, eaten with due gratitude to God. It is what women devour at their private feasts, to the enriching of doctors and beauty doctors. (509)

While the fact that Mencken felt compelled to review the text at all may be surprising, his attacks against it are not. Like other writers of his time, he sets up arbitrary limits for what can count for manly (and by extension) edible food. Like Frederick, who dismisses what he considers feminine food as un-American, Mencken's claim that it is un-Christian serves as a rhetorical tool to utterly condemn it.

By the 1930s, the idea that a division of labor was matched by a division of taste was firmly established in cooking literature for both sexes. A cookbook published in 1937 addressing single women, *Corned Beef and Caviar,* included an entire section on what to feed men and warned that at a "Ladies Only Tea," all dishes should, "of course, be dainty rather than hearty." Articles in women's magazines regularly advised women on what to cook to satisfy their men's hunger for meat and potatoes. Ann Batchelder in the March 1936 *Ladies' Home Journal* suggests as proper male food good coffee, corned beef and cabbage, beefsteak with onions, french-fried onions, baked fritters, pork chops with glazed cherries, French bread with garlic, and spoon bread, feeding into the belief that men prefer meat and strong tastes such as cabbage, onion, and garlic. But a cooking contest for men in 1937 conducted by *Better Homes & Gardens* produced different results. One third of the recipes sent in by male cooks were for desserts—ice cream, pie, strawberry short cake, and cookies. Fifteen percent of the men sent in recipes for vegetables. Only about a fourth of the recipes were meat-centered. (The remaining 15 percent included everything from egg dishes to cocktails and candies.) The recipes, the author Jean Guthrie remarked, also came with the fancy names men's cookbooks so often rejected as typically feminine: "Butterfly Salad," "Charm Tarts," "Strawberry Dream Pie," "and about a dozen Surprises, Supremes, De Luxes, and Delights" (36). In spite of the cultural reiteration of the tale of biologically determined tastes, male cooks in the end seemed to have cooked the same foods as women. This makes cookbook author Hazel Young marvel: "We are always surprised at the number of stalwart huskies who consume such effeminate dishes as chocolate marshmallow sundaes and strawberry ice cream sodas" (194). But despite evidence to the contrary, the idea that men engage in manly cooking still thrived.

Most cooking advice for men stressed the idea that men do not cook daily, as women do, but on special occasions. As Ted Shane put it, men put out "the most delectable dishes in the world. Of course they don't do this constantly—for after all, man is a foraging mind and must earn a living—but when they do do it, they prove the old adage that a man can do anything better than a woman can" (16). Women authors occasionally fought back, making fun of men's culinary ambitions. Agnes Dean, writing in *American Cookery* in 1920 in the guise of a male narrator, allegedly educated women to overlook male cooks' messiness in the kitchen. "A Sunday and holiday husband-chef should be allowed a certain latitude with the butter. And never, never should he be distracted from the business in hand by mention of the open ice box doors" (584). Men tend to use (and ruin) all kinds of linen in the process of cooking as well as producing an absurd quantity of dirty dishes the wife is stuck with afterward. While the male narrator claims that the results are worth the trouble, affirmative female voices are conspicuously silent in this article. But for the most part, articles proposed that women readers support their men's endeavors in the kitchen. In "When Men Entertain," Edna Sibley Tipton suggests that if a man wants to cook (in this case, to entertain fellow men), the woman should become "an innocent bystander," remembering "that daintiness is one of the minor virtues" (25). The male cook in this article announces that he will serve "real food" to his friends, "nothing a woman would like to serve" (which turns out to be "hogshead cooked in greens, one other vegetable, corn bread, fruit pie with plenty of juice, coffee") (25). The author acknowledges that not all men are able to produce such a meal on their own and recommends for such cases that women cooks do most of the work but involve their husbands by setting "down before him everything just ready for the finishing touches. He will have a wonderful time, and so will you while he concocts and serves his masterpiece!" (25). Byron MacFadyen advises wives of male cooks: "Lack of economy must also be overlooked.... Three-inch steaks, half-pounds of butter, and out-of-season vegetables must be enjoyed without thought of cost" ("When a Man Goes Culinary," 90). The ingenious housewife can balance the budget—a woman's responsibility—by trimming afterward, but the results (the food, marital bliss, happy husband) are well worth the sacrifice. Evidently, it was in the interest of both sexes for women to yield their authority to men's superior knowledge even in this most feminized of spheres.

HARD-BOILED COOKING, FEMMES FATALES, AND AMERICAN NOIR

It is no coincidence that the idea of manly cooking appeared in the 1920s at the same historical moment as the emergence of a new hegemonic cultural fantasy in the concept of hard-boiled masculinity. Hard-boiled masculinity is defined by Christopher Breu as "characterized by a tough, shell-like exterior, a prophylactic toughness that was organized around the rigorous suppression of affect and was mirrored by ... detached, laconic utterances" (*Hard-Boiled Masculinities,* 1). It transfers the ideal of the cowboy, hunter, and soldier from the wilderness to the jungle of the metropolis—without the healing potential of nature or the hope for salvation through individual courage because the urban environment is inherently corrupt and toxic. The hard-boiled narrative conflates women with all that ails 1920s and 1930s masculinity, including the economic crisis of the middle class, automation, and urbanization. All that inhibits man from being manly is embodied by the femme fatale, who constantly tempts the male protagonist to give in and give himself up. Only the complete abjection of everything the femme fatale has to offer can save the hero.

Like the cowboy figure, hard-boiled masculinity negotiates cultural contradictions between notions of ideal masculinities and the demands of society, notably the tension between manly ideals such as individualism and autonomy and a conformist, industrialized world.[45] Unlike the cowboy, the hard-boiled man does not offer an escape into a mythic past. Projected onto an urban landscape, the hard-boiled man demonstrates skills of survival. His ethics of reason, honor, and independence are constantly tested, and he achieves mastery over his environment thanks to his street smarts and his fists. In hard-boiled fiction, most notably in the hard-boiled detective novel, the signature genre, manliness is no longer demonstrated through weekend camping trips but in every moment of the waking day. There is no break from gender performance, and at no moment can a man let his guard down or allow his emotions to get the better of him. What is left is the unwavering trust in his own abilities and values.

Hard-boiled masculinity reflected on economic change and the reorganization of gender ideology during the late 1920s and the Depression. Sherwood Anderson in *Perhaps Women* (1931) expressed disorientation and male insecurity as symptomatic of the time:

> The machine has taken from us the work of our hands. Work kept men healthy and strong. It was good to feel things done by our hands. The ability to do things to materials with our hands and our heads gave us a certain power over women that is being lost. . . .
>
> When more men worked in the fields and when most of the goods we need to cover our nakedness against the cold, the house we live in, were made by men's hands, men were different.
>
> They believed more fully in the mystery of existence. The fact gave man a certain dignity. He was, at the same time, more sure of himself and more humble. Most of the modern assertiveness of men is due to fear. . . .
>
> They become no good for women. (41–44)

While men become disoriented "in the face of the machine" and bemoan their sense of entitlement swept away by their alienation from the work they do, women, Anderson claims, fare better, since they can develop their identities via consumption (97). In Anderson's text, women stand for the domestication of American males, and all phenomena endangering manliness. In hard-boiled literature Anderson's consumption-oriented, newly empowered women turn into femmes fatales who benefit from men's insecurity and independence and know how to move within the new world, claiming male privileges for themselves.

It is telling that this flavor of masculinity was named with a metaphor from the kitchen. While hard-boiled masculinity and cooking may seem mutually exclusive at first, the genres of detective fiction and cooking instructions for men both adapted the image of the male cook to convey the notion that true masculinity is uncorrupted by civilization, technology, and femininity. After the stock market crash, the traditional gender ideology that defined masculinity as the position of the "breadwinner" was endangered when the unemployment rate rose to 25 percent in the United States. In their famous study *Middletown in Transition* (1937), the sociologists Robert Staughton Lynd and Helen Merrell Lynd examined the impact of the Great Depression on American family life in rural small towns. They found that the economic breakdown accelerated changes in gender organization, and argued, like Anderson, that men were more severely hit. The Lynds claimed that "the women's world has been disrupted less than the men's world by unemployment" (179). In contrast to men, women did not have to struggle as much with their identity:

> The narrowed role of the male, so largely confined to moneymaking, took the brunt of the shock, with the general impairment of financial security and a quarter of the city families forced onto relief. With the man's failure of role went . . . inability to marry in many cases and the postponement of children. Men's and women's roles have in some cases reversed, with the woman taking a job at whatever money she could earn and the man caring for household and children. (178)

With employment rates for women still rising through the Great Depression, it may have seemed to some that women profited from the crisis. Across the United States, couples married later than in the 1920s. Some cities, like Middletown, saw an increase in bachelor apartments that catered directly to the needs of single men. Communal eateries were supposed to feed the unmarried, but the decrease of 36 percent in real income between 1929 and 1933 often made it impossible for singles to pay for a meal.[46] This was perhaps one of the reasons why cookbook sales were still rising during the Depression (along with the fact that they commonly addressed a less affected middle class).

The increase in cookery advice for men seems directly related to this demographic trend. At the same time, men's need to cook for themselves further added to the perceived destabilization of masculine ideals. Therefore cookbooks addressing men used narrative strategies that affirmed their readers' gender identities by evoking images of archetypical manly men, or using he-man language and a misogynist tone. They also commented explicitly on the changes in gender organization. George Frederick in *Cooking as Men Like It* laments across seventy-two pages the sad state of gender relations. In subchapters such as "Less Home Cookery, Less Marriage," "False Ideas of Some Modern Women," "Why Do Men Love Food and Cookery," and "Why Do Women Seldom Savor Food," he argues that men cook better than women since they have a better mastery of taste and more talent (for practically everything), and that women who cannot cook will not find a man to marry (2, 8–15). He blames the decline of the American nuclear family, high divorce rates, the size of shoebox apartments in urban settings, and the culinary underdevelopment of American culture on women who pursue careers outside the home or simply do not cook "as men like it." Women's alleged takeover of society extends here to the emasculation of the male body, which needs to be counteracted by manly food.

In the 1930s, both genres—the men's cookbook and the hard-boiled mystery novel—reacted to the greater economic and political independence of women with the abjection of everything feminine and by offering protection against the specter of feminization. Within this cultural context, the representation of a man cooking for himself was constructed as signifying ultimate independence from feminine influence and racial corruption; like earlier masculinity ideals, the hard-boiled ideal is pitted against women as well as men of color. Sam Spade of Dashiell Hammett's *The Maltese Falcon* (1929) is exemplary in this regard. The story narrates the twin quests for a fantastic treasure and love, both of which, according to the logic of the hard-boiled plot, must fail. Hammett sketches Sam Spade against a foil of contrasting and eventually discredited masculinities. Joel Cairo is described as foreign and exotic ("Levantine" [42]). He is small and dark skinned, which in Hammett's world makes him suspicious. The narrator lingers upon Cairo's manicured hands, perfumed handkerchiefs, well-groomed appearance, tight clothes, small frame, highbrow form of expression, and shrill voice (42–50). The feminization of Cairo signifies his ambiguous sexuality and reflects a growing concern with homosexuality in the 1930s. Before Cairo appears for the first time, he is announced by Spade's secretary: "This guy is queer" (42), and later he is referred to by Spade as a "fairy" (94). Feminization and homosexual stereotypes are bundled together in Joel Cairo, and through this unsympathetic figure safely deflected onto the body of the other and thus presented not only as un-masculine but also as un-American.

Casper Gutman's masculinity deviates in different ways. In the text, he is usually referred to as "the fat man," an epithet that, together with his last name, refer to the body, emphasizing his obesity, which marks him as weak, greedy, and lacking self-control. Gutman is described vaguely as having an upper-class background, but the elite he seems to represent has fallen prey to the pleasure of unrestrained consumption and lost any credible claim to leadership, moral or otherwise.

The superiority of the masculinity Sam Spade represents is seldom questioned in the text. *The Maltese Falcon* begins with an extensive description of Spade:

> Samuel Spade's jaw was long and bony, his chin a jutting v under the more flexible v of his mouth. His nostrils curved back to make another, smaller, v. His yellow-gray eyes were horizontal. The *v motif* was picked up again by thickish brows rising outward from twin creases above a hooked nose, and his pale brown hair grew down—from high flat temples—in a point on his forehead. He looked rather pleasantly like a blond satan. (4)

The "v-motif" corresponds to his name and suggests purposefulness as well as sharpness, edginess, and danger, concepts that are conflated in the final assessment of the "blond satan."[47] This makes him a hard-body in contrast to Gutman, and white against the foil of Joel Cairo's skin. His street smarts and ruggedness successfully balance the fact that he otherwise has a quite comfortable life: he runs a business, employs a secretary, and entertains a married woman as his mistress. As in texts referencing soldiers, hunters, and cowboys, this text, too, connects middle-class masculinities to romanticized and simplified working-class models. The other men are almost effortlessly controlled by Spade, who seldom loses the upper hand and usually only when his opponents trick him in an unmanly fashion. None of the other protagonists is a match for his superior reasoning, his strength, or his ability to control his emotions. Central to the hard-boiled character is his capacity to create his own moral guidelines and honor code and stick to them in a world full of temptations, ethical shortcuts, and corruption. Spade in the end remains true to himself in a world in which "truth" has become a floating concept.

The greatest danger to his masculinity and individuality comes to him not from alternate masculinities but from Brigid O'Shaughnessy. From the first scene, she is introduced as Spade's true antagonist. Where Spade is all v's, she is all s's—floating into the room and the text, she is described as soft, slow, shy, and slender (5). In her body and features there is no "angularity any-where" (4). The color coding—"[t]he hair curling from under a blue hat was darkly red, her full lips more brightly red. White teeth glistened" (4)—makes her a true American beauty. Like other of Hammett's femmes fatales, O'Shaughnessy has her own agenda that reaches far beyond the wish to make a man happy. In many regards she is a deprecatory caricature of the frightening "career woman" who competes with middle-class men in the workplace. Although O'Shaughnessy is not shy about protecting her inter-ests, even violently, when it comes to business, her feminine look and act confuse but utterly fascinate Spade. O'Shaughnessy is most dangerous not because of her recklessness, but because of her perfect performance of white women's ideal femininity, able to deploy helplessness, disorientation, admira-tion, sexuality, mystery, shame, and tears at the right moment. The men in the novel underestimate her, and are tempted to follow their gender training by protecting and loving her, which puts them at a disadvantage. O'Shaughnessy schemes, plots, and fights like any of the men in the story. While Spade is cautious and distrusts her, he cannot help being attracted to her. But whereas a number of tough guys have fallen for O'Shaughnessy, Spade ultimately does not.

O'Shaughnessy, Gutman, and Cairo represent what in Hammett's uni-verse ails America in the 1930s: ambitious women, a greedy elite, homosexu-als, and foreigners. This can be countered only by clear-cut, ethically mature, white, heterosexual men who do not allow themselves to be manipulated via affect. Spade's independent and undomesticated masculinity becomes evi-dent in the text's food scenes, which appear in prominent positions in the story. Two of them, a dinner and a breakfast, frame the night in which O'Shaughnessy seduces Spade into having sex with her to evade his increas-ingly urgent questions and to secure his future services.

In the dinner scene, Spade serves her sandwiches and coffee laced with brandy. Like in Hemingway and the cooking instructions of the 1920s, the male protagonist who prepares food himself is located within the long tradition of independent males like cowboys and soldiers. The fare is simple and manly and based on coffee, alcohol, and corned beef. The preparations are described with the accuracy of a recipe:

> He had put the coffee-pot on the stove ... and was slicing a slender loaf of French bread ... he spread the liverwurst on, or put cold corned beef between, the small ovals of bread he had sliced. Then he poured the coffee, added brandy to it from a squat bottle, and they sat at the table. (85)

In the kitchen Spade displays assurance and control. O'Shaughnessy, meanwhile, stands forlornly in the kitchen's door frame and unconsciously toys with a pistol. While this setting indicates gender reversal, O'Shaughnessy is nervous and indecisive with the weapon, which contrasts sharply with Spade's familiarity and effectiveness in the kitchen. This does not diminish his masculinity. The kitchen scene serves to demonstrate Spade's sovereignty in any situation. As there is no place for O'Shaughnessy in Spade's kitchen, eventually there is none for her in his life. Spade is not only in control of the situation but also of O'Shaughnessy, whom he orders to set the table, a bread knife in his hand.

Unlike the food preparation scenes in *The Virginian,* it is not O'Shaughnessy who prepares breakfast the next morning. Having spent the night together gives her no wife status like what Molly acquired in Wister's novel. In banning O'Shaughnessy from the kitchen, the text suggests that in spite of their sexual engagement, Spade remains in control over his emotions. It is Spade who shops for and prepares breakfast (only after having searched the woman's clothes and her apartment, indicating that the sexual encounter has not clouded his mind). For breakfast he serves eggs and orders her to make the bed in the meantime. This is not a manifesto for shared household duties. While tidying up the apartment is work O'Shaughnessy can be entrusted with, the preparation of food clearly is not.

The food prepared for breakfast—the sandwiches, eggs, and coffee—is again simple, masculine-connoted fare. The preparation is fast and straightforward. Spade's cooking therefore serves as a marker of his superior, hardboiled masculinity, a masculinity that climaxes in giving up the woman he has fallen in love with as ultimate proof of the total mastery over his affect. The novel ends with Spade handing O'Shaughnessy over to the police for murder, thus containing the danger she represents to men's identity, life, and privilege.

Hard-boiled masculinity, then, makes itself utterly independent from everything feminine; it abjects femininity in order to protect itself. The feminine carries the danger of weakness and softening by appealing to the emotional in men, so any affect needs to be entirely suppressed to avoid manipulation. The rejection of food, pregnant with images that express women's love as well as their status as wives and mothers, became shorthand for rejecting their power over men. It is no surprise, then, that a contributor to the *Journal of Gastronomy* in 1940 gave his motivation for cooking as wanting "to learn to be forever free of women" (Richard Stein 245).

Cooking as a means and symbol for women's manipulative powers is a recurring theme not only in hard-boiled fiction but also in American noir. The food women prepare often stands in for sexual temptation and the potential to corrupt men's moral compasses. In James M. Cain's famed *The Postman Always Rings Twice* (1934), the fatal affair between the drifter Frank Chambers and Cora Papadakis, wife of Frank's employer, begins in the kitchen with a compliment Frank makes on her cooking. The enchiladas serve as foreplay in the text, her offering him food a foreshadowing of their looming sexual entanglement. Unlike Spade, Chambers will follow his passions and go down with them, a dire warning to male readers to stay away from women and their cooking. Establishing his protagonists initially as characters deserving sympathy, Cain shows how Frank and Cora try to withstand temptation at first—again by using food imagery. During dinner, Cora refuses to serve Frank more food. Her husband, unaware of the growing sexual tension and the meaning of her rejection, chides her: "Give a man something to eat." She responds: "Can't he help himself?" But, of course, he cannot, since he is already tightly caught in the spiderweb of lust and love. She finally gives in to her husband's demands and serves Frank the potatoes, which, as it turns out, he cannot swallow, because he "wanted that woman so bad." He helps himself to Cora a few days later (6–7). In a mixture of lust, greed, and subtle xenophobia (the husband is a Greek immigrant), they kill the husband by staging a car accident and are able to escape prosecution. Weighed down by guilt and fear, they do not live happily ever after. Cora eventually is killed in a real car accident. Frank is unjustly blamed and convicted of her murder and sent to death row. In the end he is punished for giving in to his illicit desires, a fate Sam Spade managed to escape. Chambers serves as a warning to men to control their affect and desire for women. The food Cora prepares codes the sexual and emotional temptation that a man should resist. Since Cora's attraction proves to be deadly to Frank, her food turns from nourishing to intoxicating to fatal.

Cain, known as a "tough guy" writer, not only incorporated food scenes as social commentary in his novels, but also was a prolific food writer in his own right.[48] His food essays were published in *Esquire* magazine, the *Washington Post,* and the *New York World*. But he had no interest in campfire cooking, which for him held little potential for surprise. Cain wrote about spaghetti and crepes suzette, dishes that in his era could impress a crowd and befitted an urban, middle-class identity that cherished sophistication and cosmopolitanism: an early instance of "gourmet cooking" as a reaction to the premise that manly cooking must be simple and rugged.

SILVER SPOONS IN THEIR HANDS: THE RISE OF THE GOURMET

In the early twentieth century, rugged masculinities emerged as the effect of what Michael Kimmel and others have described as a major shift in how masculinity was conceptualized—no longer in opposition to boyhood, but in opposition to femininity ("Consuming Manhood," 13–15). Manly cooking defined itself in parallel fashion in terms of un-domesticated cooking. The romanticization of campfires, hardship, and nature as crucibles of manliness lost its resonance during the Great Depression, when campfire cooking connoted poverty and unemployment, resembling all too closely the ashcan fires warming desperate clusters of the ill-housed, ill-clothed, and ill-fed. Middle-class men sought other models. Gourmet cooking entered the American mainstream as an alternative way to express manliness, and as the further commodification of masculinity: manliness was now to be acquired by purchasing the right kitchen equipment and the right ingredients, which simultaneously permitted the demonstration of class distinction. Gourmet cooking advice embraced middle-class, white privilege while evoking urban living, sophistication, and cosmopolitanism.

The term "gourmet" first arrived in American popular culture in the early nineteenth century as a French import with underdetermined meaning. When it entered the English language, it connoted deep knowledge of alcohol rather than food ("a connoisseur of liquors" in Nugent, *The New Pocket Dictionary,* 162). To describe expert eaters, texts used the terms "gourmand" and "epicure." A few texts associated gourmandism with gluttony, as is common today, but more commonly the difference between the "gourmand" and the "gourmet" was one of degree and form of expertise. An article in the *American Quarterly Review* from 1827 drew on the Abbé Ange Denis M'Quin's *Tabella Cibaria* to explain to its readers:

> *Gourmand* . . . being applied to the man who, having empirically discovered the different tastes of esculent substance, is able to select the most dainty parts; in short, he is the epicure of the English. The *gourmet,* however, considers chiefly the theoretical part of gastronomy . . . discovering the nicest shades of difference and of excellence in materials set before him. . . . The *gourmet* . . . is occupied with the higher branches of the art, and is careless about practicing. (Peignot 426–27)

The celebrated culinary expert Jean Anthelme Brillat-Savarin called himself a gourmand rather than a gourmet. Gourmandism is "the enemy of overindulgence," he wrote, defining it as "an impassioned, considered, and habitual preference for whatever pleases the taste" (148). In 1825 he published his *Physiology of Taste,* in which he argued that the enjoyment of food can bring together men of all classes, since the sense of taste is given to everyone. Based on his experience in France, where after the Revolution court-trained cooks opened restaurants to earn a livelihood by cooking for the bourgeoisie, he saw gourmandism as an instrument of democratization.

In the United States, in contrast, fine dining was firmly connoted with elite lifestyles. Fine dining and French food were considered overlapping categories in the first half of the nineteenth century, and both were suspect for their un-republican values as well as for their blatant sensuality. Upper-class travelers brought back from their trips to Europe culinary souvenirs such as recipes and cookbooks, or even French-trained servants and slaves. This association with wealth alienated mainstream Americans from French food. Fine dining was not only class-based but firmly gendered. Aside from the few households that could afford a French or French-trained cook, it was available only in men's clubs, restaurants where respectable women would not be seen, and in gourmet societies, which initially admitted only male members.[49]

After the Civil War, many American culinary experts overcame their suspicion of French culture and started to show a greater interest in foreign cuisines. This was a reaction to the greater availability of international travel, increased global trade, and the emergence of cosmopolitan sophistication as a marker of class. Those who could not afford the ticket, or the growing numbers of restaurants, referred to cookbooks to bring sophistication to their tables. French cooking was thus relieved of its worst anti-democratic and anti-republican connotations, while being presented to the American middle class as an ideal tool for social advancement.

The rise of home economics took on the fashion of fine dining with a gendered challenge. Women acquired new expertise in this field, taking advantage of opportunities in higher education and new jobs as educators, publishers, and authors promoting the new science of nutrition. Home economics eased the transition for middle-class households from servant-run to servant-free kitchens: in the nineteenth century the housewife was expected to oversee a number of servants and a cook, while at the end of the century many households could no longer compete with the salaries paid by sweatshops and factories. Kitchens were redesigned and kitchen equipment invented that made it possible for one person with occasional help to run a household. Home economists developed streamlined workflows that Taylorized the homemaker's space and time. In this complicated period of transition, women gained authority over their family's nutritional intake while being firmly bound to the kitchen.

The "gourmet," I argue, became a successful narrative promising masculine capital the moment he was construed as a figure of resistance against home economics–inspired domestic cooking. The gourmet now was someone who valued taste over nutrition and efficiency, thus providing a standpoint to take on home economics and to implicitly or directly challenge women's authority in the culinary field and their political demands in the public sphere. Like other Progressives, home economists targeted immigrant foodways for reform, attacking fresh ingredients as less reliable and uniform in their nutritional value than canned foods, and traditional methods as inferior to scientific ones, whereas gourmets in the 1920s started to embrace not only the foods of the world but also the ethnic foods American cities had to offer. Cooking advice in the 1930s addressing men suggested they should cook for themselves to escape the inferior dishes women, who lacked men's culinary genius, provided. Besides French cuisine, gourmet cooks began to explore American regional cooking, dishes from other regions in the world, and ethnic cuisines, mining and Americanizing other cultures' heritages for the sake of class distinction.

During the Depression, the slowly growing genre of cooking manuals for male cooks started to suggest that men who engaged in gourmet cooking could maintain their class status by producing their own classy meals.

Gourmet cooking in this era was not necessarily bound to luxury but to the knowledge of other cultures, methods of cooking, and exotic ingredients (purchased cheaply in immigrant neighborhoods); anticipating markers of social class in postwar America, gourmet status was less dependent on the budget of the cook and more on his knowledge.

Books such as *Dine at Home with Rector* (1937) revealed the "secrets" of famous restaurateurs to those who could not afford their restaurants, while at the same time promoting gourmet cooking as manly cooking. An increasing number of famous men came forward to declare themselves amateur chefs and share their recipes in cookbooks and magazine articles, which made cooking a more accepted male hobby. But it was still a potentially dangerous area for white men's masculinity. Radio (and later TV) chef John MacPherson presented his cooking show in the 1930s anonymously under the name "The Mystery Chef" because he did not want to embarrass his mother, who thought cooking an inappropriate activity for a man.[50]

In the course of the late 1930s, however, fine dining became an acceptable and desirable part of a refined urban ideal of masculinity that no longer defined itself by simplicity. While consumption at the beginning of the century was connoted as a feminine activity, the erosion of traditional modes of production and the need for new markets led to a weakened gendering of consumption.[51] In 1933 the first men's lifestyle magazine, *Esquire,* was founded, encouraging consumption that promised increased masculine capital. It not only promoted fashion, travel, and interior design for men, but also published articles on food and cooking.[52] Men were encouraged to "invest" in their masculinity by making certain lifestyle choices guided by a taste educated by the *Esquire* experts.

In the early years of *Esquire,* authors initially promoted "hard-boiled" masculinities. "Dining without Pain" instructed *Esquire* readers on how to host a dinner party "with or without a wife as hindrance."[53] But instead of shooting dinner and then cooking it in the wilderness, *Esquire* encouraged its male readers to explore other peoples' cultures from the comfort of their own kitchens. Travel writer John Gunther wrote a column for the magazine exploring the foods of Europe ("a series of mouth-watering articles to make American men's stomachs feel at home abroad") in installments such as "Roast Beef of Old England," "Strong Stomach in Spain," "Food along the Danube," and "Life History of Spaghetti." Being knowledgeable about the world (especially the parts of the world that held desirable cultural capital) became an important part of middle-class masculine performance.

The recipes featured in *Esquire* provided cultural knowledge and culinary experience, depicting men's eating as adventurous and educated and male cooking as exceptional and spectacular. Unlike the (female) family cook, the gourmet cook appeared only for special events, and his cooking itself was staged as a special event. In January 1930, Byron MacFadyen wrote in *Good Housekeeping* about male cooks. "These men may knock the week's budget ... but what they serve is undeniably fine. And how they brag, or point out as they eat that if every cook paid a little attention to the niceties in cooking, the whole family would be happier" ("When a Man Goes Culinary," 90). The wife, overseeing the family meals during the week without paying "attention to the niceties in cooking" was urged to support her husband: "the wise woman sits back while her man is developing his sense of power in the kitchen" (90). Only seldom did authors speak against the idea of the male genius cook, such as Eleanor Pollock in 1949, who wrote in *Good Housekeeping:* "As an exhibitionist the amateur *chef* knows no equal" (38).

Authors of male cooking advice often promoted biological arguments for their superior abilities, but sometimes engaged in cultural analysis. Will Brown, for instance, claimed in 1933:

> Women have no imagination in the kitchen. Bless their hearts, why should they? This business of getting together three squares a day; of including something filling for a healthy husband and enough calories and vitamins for the babies and few enough fattening effects for herself; and all the same time staying within a budget that possibly isn't what it is used to be—there's little time left for imagination. (289)

Authors rarely suggested that men should share the burden many women had to carry, but rather encouraged male cooks to embrace the freedom that comes from not being responsible for family meals. Rather than the regular family cook, Alfred Toombs claimed, he "set out to become the family Escoffier" after his youngest daughter praised him for his apple pie. The family members in cooking instructions directed at men generally appear as claqueurs. Unlike in campfire narratives, masculinity is described here in the context of sophistication, education, and family values, fitting more easily into urban white men's lives and assuring them of the legitimacy of their entitlements.

Cooking advice for men routinely assured readers that every man could become a gourmet cook in no time, because of his inborn superior tastes. Will Brown advised men to enter the kitchen when the "mistress" is away and look in a cookbook for those recipes that appeal to him but have never been served to him: "By now you have broken the ice. The next thing you know you will have graduated into a full-fledged chef and be putting Delmonico to shame" (288). References to restaurant cooking are another staple of cooking advice for men, and they usually elide the fact that male professional cooks had decades of training in the kitchen before they rose to fame.

What keeps the talented apprentice gourmet cook from following his vocation, the same article claims, is the cryptic genre of female cookbook writing: "'fold' was a puzzler to me for a long time. In fact, for quite a while I had to yell from the kitchen to the living room to demand what 'fold' and 'sear' and 'dice' and 'cream the shortening' meant." But once this linguistic hurdle preserving women's authority through expert knowledge is overcome, men are at an advantage, since "A woman will take a recipe, follow it faithfully and religiously to the dot and set out a dish which . . . is exactly the same dish a thousand other women are setting out at the moment. . . . You as a man will never let it stop at that" (Brown 289). Another article suggests using recipes as a starting point but then dismissing them. "Learn the rules lightly and throw them away, one at a time. Only then can you take the real creator's pride in your dish and put it out as a little thing of your own" (Pemberton 54). Manly gourmet cooking therefore served as the artistic expression of a man's individuality, while women merely followed the standardized instructions of cookbooks and home economists.

Looking at the culinary articles in *Esquire,* it may seem as if campfire cooking and gourmet cooking were two incompatible extremes. But this was not necessarily always the case. Gourmet cooking became as well established as manly cooking in the 1930s, but campfire cooking continued to appear, even if it needed reformulation to disassociate it from poverty. As campfire cooking narratives borrowed from imagery associated with working-class masculinities (expressed by an iconography of muscles, strength, physical labor, danger, the fight for survival, outdoor living and labor, control of affect, and strict hierarchies), gourmet cooking borrowed leisure-class imagery such as travel, cosmopolitanism, refinement, and elite knowledge. In "Come and Get Hit" (1937), Donald Hough argued that there are two camps of male cooks: "the very tough, duck-rolled-in-clay division" and "the more effete trout-in-wine sauce group," but that these two groups are not so far apart: "They are classed together because each strives for an effect by departure from the norm, advertising its Epicurean culture with a flourish" (92). The common denominator is that manly cooking is superior to women's cooking ("the norm"), a constant in 1930s cooking instructions directed at men. This fusion rested on the argument that simplicity is at the core of each gourmet meal and a perfectly barbecued steak is the height of refinement, hence it, too, is "gourmet." Byron MacFadyen claimed that men can be connoisseurs of excellent foods and simultaneously crave "plain food." He then quotes some men engaging in a gourmet assessment of hamburgers ("Dishes Fit for Gods—and Men," 81). The knowledge and appreciation of simplicity becomes part of gourmet discourse, miraculously transforming any food men like into gourmet food.

Cookbooks directed at men, too, mixed the two discourses effortlessly. In "Gastronomy in the Woods," Stewart Holbrook collected recipes from cooks in (mostly logging) camps such as "Receipt of the Rabbit to the Wine White or the Wine Red," a garlic vinaigrette from a British cook, and *potage au boeuf*. He also mentions fruitcake with raisins and orange peel, Yorkshire pudding "light as drift and yellow as gold," and puff-paste tarts. While the food is very far from Hemingway's flapjacks, it still serves to differentiate "real" and manly food from processed and feminine food. "[T]here are some queer chefs in the timber," the narrator warns, referring to cooks who use processed foods, such as lemon extract, to feed their charges. But these experiences are the exception, the narrator asserts. "Although the menus vary in both quality and scope, they are invariably excellent. The cooking is generally of a high order and the variety of food is astounding" (341). This fusion of gourmet and camp cuisine served the reinforcement of masculinity as well as legitimizing class status. Roughed-up gourmet food, or gentrified camp food, asserted culinary as well as masculine capital for the cook.

The changes in the conception in manly cooking that occurred from the 1920s to the 1930s may be best summarized in a comparison. *The Stag Cook Book* was reedited and published as *The Stag at Ease* in 1938. The revisions were substantial and are illuminating, as they reflect changes not only in ideas of manly cooking but also in how ideal masculinity had evolved. While the subtitle of *The Stag Cook Book* read "Written for Men by Men," *The Stag at Ease* proclaimed, "Being the Culinary Preferences of a Number of Distinguished Male Citizens of the World." Of the total of 110 contributors in *The Stag at Ease,* only a handful had been part of the first edition. And of those, the majority decided to alter their recipes. The painter and author Will Deming in *The Stag Cook Book* had offered "Virginia Ham," "Lemon Pie," and "A Dressing," but in the revision replaced them with "Birds and Fish in Clay" and "Beef Deming." Booth Tarkington claimed in the first edition:

"My favorite dish is corn flakes. They should be placed in a saucer or hollow dish, then lifted in both hands and rolled for a moment, then dropped back into the dish. After that an indefinite quantity of cream should be poured upon them. They should be eaten with a spoon" (97). In *The Stag at Ease,* Tarkington cited "Panned Oysters" as a dish he favored (137). Recipes were more complicated, male cooks less defensive and more self-assured. The recipe titles reflected the changing demands of gender performance men faced.

The relationship between gourmet cooking and ethnic and non-American cuisines oscillated between colonial gestures and endorsement of cultural difference.[54] Ethnic food commonly helped to demarcate class on the basis of knowledge and education rather than wealth. While historically, good food was the provenance of the wealthy, the cosmopolitan focus of gourmet food in the 1930s helped artists and academics to establish themselves as cultural trendsetters by utilizing ethnic ingredients. While gourmets were often advised to embrace other cuisines and explore the culinary ethnic diversity of the United States, recipes were usually adjusted to fit the American palate and to simplify the process of cooking. A "Hungarian Beef Goulash" in *For Men Only* was reduced to seven ingredients: steak, onions, canned tomato soup, beef suet, beef stock, paprika, and vinegar (128). Traditionally stews in Europe did not use the best cuts, but less-desirable pieces of meat, such as shoulder or shin. A Hungarian recipe might also have included garlic, caraway seeds, bay leaves, carrots, parsnips, celery, and, most importantly, bell pepper, with wine instead of vinegar. In this regard, cooking instructions for men did not differ from similar processes in American women's cookbooks. But gourmet narratives often played up the foreign as part of food expertise, and introduced cuisines that American cookbook authors had not featured prominently. The gourmets were more ready to incorporate ingredients that were looked at askance in mainstream cooking advice. A case in point is the use of garlic, which was still viewed ambiguously by many authors of cooking advice, but enthusiastically endorsed by many male writers. In 1930 Holbrook wrote in the *American Mercury*: "garlic, according to an unofficial yet decisive survey of American home life . . . is a weed used only by long-whiskered Socialists and other foreigners. Only a small portion of the good American wives in my survey have ever seen or even smelled it" (101). The brave male cook knew no such fears and flavored his dishes as he liked.

Forays into exotic neighborhoods were a staple of gourmet writing, transferring the thrill of the hunt from the jungle or savannah to the borough next door. James M. Cain, asked to contribute to Merle Armitage's cookbook *Fit for a King* (1939), offered a recipe for spaghetti. Other cooking advice in the 1920s had established spaghetti as a good manly dish (*The Stag Cook Book* lists eight recipes for pasta). Cain's brief essay says it is perfect for a supper around midnight when a party is just about to slow down. Instead of cooking the sauce, Cain suggests that the cook purchase it in advance from an Italian restaurant. The cook is then left to prepare the spaghetti, a project more complex than one might expect. The process begins with buying the right kind:

> [T]o get spaghetti, you must go where spaghetti is. You cannot get spaghetti, or anything that goes with it, in an American grocery, regardless of what they tell you about the fine quality of goods they carry. . . . To get spaghetti you have to go to Italians: nobody else understands it. Within a mile of you, if you take the trouble to find it, is an Italian grocery. . . . You will find, arranged in wooden bins, about a hundred different sizes of spaghetti, ranging from fine sizes for soups . . . to coarse macaronis. . . . You will have to find one to suit you. . . . Stock your spaghetti several pounds at a time, as it is a nuisance to be going after it constantly. (243)

The advice on how to buy pasta makes a number of assumptions: that the reader does not live in an Italian neighborhood but within a mile of an Italian grocery store, and that he does not find himself regularly in an Italian neighborhood, as it takes trouble to find the place and it is a nuisance to return. Italians are praised for their knowledge of pasta, but this only makes them more exotic. Cain provides no cultural information, nor does he express interest in exploring Italian culture. The immigrant community serves as a provider of resources to increase one's culinary capital, as the cook can impress his guests with the foreign taste of his impromptu dish, or the unusual shape of the pasta he bought. John Burdick calls this process of entering ethnic neighborhoods solely for the pursuit of mining authentic food (and talking about it) "culinary slumming."[55]

Across a total of four pages Cain describes how to cook the spaghetti, making it an act of artistry and culinary achievement, veiling the fact that the actual labor that went into the dish, the making of the pasta and sauce, was done by somebody else. Cain suggests inviting the guests into the kitchen to observe the masterful male cook and to appreciate his labor. Like earlier advice that suggested that women do the prep work and let their men do the "finishing touches," here the invisible ethnic cook becomes the sous chef to the male white genius.

In 1941 *Gourmet Magazine* was launched, manifesting the arrival of gourmet discourses in the American mainstream. *Gourmet* employed male and female staff writers and editors, but in the first years propagated a cuisine that had many of the characteristics associated at this point with manly cooking, such as references to professional cooking, game, and alcohol, and no concern with the causes home economists promoted such as nutrition, health, and maintaining moderate weight. In the October 1941 issue, the authors asserted that "*Gourmet* is a man's magazine on food that men enjoy. No vitamins, no calories. Just good food, yes, and good drinks" (35). The magazine engaged in equal-opportunity denigration of women's abilities: its illustrations often made fun of women who cooked, and of those who did not. An illustration in the May 1942 issue shows a daughter asking her mother, "Last night Bill asked me if I could cook. What's cooking?" (66). Another illustration from February shows a female restaurant diner negotiating with a waiter: "If the Chef will give me his recipe for his Bisquit Tortoni, I'll give him mine for apple jelly" (66), evidently a ridiculous proposition. In the same issue a woman staring at a bottle asks a wine dealer incredulously: "Jeepers! Nothing fresher than 1928?" (66). In articles such as "Pioneers of Gastronomy," the magazine promoted all-male lines of tradition for gourmet cooking (Carniol 20).

The "Gourmet Chef" or culinary director of the magazine, Louis DeGouy, was a French professional cook. Employing him to provide signature dishes for the magazine created a profile that differentiated *Gourmet* from magazines directed at women and housewives, which touted the expertise of home economists rather than chefs. Before joining *Gourmet,* DeGouy had published cookbooks that provided recipes for fowl and fish to wealthy hobby hunters who wanted to prepare their bounty (or have it prepared) European style.[56] This was the spirit DeGouy brought to his column. He offered recipes for game, fish, and venison, all of which, it was suggested, had been hunted by the cook himself. DeGouy's recipes were also published in *The Gourmet Cookbook* (1950). Barbara Haber recalls how alienating the cookbook was for female domestic cooks. In *From Hardtack to Home Fries* she tells the story of how as a teenager she gave her mother *The Gourmet Cookbook* in the hope, she confesses, that the fancy recipes would help to transform her modest middle-class background into something more exciting and cosmopolitan. For her "that thick brown classic with its gold lettering represented a sophisticated, elegant world of food that could have been easily available to our family if only my mother applied herself and learned to prepare the dishes" (210–11). After a few weeks went by with no culinary change to the Haber household, she confronted her mother, who claimed not to be able to understand the book. Haber, to prove her mother wrong, opened *The Gourmet Cookbook* at a random page and read aloud: "Marinate the ham of a bear for five days in cooked red wine marinade." Dumbstruck, she looked at her mother, who held her gaze and said, "See?" After that mother and daughter dissolved in laughter at the "notion of my mother cooking anything that had to be hunted down in a forest. . . . The earliest issues of *Gourmet* magazine . . . were never intended for a female audience" (211).

Nonetheless, during the war, the female readership of *Gourmet* grew due to the social mobility and luxurious lifestyles the recipes promised. The magazine also acted as a counterweight to the narratives of sacrifice on an individual and national level that, as Harvey Levenstein has argued, undermined an American sense of entitlement to abundance (*Paradox*, 80–100). The magazine also drew in women readers by changing its strategy to suit wartime conditions, recognizing that military mobilization had taken many of its potential male readers out of the market for magazines about cooking, while requiring new skills of family cooks; enforced food rationing asked home cooks to think creatively. In the war cookbook *Cooking on a Ration: Food Is Still Fun* (1943), for instance, Marjorie Mills wrote: "We're stumped. We need cooking procedures that are not in any of our books. We need good meatless main dishes, recipes low in fat and sugar, hearty soups and chowders, and above all meals that won't take too much time to prepare. Yet we want to be satisfying and a joy to our families in difficult times" (ix). Focusing on the difficult position women faced as wartime propaganda made them responsible for making food rationing palatable to their families ("Mother has to cushion the shock of transition" [57]) while also working outside the house, regular cookbooks promoted a doing-without philosophy and an ethic of duty. *Gourmet,* on the contrary, promised gains in social status and patriotic service at the same time.

As its wartime strategy, *Gourmet* carefully avoided all associations with excess and promoted ingredients that were not rationed, such as offal (Strauss 150–55). The "other meats," non-muscle meat or meat from undomesticated animals, were not rationed and widely available. Offering French recipes for them allowed necessity to be the mother of cosmopolitan refinement: David Strauss argues that the magazine attempted to beat "the Nazis with Truffles and Tripe" (134). Despite the heavy promotion of French cuisine, the magazine now established gourmet food as American. Instead of hard-to-get

French wines and other imported products, the authors concentrated on domestic products. And while they paid attention to the cuisines of allies (French and Russian), tellingly, they left out the German recipes that had been a regular part of earlier gourmet literature (160). The gourmet lifestyle was presented as the quintessence of Western civilization, now threatened by Nazi domination. In this context, eating well was recast as good citizenship (149–50).

After DeGouy's death, Louis Diat became the new "Gourmet Chef." Diat targeted a market that was more inclusive of female readers. He came up with recipes that were easier to re-create in the home kitchen than bear steaks, and gave detailed information on methods and procedures that had often been missing from DeGouy's instructions. Most importantly, he acknowledged women's expertise respectfully, paying tribute in an article to "My Mother's Kitchen" and crediting his knowledge to French home cooking rather than his own haute cuisine experience as head chef at the Ritz-Carlton. Welcoming women into gourmet discourse came at a price. Diat depicted a conservative ideal of motherhood and femininity, one out of reach for many of his readers. "More important was the spirit of my smiling, friendly mother who was the queen of this little domain" ("My Mother's Kitchen," 10). He sketched his mother's character by describing her cooking, "her capable hands on the rolling pin flattening out a fat ball of pastry, or carefully skimming the *pot-au-feu,* or perhaps carrying a soufflé to the table, carrying it so very gently lest its magic puffing collapse too soon" (10). Not only is this female gourmet not a professional chef, she seems not to work for pay at all, focusing her time and care on pots-au-feu and soufflés.

This image of an impossibly ideal mother was told to a generation of women who had just helped win a war with hard work in factories and other positions that were traditionally closed to them, and were now asked to yield their jobs in the industrial and service sectors to returning veterans. Texts such as this tried to lure them back to their kitchens with images of filling them with sunshine, smiles, and irresistible aromas and thereby claiming their rightful heritage as "queens of their little domains." Non-gourmet cookbooks such as *How Mama Could Cook* by Dorothy Malone (1946) carried similar messages. The cover shows a woman in Gibson girl attire, which would more befit the author's grandmother than her mother, cooking in an old-fashioned kitchen without the gadgets and electronic appliances that were associated with progress, thus creating a similar setting to Diat's mother's French kitchen filled with love and good spirits, and concealing the labor women do in it. Choosing these illustrations transposed an almost Victorian ideal of femininity onto postwar America. But what had changed for men since the adventurous gourmet had been mobilized for military service? After the war was over, suburbs grew rapidly thanks to low-interest federal home mortgages the government provided for veterans to buy new houses. And with suburbanization grew a highly commodified, middle class–dominated culture that organized masculinity ideals around maturity and responsibility to the family. Cooking for men was carefully crafted as a hobby and mostly concentrated on barbecuing in suburban backyards, faintly echoing earlier images of cowboys and hunters cooking over open fires, but with any sense of danger thoroughly tamed through domestication. Gourmet cooking, with its connotations of upper-class sensibilities and travel, in the 1930s may have initially served as a point of resistance against pressures to conform to society's expectations, but in the end gourmet cooking, or its pale imitation, was so thoroughly incorporated into middle-class life that it became a marker of conformity.

Supported by a gourmet discourse that had by now established the idea of male culinary expertise in American culture, the 1950s also saw the rise of two male culinary superstars. Craig Claiborne had served in World War II and attended a Swiss hotel school on the G. I. Bill before he returned to the United States and wrote for *Gourmet Magazine.* In 1957 he became the food editor of the *New York Times,* a perch he used, along with his many cookbooks, to acquaint American readers with ethnic cuisines ranging from French haute cuisine to Asian and Latin American styles. James Beard was a pioneer in the gourmet food industry. In the late 1930s he opened a catering business that specialized in cocktail parties. In 1946 he hosted a TV cooking show that, tellingly, was not called *I Love to Cook,* but *I Love to Eat,* and he became the embodiment of the male gourmet. In the perception of his audience, his bearlike stature and guy persona (wrongly) assured his heteronormativity. A forerunner to Julia Child, Beard promoted French cooking to an American audience in the 1950s, but in his dozens of cookbooks and cooking performances around the United States, he also urged Americans to enjoy taking the time to cook well, and to cook with ingredients available in their own country. While Beard and Claiborne did not address an exclusively male audience, they were crucial in establishing male culinary expertise via gourmet cooking in the American mainstream—helping to make the kitchen a safe place for male ambition.

PLAYBOYS IN THE KITCHEN: MANLY
COOKING IN THE 1950S AND 1960S

One of the ongoing concerns in cooking instructions for men was that cooking could be seen as effete, and, in an increasingly homophobic climate, a sign of homosexuality. In the 1950s, white male authors of cookbooks, always vigilantly patrolling the boundaries of appropriate masculine behavior to avoid the stigma of inadequacy in any way, started to include blatant (hetero) sexual references in their texts.

Such references had been a staple of cooking instructions for men before, but were less explicit. In *The Bachelor and the Chafing Dish* (1896), the narrator and protagonist described making lunch for a female guest. The scene is full of sexual innuendo, as the woman is not chaperoned and the setting is intimate (120). Since the 1930s, texts claimed that men who cook have an advantage in pursuing women. In 1935 James Cain published "Oh, les Crêpes Suzettes!" in *Esquire*. With a wink, he observed that "she likes to 'blow out the fire,'" and promised: "If you have done it right you ought to rate an even break" (*Cookbook,* 59, 63). After serving the female guest, he instructs: "Serve your own plate. Smack your lips. Make one or two technical criticisms. Be evasive as to where you learned the art. Sit back. Look at her. Forget to turn on the lights. Estimate your chances" (*Cookbook,* 63). Gourmet cooking, as a means to sexual conquest, becomes a safe, manly tool that implies social cachet. Gourmet cooking instructions thus create a legitimization for the male cook, and safely anchor cooking within a heterosexual order.

While bold for mainstream writing in the 1930s, by the 1950s such references to premarital sex became commonplace in cookbook literature for men. *Wolf in Chef's Clothing* (1950) by Robert Loeb is a case in point. The "Picture Cook and Drink Book for Men," as the cover page reads, presents cooking instructions in comic-strip form. The text contains many of the staples of men's cookbooks of the time, such as spaghetti bolognese, crêpes suzette, barbecue, omelets, and roasted bananas. The gender-affirming strategies the book uses are similar to texts in the 1930s and 1940s, too. For instance, the notion of men as victims of women's cooking can be found in the first pages, in the dedication to a generation of men, who, the author claims, were "victims of feminine culinary caprice—from the first apple to apfelstrudel." What is new is the implication that men no longer cook for themselves or their buddies; the intended target for a man's culinary efforts is a woman who needs to be wowed or wooed. The text expects the reader to cook for his wife, his lover, or a candidate to become one or the other. Within this framework, cooking skills can come in handy, Loeb promises, for "guilt and appeasement days" and "Gastronomic Foreplay." The breakfast section starts with a poem of sorts that betrays its inspiration in the Burma Shave advertising slogans:

> If you want to rise and shine—
> Make her breakfast.
> If your conscience is bad—
> Make her breakfast.
> If *her* conscience is bad—
> Make her breakfast.
> If you want to breakfast her—
> Read on (12)

The section called "Her majesty's breakfast service" teaches men how to set a breakfast table or bed tray, promising that this is a good investment, since it will "make a queen eat out of your hand next time" (30). The dinner section (tastefully named "Sup-Her") offers a taxonomy of womanhood to help men understand whom they are dealing with: the athletic type, "long, lean, and limbsome, who prefers a game of tennis to a shot of 3-star Henness(ey)"; the "indoor type," "soft, round, and fluffy"; the intellectual type, "more an I. Q. than a Q. T."; or the "3-B" type, "brains, bonds, and beauty—don't believe it" (31) (fig. 7). According to this logic, women cannot be smart *and* cute, but they all can be caught with the right bait. The recipes provided are for two adult eaters or for parties. It is never suggested that the male cook may find himself in a situation where he has to provide family meals or school lunches.

In 1953, *Playboy* magazine made its scandalous debut. From its initial issue on, it featured a cooking column that utilized the newly sexualized rationale of men cooking in the pursuit of sexual conquest. The reader implied in these texts was the refined, urban, white male, a man of gourmet appetites and expert skills, an image that the reader purchased together with the centerfolds and that was as important to the success of the magazine as the playmates. With cooking still implicated with domestic femininity in the 1950s, *Playboy*'s commitment to food instruction may come as a surprise, but the column featured cooking as a crucial part of the playboy lifestyle. Borrowing from earlier conceptualizations of manly cooking, the playboy cook demonstrated his independence from women (especially wives and mothers) with pots and pans. Barbara Ehrenreich has argued that the economy of a nuclear family, what she

sup — her

Here are four $10 specials graded for type:

menu #1	**menu #2**
If she's the athletic type—long, lean, and limbsome, who prefers a game of tennis to a shot of 3-star Henness(ey): tomato juice `a l'ocean—mignon et béarnaise—baked potatoes—salad Roquefort	If she's the indoor type—soft, round, and fluffy, who thinks Alexander the Great the best cocktail ever made: broiled grapefruit—lamb chops—potatoes fried `a la France—salade Walt Whitman
menu #3	**menu #4**
If she's the intellectual type—more an I.Q. than a Q.T.—if she prefers Gounod's *Faust* to getting soused: orange Hawaiian—spaghetti da Vinci—les choux froids	If she's the 3-B type—brains, bonds, and beauty—don't believe it—but it's fun pretending: strawberry loving cup—poulet maison dixon—potatoes `a l'onion—salad subversive

31

FIGURE 7. "Sup-her," from Robert H. Loeb Jr., *Wolf in Chef's Clothing* (Wilcox and Follett Co., 1950).

calls the "family wage," is based on the idea that a family lives on the male breadwinner's income while wives provide unpaid labor such as cooking, child rearing, and cleaning. This model leads not only to limited outlets for women's self-expression but also to great pressure on the sole earner of the family income. In the 1950s this led some fathers to see their families no longer as an asset but as a burden, and to an underlying resentment of women's perceived exploitation of male labor (4). Although a great number of middle-class mothers did work, women were blamed for forcing men into nine-to-five jobs and for all the downsides of suburban conformity (6–9). *Playboy* showed that many of the tasks that were traditionally connoted with women's authority and labor, such as cooking, could be easily taken over by men (who, if they set their minds to it, would also do a much better job). Although the column typically addressed its readers as "bachelors," the magazine's actual readers were older and married.[57] Thus the cooking advice as well as other parts of the magazine suggested that the instructions and products the magazine featured would allow the reader a lifestyle of pleasure and leisure.

Masculinity, heterosexuality, and economic success were fused together in *Playboy*'s philosophy, especially in its food and drink section. The cooking instructions, later collected in *Playboy's Gourmet* by Thomas Mario, *Playboy's* food and drink editor since 1954, were heavy with sexual innuendo, either directly ("The bachelor who attempts to make a hamburger should have a thorough orientation in the art of petting" [162]) or indirectly, as in references to the imagined "sex life" of the ingredients used (such as crabs) or by sexualizing food. Mario prefaced a recipe for lobster, for example: "Lobster is the playboy of the deep; he is a night person, an epicure, a traveler. During the daylight hours, he remains relatively stable on the ocean bed, but after sundown he becomes noticeably restless. . . . He has the true gourmet's fondness for seafood, being partial to clams in the shell" (65). Digesting a "playboy of the deep" is safe for those who do not want to (or cannot) engage in the racier aspects of playboy life, and while not affordable for everybody, it is still cheaper than buying a penthouse apartment or driving an Aston Martin. The magazine suggested that sexual and financial success were inevitably linked. *Playboy's* recipes for gourmet chick bait insinuated that cooking reflecting elite tastes, expert knowledge, and upper-class income indicated virility and flashier playboy lifestyles, and would impress women sufficiently that they would succumb to the cook's charms.

Playboy's cooking column invoked bachelor lifestyles in luxurious urban apartments (penthouses if possible), fast cars, and intellectual stimulation, all of it without the responsibilities to wives and families mainstream culture demanded of grown men. Despite the clichéd masculinities *Playboy* offered, it represented points of potential resistance against the normative masculine identities of American middle-class culture. Ehrenreich writes, "The magazine encouraged the sense of membership in a fraternity of male rebels" (43), allowing men to reclaim domestic space as a space for personal expression (as exemplified in the many stories it devoted to interior design and manly gadgets) and to criticize marriage as an institution. But this resistance happened within clearly confined limits, and at the expense of wives who were deemed responsible for the pressures men felt.

Playboy's playboy wholeheartedly embraced consumerism and a white-collar economy. The magazine insinuated that the ideal reader had financial resources that were not only abundant but also at the male consumer's free disposal (without worries about mortgages or college funds).[58] Even if the financial resources were wanting, abundance could and should be faked, the magazine's writers suggested, by investing in the right products to mimic upper-class tastes and resources. After two decades of frugality and sacrifices, a booming industry now encouraged Americans to find pleasure in consumption, regularly equating it with well-earned fun. *Playboy* thus provided men with a new motivation to engage in the workplace by stimulating their desire to consume. In this way the magazine participated in keeping men functioning within the capitalist economy (unlike the Beats, who also rejected suburban living and promoted new sexual frontiers, but rejected consumption and traditional careers). *Playboy* founder Hugh Hefner later claimed that it was this commitment to American capitalism that protected the magazine against more radical criticism and censorship.[59]

The obsession with consumption played an important role in the magazine's food and drink section. The writers suggested that men could not cook with the same tools and gadgets as women, but needed their own set of instruments. This included seemingly gender-neutral items such as salad bowls. "Gear and Gadgets for the Bachelor's Buffet" warned of the perils that came with items purchased by women, and promoted manly devices: "Not for him the embellished and decorated gear that floods the shops and warms the heart of the housewife. The gourmet uses handsomely wrought, masculine gadgetry, functional ware that's fine-lined and clean-limbed, that gleams with the colors as felicitously as it does his job."[60] Manly gadgets kept men's masculinity intact, even in the ambivalent space of the kitchen, demonstrating the power objects were believed to have over masculine identity.

Joanne Hollows, Bill Osgerby, and others have found that much of *Playboy*'s rhetoric was an attempt to masculinize the private and the domestic sphere that during the 1950s was again firmly associated with women's authority. War propaganda and postwar discourses claiming the homemakers' importance to society had reinforced women's authority over the domestic. These strategies were meant to help women embrace their status as homemakers, but they made it more difficult for men to find a place and role within their own homes. *Playboy*'s manly take on kitchen chores was represented not only in the extra tools they demanded, but also in kitchen design. *Playboy* designers recommended open kitchens that allowed the cook to talk to his guests while cooking (presumably collecting some praise in the process), making his cooking a visible and impressive performance, while women's domestic labor was still hidden in closed kitchens. The TV show *Playboy's Penthouse* (1959–60), hosted by Hugh Hefner and shot in a presumably perfect playboy apartment, went even further by presenting in the first episode the "kitchenless kitchen" specifically designed for that space. It was a cube-shaped, bar-like construction with a strip of outlets and a sink, situated right in the living room, which removed it as far from the feminine-connoted regular kitchen as possible.

Despite its manliness, when Hefner orchestrates the big reveal of the "kitchenless kitchen," he does not present it to some ambitious male cooks, but to two playmates, Joyce Nizzari and Eleanor Bradley. After claiming that he likes to see that being a centerfold jump-starts the careers of young women, he has the kitchen explained to them by editorial director Auguste Comte Spectorsky (who is credited with its design). After staring at the blank, empty surface, the women ask simultaneously "Where is the stove?" and "How do you cook?" As it turns out, Spectorsky had omitted the stove and oven and imagined meals prepared on appliances such as a waffle iron and a deep fryer. The entire kitchen is thus a big toolbox, full of specialized gadgets—an automated place that is very different from the soft pastels of suburban kitchens fashionable at the time. It also suggests that such a highly automated kitchen needs a technologically savvy, and therefore male, cook. With the help of gadgets, *Playboy* repeatedly argued, kitchen work was no longer labor but pure pleasure. Tedious tasks such as dishwashing were to be done not by the male cook but by his high-tech dishwasher.[61]

It is remarkable how the scene ends: Hefner steps aside to take a (fake) call (Ella Fitzgerald rings to let him know that she will drop by later). From offstage, Spectorsky says: "Hef, why don't you go ahead and take care of your guests and I'll help the girls rustle up something to eat." In the end, it seems that none of the men present can or is willing to operate the kitchen, and even the perfect playboy kitchen is relinquished to women, who now are expected to nonchalantly produce a meal for twenty-plus guests on single-serve gadgets. This is a good example of the inherent discrepancies in playboy cooking advice, where the idea of manly cooking is more important than the act.

Playboy appeared to offer alternative, liberated masculine identities, but always strictly contained and heavily regulated. Popular authors of the 1950s such as William H. Whyte and David Riesman claimed that masculinity was in crisis from conformity, overconsumption, "Momism," and domineering women. Arthur Schlesinger, spokesman for American centrist establishment thinking, in a 1958 *Esquire* essay saw nothing less than "The Crisis of American Masculinity": "Today men are more and more conscious of maleness not as a fact but as a problem. The ways by which American men affirm their masculinity are uncertain and obscure" (292). Blurring gender roles, Schlesinger argued, had kindled the crisis, and it is striking that he sees this most prominently represented within the home:

> The roles of male and female are increasingly merged in the American household. The American man is found as never before as a substitute for wife and mother—changing diapers, washing dishes, cooking meals, and performing a whole series of what once were considered female duties. The American woman meanwhile takes over more and more of the big decisions, controlling them. . . . Outside the home, one sees a similar blurring of function. While men design dresses and brew up cosmetics, women become doctors, lawyers, bank cashiers, and executives. (293)

Schlesinger conceded that men's identity was threatened by women's drive for equality, but even more so by the general pressure to conform to a broad range of social expectations. The fear of women taking political and economic power and sending men back into the kitchen was an ongoing theme in the 1950s. Within this broadly propagated sense of crisis, *Playboy* showed not the problematic but the pleasurable sides of masculinity, providing an escape from the sense of doom, the Cold War, and the suburbs by endorsing pleasurable spending and engaging in fantasy. While masculine sexual desires were seemingly openly discussed and lived in the securely contained spaces of the magazine's pages and in blueprints of the *Playboy* apartment, penthouse, townhouse, and other dream spaces the magazine featured over the years, they had no room in the familial suburban home.[62]

In Hugh Hefner's introduction to the first issue, *Playboy* distanced itself from women's magazines and "family magazines," claiming to be a new kind of magazine for men: "Most of today's 'magazines for men' spend all their time out-of-doors—thrashing through thorny thickets or splashing about in fast flowing streams. We'll be out there too, occasionally, but we don't mind telling you in advance—we plan on spending most of our time inside."[63] Spending time inside, motivated by the possibility of sexual encounter, was Hefner's idea of performing superior masculinity: "We like our apartment. We enjoy mixing up cocktails and an *hors d'oeuvre* or two . . . and inviting in a female acquaintance for a quiet discussion on Picasso, Nietzsche, jazz, sex."[64] Earlier masculine ideals had referred to nature as a space to demonstrate one's superior skills. In *Playboy* this notion was subsumed by the idea that masculinity is best proved by mastery over women, technology, consumption, and social entertainment. The pronounced upper-class masculinity presented there, including food preparation competence, was rewarded with sexual satisfaction.

As in gourmet discourses, *Playboy* made fun of campfire cooking, deeming it old-fashioned and insufficiently bourgeois. *Playboy's Penthouse* joked at the expense of men's magazines such as *Field and Stream* that concentrated on adventures in nature by claiming that "their playmate for December has a duck in her mouth" (S1 E1). In "Fishing for Compliments" Mario makes mild fun of narratives of fishing adventures found in other magazines of that time: "You needn't go spearfishing by torchlight or take rod and line and go hunting for tiger shark in tropical waters. Merely walk to the nearest fish stall . . . and shanghai the freshest specimens you can find" (*Playboy's Gourmet*, 52). His column on "Fair Game" begins, "Once a year, men in practically every state of the union tromp out of the woods with dogs and guns, their game bags filled to the legal limit with things furred and feathered." Thoroughly unimpressed, he claims that game bought in gourmet butcher shops and from mail-order game farms is superior, as the game was raised under "controlled conditions" (182).

The cooking column preferred class-marked urbanity over natural and rugged settings, but favored foods that were well established as masculine. The manliness of meat was emphasized with the usual references to sports, warfare, and (one of Mario's favorite historical/mythical references) Sparta. "In Sparta during the Fourth Century [*sic*], if you were male and over 20 years of age, you were required by law to eat two pounds of meat a day. It was supposed to make you brave" (122). Mario goes on to assert that "Meat-eating Tartars" were aggressive and "vegetable-eating Brahmans" peaceful. He concludes that steak eating is good for one's virility, and that therefore men should run the grill. It "has always been a male art. A woman may make the greatest chicken patty in the world but it seems to take a man to place a thick shell steak over a bed of live ashen-white charcoal, season it, brush it with butter and finally carve it properly" (123). Mario calls meat cooking the "aggressive art" (123), conflating not only meat eating, but also meat cooking, with masculine performance.

Women's cooking is dismissed as unfit for the male palate, echoing earlier tropes. Mario warns against "feminine bunny food," which includes most vegetables, also known as "tasteless wet shrubbery" (210), and dishes such as "Frozen Tomato Salad in Cucumber Boats" and "Jellied Ginger Ale and Grape Salad," which women apparently prefer, the "savorless fabrications originating in the minds of congenital spinsters, Home Economics teachers and amateur food demonstrators" ("Playboy at the Salad Bowl," 32).

But *Playboy*'s cooking advice also contested traditionally permissible arenas of male cooking; cooking advice for men rarely acknowledged holiday cooking, since the preparation of Thanksgiving and Christmas dinners was firmly associated with family and children. The *Playboy* food and drink section innovatively included recipes for holiday cooking by reformulating its significance. In the November 1956 issue, Mario opens "The Holiday Dinner" by stating that the family holiday dinner and *Playboy*'s romantic Thanksgiving or Christmas tête-à-tête were so different in intent that they needed entirely different dishes. This removes male preparations of holiday feasts safely from the realm of the family home. The accompanying illustration shows an intimate scene: a male and a female diner, she having opened her present of a gold bracelet. Between the two are multiple dishes of a festive dinner accompanied by coffee and red and white wine. The table is understated in its decorations and colors (no tablecloth, dark wood, modern dishware), endorsing *Playboy*'s idea of manly aesthetics. The menu includes "Iced Spanish Melon with Lime" and "Roast Rock Cornish Game Hen, Truffle Sauce" to be accompanied with "Quince Jelly, Buttered Asparagus, Chestnut Puree" (40). Mario notes that the expense of the dinner as well as the effort involved is well worth the investment. In "The Gourmet Gobbler," he liberates the turkey ("rich with breathtaking curves") from its association with Thanksgiving family dinners and women's cooking by framing it with some American history and the turkey's involvement and importance in it, followed by a discussion on carving techniques. The recipes appear almost as an afterthought, a reminder that the turkey also needs to be cooked, although (as Mario points out) not necessarily by the reader, as turkeys can be bought roasted (178).

Playboy helped to mainstream the idea that men cook with sexual innuendo and conquest in mind. In the late 1960s, the playboy cook appeared in a new incarnation in Graham Kerr's *The Galloping Gourmet,* a TV show that ran with great success from 1969 to 1972 and was accompanied by a number of cookbooks (it was produced for Canadian TV but syndicated in the United States). Unlike *Playboy, The Galloping Gourmet* was produced for a mainstream, coed audience and the cookbooks addressed the larger housewife market. Still, Kerr appropriated for his public persona elements that had been established as typical for playboy and gourmet cooks, renegotiating them to be palatable for family TV.

In the early episodes, Kerr greeted his live studio audience in a tuxedo, drink in hand, on a stage that resembled the *Playboy* apartment, channeling Hugh Hefner. The studio featured exposed-stone walls, earthy colors, a reading nook with a single armchair and a small table to hold a drink, and an open bar. A prominently displayed antique map, crossed swords, and family crest served as wall decorations, reproducing the *Playboy* aesthetic of manly interior design. The kitchen, while not "kitchenless," featured a brown and green palette, modern appliances, and minimalist decoration. A big wine shelf dominated the background of most shots, supporting the important role alcohol played in the show.

The Galloping Gourmet offered rich and luxurious recipes from restaurants all over the world, in line with a new interest in international cuisine no longer restricted to French cooking. Recipes included "Jamaican Pepper Pot Soup," "Feinschmeckerrolle," and "Gateau St. Honoré." The show encouraged viewers to experiment with new ingredients and not to be afraid of unknown dishes. Episodes started with some short footage of Kerr eating the recipe he presented in its supposedly original setting, a restaurant in a European capital or some exotic locale. Kerr therefore freely borrowed from ideas of manly cooking as aspirationally upper-class, adventurous, and cosmopolitan. He employed the gourmet and the playboy cook discourse also in promoting the use of ample amounts of alcohol, clarified butter, and cream, and by defying the calorie-conscious food advice of the day that was also increasingly concerned with heart health. He followed in the tradition of other male food instructors by objecting to accurate measurements.[65] In the episode "Bacon Fish Rolls" he stamped on a set of cup measures to make his indignation known. Sometimes a female voice from offstage corrects details or reminds Kerr of ingredients he has forgotten. Occasionally, he makes fun of the instructions he receives and dismisses them as nitpicking. He stages himself as a bohemian cook, mildly rebelling against his invisible prep and production team (and his wife, the producer of the show), thus echoing earlier narratives in which all men would be geniuses in the kitchen if their wives and mothers would only let them. In *The Graham Kerr Cookbook,* although addressing women, Kerr reverts sporadically to well-worn binaries such as the ignorant hostess versus the "great restaurateur" (8), or invokes women's irrationality and obsession with their weight (216).

The show, a mixture of slapstick, stand-up comedy, and cooking instruction, where the host might break out in song and dance at any moment and imitate accents and dialects, thrived on the mishaps and mistakes Kerr made (many of which seemed planned and carefully staged, while others were well-exploited genuine accidents). Similarly to Julia Child's *The French Chef,* the unpredictability that came with the format of the broadcast cooking show turned out to be an asset, making fine cooking not only entertaining but also accessible. Kerr's gourmet cuisine was mostly free of snobbishness. The episodes do not show the same reverence for foreign, especially European, cuisines that earlier gourmet narratives did. Often they openly make fun of the cultures the recipes originate from, encouraging New World cooks to become more self-confident at the expense of others.

The tuxedo of the first season, the playboy-style apartment with its bachelor interior design, and the party-like atmosphere were not the only references to the playboy cook. The show leaned heavily on sexual innuendo. Handling an onion, Kerr gave its measurement as a "size D" ("Jambalaya"). Peeling a tomato became "stripping" it and resulted in a "naked" tomato ("Grillards"). While the earliest episodes of the show ended with Kerr sitting down at a table set for one and tasting his dish with a rapt facial expression for the camera, later episodes ended with him sitting down at a table set for two, tasting the food, and then inviting someone from the audience, usually a woman, to join him. While the credits roll, we see and hear the two talking and the female guest praising Kerr's food. The scene is set to resemble an intimate dinner for two, Kerr seducing his guest with his extraordinary cooking.

Kerr did not wear a wedding band on the show, perhaps in line with the playboy persona he embodied. But he referred to his wife, Treena, and more often as the show continued. In much of the footage in foreign locales, Treena could be seen too, casting them as a young, glamorous, jet-setting couple.

Often she was on the receiving end of jokes and sexual insinuation (in "Bacon Fish Rolls," he "discloses" that Treena likes a "hot nibble" late at night). But her representation clearly departs from the depiction of wives as man's natural enemy, as in *Playboy*. Kerr's persona changed the figure of the playboy cook in such a fashion that he appealed to female viewers, too. He appropriated the authority of the manly cook over meat, exotic foods, and alcohol, as well as the glamour and evident heterosexuality of the playboy, together with the social status and cosmopolitanism of the gourmet, and mixed it with self-mockery, humor, and racist and sexist stereotypes, creating a successful TV cooking show that brought manly cooking into the American mainstream—a mainstream that hoped to absorb other cultures without friction by appropriating the ethnic diversity that was a central characteristic of society.

Such blatant misogyny and sexual objectification of women was missing from the newly emerging cookbooks written by African American male authors in the 1960s, when interest in soul food opened a market for cookbooks with a specific focus on African American cooking. The texts were directed at a coed audience and therefore serve as a contrast to the texts by white authors discussed earlier. Soul food cookbooks understood food as an intensely political topic, following a long tradition of using food to express racial pride and communal belonging in texts by African American authors.[66] Andrew Warnes argues that foodways in African American cultures are more politicized than in others. One reason is the history of hunger, poverty, and exclusion from the nation's abundance. Another is a sense of power, pride, and self-assertion in the many culinary strategies designed in response.[67] bell hooks explains, "Historically, African-American people believed that the construction of a homeplace, however fragile and tenuous (the slave hut, the wooden shack), had a radical political dimension."[68] Physical deprivation and hunger were a central aspect of the experience of slavery, and in many cases extended well into the next century.[69] Food served to define, redefine, and contest representations of racial and ethnic difference. "I yam what I am," exclaims the protagonist of Ralph Ellison's *Invisible Man* (1952) after giving in to a craving for yams that he had considered below his status as an educated African American living in a Northern metropolis. The yam he associates with poverty, provincialism, and the legacy of slavery, all of which he wishes to escape. Ellison joined other African American writers who described the choice of foods as a political act. Biting into the yam after trying to resist it, Ellison's protagonist literally incorporates his black

Southern roots, declaring allegiance to a culture from which he had wished to be disassociated. It is a powerful image that is followed by the character's commitment to work for social justice. Soul food authors could draw on a tradition of seeing food as a political rather than a domestic topic.

The advent of soul food in the 1960s gave authors the opportunity to reclaim their commodified African American culinary heritage and put it into a nationalist context. Soul food was established during the Black Liberation movement as the prototypical African American cuisine, consisting of canonical dishes and ingredients such as greens, "chittlings," yams, and pigs' feet that, soul food proponents argued, had their roots in African origins and the experience of enslavement. Foods that before had been understood as markers of slavery, poverty, or rurality were reformulated and appropriated as a valued heritage and source of racial pride. In this fashion, racist assumptions about African American cookery as simple, poor, and uncivilized were opposed with the counter-concept of a long, rich culinary history and the expertise of generations of cooks who, against all odds, created nourishment and delight. For instance, soul food authors claimed, chitterlings were eaten by slaves because when a pig was slaughtered, the slave master's family received the good parts and the slaves the rest: feet, intestines, tails, snout.[70]

The concept itself first appeared in print in 1962 in an article by LeRoi Jones, "Soul Food." Jones, a poet, playwright, essayist, and activist who would later become Amiri Baraka, was reacting to a "young Negro novelist writing in *Esquire* about the beauties of America" (101) who claimed that African American culture had not developed a specific language or a specific cuisine, to which he answers: "No language? No characteristic food? Oh, man, come on" (101). In his essay, Jones attempts to level class distinctions and regional differences within the African American communities and form one common culture, cuisine, language, and history, with the intention of improving the political potential of African Americans as a unified group. Jones describes chitterlings and sweet potato pie as tasting "like memory"; although they were dishes eaten in the South, he claimed them as part of a history that *all* African Americans shared (101). The concept of soul food constructed a culinary agency of slaves, undercutting discourses of disempowerment and victimization. It allowed a positive identification and intended to contribute to the creation of a modern collective identity.

But soul food also created a gendered conflict when men, within the newly emerging gendered labor paradigm after World War II, expected women to cook it. Being labor intensive (cleaning and cooking chitterlings, for example, can take five hours or more), soul food assigned politically engaged women back to the kitchen, defining their most important responsibility as cooking, excluding them from more prestigious, openly political endeavors, and then not valuing their work. Vertamae Smart-Grosvenor describes in *Vibration Cooking: Or, the Travel Notes of a Geechee Girl* how the jazz saxophonist Archie Shepp asked her to cater a "soul food party" for his opening night at the Chelsea Theater. Smart-Grosvenor and a friend cut up fifteen pounds of collard greens ("We got calluses on our fingers"), just to learn that the event had been postponed and they had not been informed.[71] Doris Witt posits in "My Kitchen Was the World" that soul food was constructed by the predominantly male Black Arts Movement as a safe haven from which men departed on their adventures while the women stayed home to prepare more soul food to celebrate their return (244).

When male authors of soul food cookbooks did claim the cooking for themselves in the 1960s, they could choose among a number of strategies that allowed them to negotiate the complex interplay of gender and racial identity. Soul food writing was not entirely free from gender-exclusionary mechanisms when citing homosocial solidarity and classically masculine vocations involving adventure, physical courage, and frontier environments in which women are notably absent. Jim Harwood and Ed Callahan argued in their *Soul Food Cookbook* (1969):

> Soul Food takes its name from a feeling of kinship among Blacks. In that sense, it's like "Soul Brother" and "Soul Music"—impossible to define but recognizable among those who have it. But there's nothing secret or exclusive about Soul Food.
> The Black man does have a right to feel close to Soul Food; after all, Blacks have been the caretakers of Soul Food from the beginning. But Soul Food is not exclusively Black. The Redman and poor White Southerner had an important share in its development, too. Not to mention any number of soldiers, explorers, settlers, traders and others of varied nationalities. (1)

Whether partaking in the gender-exclusionary brotherhood of Soul or following a trail blazed by armed adventurers and successful entrepreneurs, men who cooked soul food, according to this narrative, might forge links to other oppressed men, while relieving cooking of its feminine and domestic associations.

In the 1960s soul food was not embraced by all black nationalists. The pork-based dishes at the heart of soul food alienated radical young African

American men who had converted to Islam. Doris Witt's chapter on "Pork or Women" in *Black Hunger* (2004) points out that Elijah Muhammad, the leader of the Nation of Islam, published two dietary manuals in 1967 and 1972 condemning what he called the "slave diet" and excoriating eaters of "dirty" hogs. His followers hawked their signature pork-free bean pies along with the Nation of Islam newspaper and championed male self-discipline against the temptations of unclean food and promiscuous women. Muhammad "used food as part of his effort to formulate a model of black male selfhood in which 'filth' was displaced not onto white but black femininity," Witt writes. The traditional ban on pork in Muhammad's adaptation became a stigmatization of rival soul food's Christian or secular culinary symbolism, again at the expense of women. Witt reads Muhammad's dietary advice as "intended to purify the black male self of black female contamination."[72]

Soul food's potential to serve as a site for gender negotiations beyond the 1960s is illustrated in texts such as Bob Young and Al Stankus's *Jazz Cooks* (1992), in which the authors urge their readers to "improvise" when cooking, following the lead of the African American male jazz greats who provided the recipes. The volume echoes Carroll Mac Sheridan's 1922 *The Stag Cook Book,* which had solicited recipes from famous men. Jazz was a prestigious field of reference that elevated cooking from the quotidian work of food preparation into the realm of art.

Another example is George Tillman Jr.'s film *Soul Food* (1997). Here soul food is depicted as a means to keep African American families strong, and to connect them to a wider community, as a safe space against racism and the challenges of life. In the film, it is clearly assumed that the women of the family are responsible for the cooking as a means of keeping the family together. After Big Mama, the matriarch, can no longer provide the Sunday dinner, the void is temporarily closed by her grandson Ahmad, but only as long as it takes to figure out which of her daughters, Teri, Maxine, or Bird, will follow in her footsteps. While the movie may have been intended as an homage to strong black women (a stereotype in itself), it is evident that successful lawyer Teri is a negative model. Unhappy in her second marriage, cheated upon, and childless, she is a dire warning to women looking for fulfillment outside the home. Maxine, on the other hand, who has a career as a mother and housewife and a happy marriage, is deemed worthy of becoming the family's new matriarch.

While soul food, family, love, loyalty, and healing come together in *Soul Food,* it promotes a conservative message with respect to gender: it is African

American women's duty to provide their families with time-consuming dishes, to comfort their husbands' hurt egos, and to save their marriages by swallowing their pride. Soul food stands here for traditional femininity. The film reinforces these images in the name of a concept of the family as a safe place protected from a racist society and the pitfalls of life—a safe place that is women's work to build.[73]

Male authors of soul food cookbooks did not address an exclusively male readership, which may explain why many patterns found in other cookbooks written by men are not present in them. Soul food cookbook writers used the political dimension of food to legitimize their expertise in the kitchen mostly without engaging in misogynist rhetoric. The explicitly nationalist and political underpinnings of soul food may have allowed male authors to forgo some of the emasculating potential that cooking was connoted with. Still, some texts displayed a similarly gendered dynamic as is typical for cooking advice for men that is celebratory of male pursuits, and reluctant to recognize female labor and contributions.

"WILL COOK FOR SEX":
RECIPES FOR MANLY COOKING

Cookbooks for men have been a site in which meanings of masculinity circulate and are negotiated. Their advice demonstrates the potential to subvert gender ideology, as it seems to challenge the gendered division of labor, but it usually propagates hegemonic constructions of masculinities, male supremacy, and binary conceptions of gender. Cookbooks and magazine articles geared to male audiences claim that cooking can actually emphasize a man's masculine capital by making him more independent from women, their emasculating foods, and civilizing practices thought to be also feminizing.

In the twentieth century, cooking advice for men as well as literary texts that featured a male cook routinely employed misogynist images, blaming whatever ailed white hegemonic masculinity at certain cultural moments on imaginary femmes fatales, overly demanding wives, or career women. That involved dismissing or belittling women's labor, often claiming that kitchen work was no work at all. Consequently, cooking instructions for male cooks emphasized fun and sensual pleasure in the kitchen. As Malcolm LaPrade, author of *That Man in the Kitchen: How to Teach a Woman to Cook* (1946), put it:

Man does not cook by recipes alone. Secure in the knowledge that all the world's greatest chefs have been men, he relies on his natural talent. Despising rules and regulations, he approaches culinary problems as a creative artist and avoids the use of measuring spoons or other gadgets that take the sporting element out of cookery. If the result is unexpected, he can always say he planned it that way. (xi)

Across the past century of American culinary culture, men's cooking advice lacked the admonitions that general cookbooks so often featured to follow the recipe accurately to ensure success. Cooking advice for men did not discuss the dangers of malnutrition, obesity, or poor hygiene highlighted in other cookbooks. Advice literature for men in fact openly criticized the normative and homogenizing effects of general cookbooks. In this regard they appeared as renegade texts that disclosed authoritative structures in recipes and challenged the exclusionary mechanisms in these texts that extended not only to men, but historically also to immigrants, the working class, and sometimes people of color. In this way, cookbooks for men laid bare the ideological and disciplining power that dietary advice, table manners, and food fads could carry.

Yet if men were aware of the power women held in the culinary realm and in the kitchen, they seldom commented on men's own privilege outside the kitchen. Just as these texts were often sensitive toward the power relations in cookbooks that equip the female expert with authority, they were oblivious toward their own status as expert and normative authorities in almost every other domain.

Many of the texts analyzed in this chapter raised the idea of taste as gendered; in fact, the idea of gendered taste was used as an argument for the need for cooking advice for men. While the question of what constituted male taste changed over the decades, the belief that it was fundamentally different from what women liked remained broadly uncontested. Taste thus served as an apparent biological underpinning for gender difference, stabilizing an increasingly questionable binary. Food that women prepared allegedly to satisfy their own tastes was either too complicated and dainty, too simple and uninspired, or too healthy and fat free; in any case, it was not pleasing to the male palate. The difference in taste was not without grave consequences: women's cooking, depending on the text, was disappointing, emasculating, or even toxic to the male eater.

The myth of a taste all men shared helped to hold together the contradictory notions of ideal masculinity that cooking advice for white, middle-class men produced over the decades. The bachelor's chafing dish recipes, Hemingway's flapjacks, Marlowe's liverwurst sandwiches, Cain's midnight spaghetti, and cooking columns in *Gourmet* and *Playboy* all presented very different ideas of how men were ideally supposed to be. But all the texts held onto the underlying concept that what men like is different from what women like, thus creating an allegedly transcendent masculinity that was either rooted in the biological body or at least went back to the Stone Age, when men were hunters and women gatherers (itself a tenacious myth). Cooking advice for men, disregarding the dramatic changes in gender organization during the twentieth century, attempted to hold onto claims of male primacy. In this way, taste helped men to differentiate themselves from women, and to build camaraderie around the chafing dish, the grill, *Playboy's* kitchenless kitchen, and more recently the tailgate, creating the fiction of a masculinity that transcends not only time but class, too.

The bachelor, the rugged, the gourmet, and the playboy cook are examples of the changing ideals of white middle-class masculinities over the course of the twentieth century, reminding us that hegemonic masculinity is constantly contested and in flux. Not knowing its own history has allowed every generation to reinvent the manly cook, each time making fresh claims as to how cooking can be testimony to manliness. In 2000 W. J. Rayment published *The Real Man's Cookbook,* in which he declared: "Most cookbooks are written for women, and . . . do not account for the delicate tastes and abilities that make up the part and parcel of a man. With the exception of barbecue, the domestic culinary arts have been closed to the . . . American male" (9). A century of publishing has not changed the assertion, first made at the beginning of the twentieth century, that there are no cookbooks for real men. And like in earlier times, it is women's struggle for equality that forces men into the kitchen: "Many men, in these trying times of feminism, are forced to fend for themselves." (9). Other well-worn strategies can be found in this recent cookbook, too, namely the fear of being seen as homosexual and the references to sports: "I . . . feel an urgent need to lay to rest notions of cooking as a pansy sport. In manly circles, it is thought of in the same light as badminton or croquette [*sic*], fit only for the effeminate. . . . Cooking is more akin to the rough-and-tumble sport of baseball" (9). This leads to the question of what it means to cook as a man in the twenty-first century, after more than forty years of feminist activism, male celebrity cooks, a growing number of dual-income households, and a foodie revolution. In an exploding cookbook market that has created ever-more-specialized niches, the tone of cookbooks for men has, if possible, become rougher and in some cases more angry and aggressive. On the other hand, it has enabled the proliferation of hegemonic masculine models adding new narratives to old tropes, including the bachelor (Lunt, *The Man Without a Mate Cookbook*, 1991), campfire (*The Marlboro Cook Like a Man Cookbook: The Last Male Art Form. Grill It. Smoke It. BBQ the Heck Out of It*, 2004), hard-boiled (Joachim, *A Man, A Can, A Plan*, 2001), gourmet (Steiman and Kita, *Guy Gourmet: Great Chefs' Best Meals for a Lean & Healthy Body*, 2013), and playboy cook (Fino, *Will Cook for Sex: A Guy's Guide to Cooking*, 2005). Some of the newer trends in manly cooking are twists on well-established concepts. One example is the reincarnation of the postwar barbecuing craze in the form of tailgating.[74] This pre-game practice, typically conducted in the masculine-connoted space of the sports stadium parking lot, features men cooking, usually, but not exclusively, for other men. In *A Man, A Can, A Tailgate Plan* (2006), author Zachary Schisgal writes that "A car, a game, food, friends, and . . . a parking lot" are the ingredients "in one of modern manhood's rites of participation" (introduction, n. p.). But unlike earlier cooking instructions for men, this one includes nutritional guidelines and warnings: "Use the nutrition evaluation to keep your fat intake no higher than 30% of the total calories in your overall diet" (introduction). This nutritional advice speaks to a general trend in men's cooking literature toward promoting healthy food, often promising the semblance of athleticism through proper consumption.

At the same time, perhaps as a reaction against the "healthification" of manly cooking, some cooking instructions for men take a pronouncedly calorie- and fat-friendly standpoint, suggesting that the greater the health hazard, the manlier the food. In *Eat What You Want and Die Like a Man* (promising in its subtitle to be "The World's Unhealthiest Cookbook"), author Steve Graham writes, "I wrote this book because I was tired of being told what to eat" (vii). It is a self-published book of presumably limited reach, but cooking that is explicitly staged as "dangerously" unhealthy and therefore manly cannot be dismissed as a fringe phenomenon. When the Canadian YouTube show *Epic Meal Time* went online in November 2010, it received global attention. The overnight success offers dishes in an ironic attempt to combine as much fat, protein, and calories as possible, while using a maximum amount of meat, especially bacon, as well as alcohol. *Epic Meal Time*'s infamous Thanksgiving recipe for "Tur-Bacon," for instance, consisted of a pig stuffed with a turkey stuffed with a duck stuffed with a chicken stuffed with a Cornish hen stuffed with a quail, all of which is further adorned with generous amounts of bacon and croissant stuffing, glazed in Dr. Pepper and butter, then cooked in a smoker. The producers claim that the result contains close to eighty thousand calories. This episode had been clicked on some eighteen million times.[75] In an interview with *ABC News,* Harley Morenstein, the brains behind *Epic Meal Time,* explicitly stated that the show is a reaction against dominant food trends: "In this day and age, I feel like there's a big emphasis on organic food or a lot of negative media in regards to obesity and [viewers] are eating vicariously through us."[76] These examples show that there is still a diffuse sense that nutritional and cooking advice (and table manners, judging from some of the freestyle eating scenes shown in *Epic*) discipline the male body in emasculating ways. *Epic Meal Time's* logo is the Jolly Roger with a cooking pan on the skull and cooking knives for bones, emphasizing the insurgent status its cooks covet.

The recently emerging foodie culture discourse may seem to be more gender-neutral, with connoisseurship and expertise generally more evenly distributed between men and women. Foodie culture, often blissfully unaware of its own middle-class privilege, seems oblivious to issues of race or gender, as if middle-class status were the great equalizer. Few foodie blogs seem to find it necessary to explicitly address a male audience; more commonly, men and women are assumed to have similar skill sets. But here, too, gender differentiation can be found in surprisingly numerous places. Despite the exceptions, cupcakes and lunch boxes are still the province of female authors; beer brewing remains a male domain.[77]

Historically, culinary discourses helped establish the boundaries of masculine identity, of legitimate behavior, and of differentiation from the feminine or the effeminate—even, or perhaps especially, in the realm of daily life most associated with femininity. They carefully legitimized and perpetuated the idea of a natural, binary gender order, relying on biologisms and stereotypical thought, proving over and over again to their own satisfaction that women are cooks, but men are chefs.

THREE

"The Difference Is Spreading"

RECIPES FOR LESBIAN LIVING

Finally we can tell you: this is what lesbians do, we cook.
—LEE LYNCH, The Butch Cookbook (2008)

SERVING HETERONORMATIVITY—
QUEERING THE MENU

"THE CONNECTION BETWEEN food and sex can be a cliché," writes Antje Lindenmeyer; indeed, it is a connection that has been lavishly exploited by cookbooks and cooking throughout the last century, and with decreasing subtlety in the last decades.[1] But the normative implication of the interrelation of food and sex is still under-researched. In 2006, Julia Ehrhardt appealed to scholars to investigate "how food and foodways shape the gender and sexual identities of people who are not heterosexual in addition to those who have not been extensively investigated by food studies scholars working on gender" (92).

It is well documented that historically, cookbooks and household manuals have featured a heteronormative organization of gender and society.[2] Since the late eighteenth century, American cookbooks have presented the gendered division of labor as natural and desirable, and masculinity and femininity as two complementary principles, which in their interplay constitute a whole—be it the family, the community, or the nation. Societal changes only reinforced this notion: increasing urbanization and the atomization of families, the emancipation of slaves and dwindling numbers of servants, the naturalization of a gendered organization of knowledge, the fear that with the growing numbers of women in the labor force, there would be no one left to do household work. This all contributed to cooking becoming firmly associated with a woman's love and her performance of femininity. This connection functioned as a cultural strategy, ensuring that the cooking would still get done even when women found employment and/or fulfillment outside the home. Women's journals, food advertisements, and household manuals have long claimed that food preparation is a central part of what it means to be a woman. They also have constructed cooking as satisfying (even producing "the Joy of Cooking"), a means to gain recognition, and an appropriate demonstration of a woman's creativity and affection.³ Cooking advice implied, if not explicitly stated, that women cook for their men as an act of love.

But for the last hundred years, texts have also undermined and subverted the heteronormativity of cookbooks and have used the well-established connection between food and sex to reinscribe marginalized forms of love and desire into the practice of cooking. While cookbooks warned against inappropriate feminine behavior and excluded or condemned any non-heterosexual family organization, in the late twentieth and early twenty-first centuries, a growing number of authors used the genre and its stylistic characteristics to subvert its normative force as well as to promote alternative identities and family structures. Texts by lesbian authors on cooking and cookbooks directed at lesbian audiences often positively represent non-normative lifestyles while adapting or challenging the ideological implications of cookbook writing when it comes to gender and sexuality. Analyzing these texts, as Ehrhardt called for, sheds light on dominant and resistant forms of gender organization also beyond the realm of food, and expands food studies by exploring the possibilities of resisting gendered and sexual normativity when it comes to cooking and eating.

In the following, I will explore some of the texts that have written against the traditional normative claims of cooking advice over women's gender performance and sexuality. As cooking advice was a genre directed at women, depicting their labor as acts of love, it lent itself as an apparent space to challenge these dominant notions. Rewriting it presented an opportunity to express same-sex desire and to represent non-normative structures of family or other forms of community in one of the very places in which these exclusions were historically produced. Literary texts and memoirs disentangled or rearranged the close association of feminine performance, cooking, and food to create alienating effects that made this seemingly natural association visible in its arbitrariness, or to create gaps in which alternative gender performances and expressions of desire found space. Juxtaposing these texts with cookbooks addressing a lesbian audience shows that there is a loose and by no means linear tradition of challenging or renegotiating the claims cooking advice historically made.

Gertrude Stein's first radical experimental text, *Tender Buttons,* employed some of the linguistic and structural devices of cookbook discourse, coded as a source of female authority, to challenge the scientific and medical discourses that depicted same-sex relations as degenerate, while simultaneously subverting the heteronormative authority of the household manual. Fragmenting the discourses holding power over women's sexuality and desire, she not only made their constructedness visible, but also destabilized the power they claimed over women's lives.

In contrast, *The Alice B. Toklas Cook Book* by Stein's partner, Alice Toklas, embraced cookbook writing, utilizing it to document her life with Stein. One of the forerunners of the "literary cookbook," her text merged recipes with memoirs, bending the conventions of the genre to present another form of family structure. She chose the traditional form of recipe exchange, a practice commonly connoted as a female form of knowledge production ("gendered discourse," as Susan Leonardi terms it), to narrate a nontraditional life. Since the introduction of the genre in the United States, cookbooks have helped to create an imagined community of women who support and encourage one another in the fulfillment of their daily tasks. Marion Harland, for instance, a popular and best-selling cookbook author of the nineteenth century, addressed her readership as "sisters," thereby creating not only a vision of family or friendship between narrator and audience but also an exclusively female economy of knowledge exchange.[4] Toklas used the inconspicuousness of the genre that had helped to conflate love and cooking to produce her own record of her life with Stein, and to write a lesbian relationship into the American mainstream.[5]

Following in the footsteps of Stein and Toklas, in the twentieth and early twenty-first centuries, lesbian authors of memoirs, cookbooks, and recipes used cooking as a trope for coming out as female "with a difference." As cooking and normative performance of femininity are closely interlinked, some protagonists became aware of their difference when they learned that they cook differently from other women, or do not enjoy cooking at all. The description of cooking for women, rather than men, can be an expression of same-sex desire. The kitchen, therefore, is in many texts the closet from which lesbians must come out to develop their own understanding of gendered and sexual identities.

A small corpus of cookbooks and cooking blogs written by self-identified lesbian authors published since the 1980s imagines lesbian cooks as their audience, thus often dealing with questions of identity: What is a lesbian cook? And how can a multitude of same-sex subjectivities form political alliances and communities without reverting to clichés? Texts such as *The Butch Cookbook* (2008) or *The Lesbian Erotic Cookbook* (1998) reflect a growing concern with identity politics and their normative force at the end of the twentieth century. The texts struggle to define what it means to be a lesbian, often by reverting to memoirs and individual experiences rather than universal claims, but occasionally falling back into stereotypes and normative claims, unable to entirely escape hegemonic definitions of lesbian identities. Cookbooks for lesbian audiences provide fertile terrain for challenges to the dominant culture, but it is evident that they are not always liberating, as they produce new normative claims over women's sexuality and gender performance.

While cookbooks for lesbians commonly address a minority audience, culinary memoirs, even those written by women whose sexuality does not follow heteronormative expectations, aim at a bigger, mainstream market. With everything food-related so highly promoted and visible in the last two decades, culinary memoirs by food critics, cooks, and amateurs have blossomed. The interest in food bridges the divide between lesbian special-interest and mainstream literature. Descriptions of food experiences, extraordinary meals, and delicious dishes thus help to normalize non-heteronormative experiences, making them palatable, so to speak, to the heterosexual reader.

As a phenomenon, cookbooks for lesbians and texts featuring lesbian cooks are not a coherent body of texts. The texts discussed below present their own agendas, strategies, and even food preferences. But they have in common their revolt against the normative authority that cooking advice (by no means a unified or homogenous genre itself) traditionally wielded over women's lives and desires, and their intention to rewrite the genre to render it more inclusive and open to many cooks' experiences.

LABOR OF LOVE: GENDER NORMATIVITY AND CONTRADICTIONS IN NINETEENTH-CENTURY COOKBOOKS

Cookbooks of the nineteenth century assumed there is a biologically rooted gendered division of labor. Yet, contradicting the asserted naturalness of such a division, the same texts found it necessary to explain and reiterate this difference until young women absorbed the lesson and complied. In *The American Woman's Home* (1869), Catherine Beecher, together with her sister Harriet Beecher Stowe, listed the following as women's duties:

> She has a husband, to whose peculiar tastes and habits she must accommodate herself; she has children whose health she must guard, whose physical constitutions she must study and develop, whose temper and habits she must regulate. . . . She is required to regulate the finances of the domestic state. . . . She has the direction of the kitchen, where ignorance, forgetfulness, and awkwardness are to be so regulated that the various operations shall each start at the right time, and all be in completeness at the same given hour. She has the claims of society to meet, visits to receive and return, and the duties of hospitality to sustain. She has the poor to relieve; benevolent societies to aid; the schools of her children to inquire and decide about; the care of the sick and the aged; the nursing of infancy; and the endless miscellany of odd items, constantly recurring in a large family. (221)

The Beecher sisters meant this list to be evidence of women's value to society and the nation, and they claimed that in the "domestic state," the housewife is the "sovereign of an empire" (222) who must carry out endless work and care for others—skilled labor and expert management that, it goes without saying, is unpaid. Conventional political engagement, such as the struggle for suffrage, is dismissed as a distraction from women's true calling. But women's extensive and demanding duties, the Beechers claimed, call for appreciation, education, and self-confidence: "every woman should imbibe, from early youth, the impression that she is in training for the discharge of the most important, the most difficult, and the most sacred and interesting duties that can possibly employ the highest intellect" (221). The book fervently spoke in favor of women's education, arguing that only substantial knowledge would allow women to perform their duties and to educate children to grow up as worthy American citizens. This agenda's prominence is visualized on the first page of the text in an illustration of a woman within the circle of her family, reading with her children (fig. 8). While the image stresses her role as educator, the woman is also presented as the intellectual equal of the men present, presumably father, husband, and grown son, who listen to her, having shut their own books. The housewife's work is defined as important beyond the realm of everyday tasks, as she wields a "long train of influence which will pass down to thousands, whose destinies, from generation to generation, will be modified by those decisions of her will, which regulate the temper, principles, and habits of her family" (212). Women's

FIGURE 8. Frontispiece to Catherine Esther Beecher and Harriet Beecher Stowe, *The American Woman's Home: Or, Principles of Domestic Science* (New York: J. B. Ford and Company, 1869).

influence therefore reaches far beyond the family, the home, or the domestic, as it reaches into society at every turn.

The authors sketch a hierarchical and heteronormative power structure of the household, placing the father at the top "by the force of his physical power and requirement of the chief responsibility; not less is he so according to the Christian law, by which, when differences arise, the husband has the deciding control, and the wife is to obey" (203). But they also state that women live in a time when they can support themselves independently, and should not consider marriage unless the couple is in love. Love, they argue, brings an equilibrium of power to a marriage, since it is the husband's duty to love his wife and his love that protects her: "The husband is to 'honor' the wife, to love her as himself, and thus account her wishes and happiness as of equal value with his own. But more than this, he is to love her 'as Christ loved the Church'; that is, he is to 'suffer' for her, if need be, in order to support and elevate and ennoble her" (204). Husbandly love prohibits the abuse of a man's power over his wife. Women have not only to submit to his power, but do so cheerfully. The Beechers admonish their readers to be gentle and kind in whatever duties they are performing. Constant agreeability is the housewife's first duty. She needs to control her temper, must not raise her voice, and can never show frustration, anger, or worry (212). "Perfect silence," the Beechers advise, "is a safe resort" in times of crisis (212). The heteronormative structure the Beecher sisters promote here is intended to create social order and peace on a larger scale. Therefore, love and respect for women is to be taught to boys beginning in early childhood (204). Girls, on the other hand, need to be taught to devote their lives to their families. Love is best expressed by the unpaid labor a woman devotes to her family, such as the daily preparation of meals.

But even cookbooks endorsing gendered labor and behavior occasionally challenged their own parameters. In *The American Woman's Home,* although women were counseled to marry only for love, were they not to find it, women could consider managing their own lives rather than agreeing to a loveless marriage. Then they are also entitled to form their own fatherless families:

> Here it is needful to notice that the distinctive duty of obedience to man does not rest on women who do not enter the relations of married life. A woman who inherits property, or who earns her own livelihood, can institute the family state, adopt orphan children and employ suitable helpers in training them; and then to her will appertain the authority and rights that belong to man as the head of a family. And when every woman is trained to some

self-supporting business, she will not be tempted to enter the family state as a subordinate, except by that love for which there is no need of law. (205)

This idea of women's inherent independence and their right to a family beyond heterosexual norms is further developed in the chapter "The Christian Neighborhood," in which the Beechers describe how women can not only contribute to but change their communities, expanding the sphere, structure, and organization of the Christian household to the community, the nation, and—via the logic of setting a good example or creating "a City upon a Hill"—the entire world. Here traditional notions of women's rightful sphere are subverted without disturbing contemporary notions of feminine propriety. After giving detailed plans for how to build tenement houses, how to decorate the apartments of the poor, and how to educate them within the spirit of Christian mission, they describe unmarried women's true calling. Women, they claim, if not devoting their lives to their families, should commit their lives to the uplift of their communities. Inspired by Roman Catholic nuns, they detail how women living together can establish the "true Christian family" when not distracted by the needs of a husband:

> The woman who from true love consents to resign her independence and be supported by another, while she bears children and trains them for heaven, has a noble mission; but the woman who earns her own independence that she may train the neglected children of her Lord and Saviour has a still higher one. And a day is coming when Protestant women will be *trained* for this their highest ministry and profession as they never yet have been. (452)

Although the Beechers do not challenge notions of appropriate feminine behavior in using metaphors of motherhood and care to describe women's work for their communities, they nonetheless subvert the idea that only a traditional family can be a woman's ultimate fulfillment and claim that there can be a meaningful life for a woman beyond marriage. They suggest that communities will collect money to build a community center that triples as church, schoolhouse, and home for unmarried women who start "true Christian families": "Two ladies residing in this building can make an illustration of the highest kind of 'Christian family,' by adopting two orphans, keeping in training one or two servants to send out for the benefit of other families, and also providing for an invalid or aged member of Christ's neglected ones" (457–58).

This unconventional family model of two women living together and with their adopted children and servants receives the highest praise in the

Beechers' estimation and sets a counterpoint to the structures of heterosexual families promoted before, as well as to the gendered division of labor they had presented above. The two-woman family is not only an imitation of the heterosexual family, but may even be a superior alternative. But as this passage also shows, a life for a woman beyond any family structure was not thinkable for the Beechers.

Although cookbooks typically promoted women's complete devotion to their families, these texts were often written by women who had successful careers. Cookbook authors published their texts to earn money. They benefited from the acceptance of female expertise in this field as well as from the fact that cookbook writing neither ruined their social status nor endangered their gender performance. Often authors claimed that they had lost their former privileged status because of some misfortune and now had to contribute to the family's upkeep, so they traded in the tastes and expertise acquired from their upper-middle-class upbringings.[6] Some authors of cookbooks had successful careers as writers, journalists, and political activists.[7] Indeed, cookbook writing could serve as their entrée to other, more prestigious genres. The best-selling author Eliza Leslie used her success on the cookbook market to venture into children's books and other genres, and started a successful writing career that granted her an income and made her a celebrity.[8] Sarah Josepha Hale, who exhorted women to recognize being wives and mothers as their highest calling, herself had a career as an editor of women's magazines such as *Godey's Lady's Book,* and she published more than fifty books, among them numerous cookbooks and children's books.[9] Nonetheless, most cookbook authors condemned middle-class women who aspired to careers outside the home and demanded that they direct their complete attention to their families.

Since these cookbooks and household manuals often bore an ideology of devoted motherhood and committed wifeliness, they steered themselves into a narrative dilemma: the ideal woman they promoted had neither the time for, nor any business writing, books. If the expert was apparently less than ideal, her expertise was questionable. To circumvent this dilemma, some cookbook authors introduced narrators, preferably a spinster. The spinster, perhaps in the form of an older unmarried aunt keeping house for more fortunate relatives, had the expertise, the time, and a credible motive in instructing others how to avoid her fate.[10]

A few cookbooks, most notably Catherine Beecher's texts, occasionally criticized conventional ideas of femininity, for instance when she denounced the use of the corset and the lack of exercise for women. But she never questioned that the household is a woman's natural place, since, as she says in *The American Woman's Home,* "any discussion of the equality of the sexes, as to intellectual capacity, seems frivolous and useless, both because it can never be decided, and because there would be no possible advantage in the decision" (220). In an afterword, Catherine Beecher attacks women's suffrage on the grounds that women have more urgent matters to attend to (467–68).

The Beechers, as well as other authors of cooking advice, presented normative notions of family structures and gender, yet at the same time the texts produced some incoherence and contradictions that invited resistant readings. This trend would continue into the twentieth century, when authors began to appropriate the genre, with its strong normative tendencies, and let it serve as shorthand for the dominant gender ideology they wished to write against.

TENDER MUTTON:
GERTRUDE STEIN'S HOUSEHOLD ADVICE

The year 1870, according to Michel Foucault, was the birth year of the modern concept of "homosexuality." Until then, same-sex practices had been understood as single, isolated acts—or sins—that could be committed by anyone in a moment of temptation. In the late nineteenth century, the newly emerging field of sexology ordered and structured sexual behavior, established profiles for what constituted abnormal behavior, and created a narrowly defined homosexual identity that made desire a crucial determinant of the self. Homosexuality, together with other sexual behavior classified as "abnormal," was constructed as heterosexuality's other and acquired normative effects on heterosexual and non-heterosexual sex and identities alike. Eve Sedgwick summarizes: "every given person, just as he or she was necessarily assignable to a male or a female gender, was now necessarily assignable as well to a homo- or hetero-sexuality . . . for even the ostensibly least sexual aspects of personal existence" (2). The development led, Sedgewick notes, to new "institutionalized taxonomic discourses—medical, legal, literary, psychological" around the binary opposition of hetero/homosexual (2). The abjection of deviant sexual behavior and bodies aimed at stabilizing the normalized heterosexual body.

Early explanations of same-sex desire were not centered on sex acts but on an assumed confusion and contestation of gender identities. The notion of gender inversion was picked up by sexologists such as Richard von Krafft-Ebing (1840–1902) and Havelock Ellis (1859–1939), who also believed homosexuality to be inborn, but diagnosed it as a disease or, in the context of the popularization of Darwinism, as a sign of degeneration.[11] Medical discourses in alliance with juridical ones tried to implement clear-cut categories and to prevent their subversion by criminalizing and pathologizing gender transgression by connecting it to prohibited sexual practices. The effort to establish clear gender categories mirrored the efforts to keep the races "pure" and to prohibit and discursively regulate interracial mixing. Deviant sexual behavior was therefore often located in racial difference, since both phenomena were seen as symptoms of degeneration. Like the figure of the mulatto, the homosexual was commonly thought to be desperate or melancholic, torn between two identities.

Science concentrated at first almost exclusively on male same-sex desire. The history of homosexuality, too, has been strikingly gendered. The formation of a discourse on female homosexuality followed its own timeline and patterns. It also had different consequences for women diagnosed as homosexual: they were less often persecuted. During the first decades of sexology, female homosexuality was widely ignored in scientific writing, but, as Claudia Breger observes, the lesbian entered literary discourses more prominently than her male counterpart (76–77).

Writings on lesbianism in American medical journals at the turn of the century conflated women's sexually deviant behavior with gender-deviant behavior. Karin Martin found in her investigation of early writings on women's same-sex desire that it was thought to accompany "masturbation, nymphomania, feeling superior to men, or being a suffragist" (248). Lesbians, experts claimed, could be recognized easily because of their short hair, their desire to be on top in the (heterosexual) sex act, and their preference for masculine attire. Women who demanded equal rights to men were dismissed as degenerates, as in an article published by Dr. William Lee Howard in the *New York Medical Journal* in 1900: "The female possessed of masculine ideas of independence; the viragint who would sit in the public highways and lift up her pseudo-virile voice, proclaiming her sole right to decide questions of war and religion, . . . and that disgusting antisocial being, the female pervert, are simply different degrees of the same class—degenerates" (qtd. in Katz 303).

Women who failed to perform their domestic duties also came under suspicion. In *The Intersexes: A History of Similisexualism* (1908), in which author Edward Prime-Stevenson tried to defend homosexuals, he described a single case of a lesbian woman as typical: "she dislikes all sewing and fancy-work, knows little of cookery, and does not like to make use of what little she knows" (qtd. in Katz 331). Martin concludes that the awakening interest of sexologists in women's homosexuality at the beginning of the twentieth century was "a response and resistance (at least in part) to the suffrage and early women's movement" (248) and a means for discrediting politically active women. "Normal" women, the texts argued, would never participate in women's rights movements.

Male authors, Sandra Gilbert and Susan Gubar write in *No Man's Land: The Place of the Woman Writer in the Twentieth Century* (1988), have often taken up the topic of women's same-sex desire, typically depicting "lesbian desire as morbid and destructive" (221). In the early twentieth century, women authors presented friendlier renderings of homosexual lifestyles and individuals, often explicitly referring to scientific discussions of the topic, but also presenting the ambiguity of empowering and oppressive moments in the sexologists' establishment of pervert identities.[12] These texts try to appropriate lesbian identity as well as to redefine it. Texts dealing with female homosexuality follow the idea of gender inversion as explanation for same-sex desire, but do not adapt the notion of degeneration or disease. Sometimes they challenge the assumption that homosexuality must produce a subject conflicted and torn by gender indifference.

A playful approach to lesbian identity is chosen by Djuna Barnes in her early *roman à clef, The Ladies Almanack* (1928).[13] She presents diverse explanations for same-sex desire, some of them in deliberate contrast to dominant medical discourses. *The Almanack* is testimony to a phenomenon at the beginning of the early twentieth century in which a few well-off and artistically inclined American women escaped the confines of gender norms and appropriate sexual behavior in the United States as well as the expectation that they get married, and chose to live as expatriates in Paris, where they experienced far less social supervision and enjoyed a limited freedom to experiment with gender performance and sexuality. *The Almanack* is a faked and comical biography of the wealthy socialite Natalie Barney, who, although she herself failed as a writer, inspired and mentored many other authors and successfully built an artist community in Paris that supported female writers, painters, and photographers. Barney's salon also served as her hunting ground for sexual partners and as a safe space for women to experiment with their sexuality or act upon same-sex desires.[14] Barnes uses *The Almanack* to present thinly veiled caricatures of the women in Barney's circle. But she also uses the opportunity to display an array of different forms of desire and sexual practices, among them homosexual, heterosexual, and bisexual ones, pushing back against the simplified models scientists offered to explain female sexuality.[15]

Stein's first novel, *Q. E. D.*, written in 1903, takes a different approach from that of Barnes.[16] Stein, who studied psychology at Radcliffe and medicine at John Hopkins Medical School, said of herself that she was most interested in pathological psychology; the novel's title refers to the carrying out of a scientific experiment.[17] She integrates a number of sexology's prejudices of the time into her story of a complicated love triangle between three young Americans. In the description of her protagonists, Stein works in motifs of degeneration, inversion, and inborn moral depravity. Sophie, the dark and unpredictable force in the story, has the body of a spinster, the manners of a gentleman, and the complexion of a mulatta, features that place her outside the norms of gender and race (55). As the story shows, however, these traits do not reflect her same-sex desire but her general moral degeneration, attributed to her upper-class background. Adele, the protagonist whom the reader follows through the course of events, is from ordinary American middle-class stock. To her surprise, she is confronted with her passion for another woman. Nothing in her childhood, her general behavior, or her appearance has prepared her or the reader for her to fall in love with Helen. Curiosity and naïveté lead her deeper and deeper into her own feelings, as well as into the relationship between Sophie and Helen, presented as unhealthy because of its imbalanced financial power distribution that Adele calls "prostitution." While Adele recognizes her same-sex desire and comes to terms with it, she remains almost unaltered by the revelation. She is not discovering the male soul in her female body, nor does she appear to be mentally unstable. Loving another woman is not differently represented from loving a married man: it is forbidden, complicated, secretive, and painful, but it does not make Adele a different person, a "degenerate," a "pervert," or a "racial other." Until the end she remains her middle-class American self.[18] The story concludes without a resolution, "very near being a dead-lock," but Adele has not bent, fallen, or failed (262). In the end, Stein dismisses the scientific definitions and explanations of her time. The changes happening in Adele's life are not caused by her pathological, immoral, or degenerate character, nor are they accompanied by specific physical traits or melancholy.[19]

In 1914, the same year in which Magnus Hirschfeld's landmark study *Die Homosexualität des Mannes und des Weibes* appeared, Stein published *Tender*

Buttons. It had been four years since Alice Toklas moved in with her into her apartment in the Rue de Fleurus. In this text Stein used linguistic and stylistic fragments of nineteenth-century cookbook discourse in a kind of literary inversion, to challenge their own normative force and use them against the claims of scientific heteronormativity.

The title of *Tender Buttons*, like the whole text, is rich in multilayered meanings, referring to women's sexuality as well as fashion—like cooking, a practice that is highly gendered and has been the subject of domestic advice since the nineteenth century. This becomes apparent in passages such as "A Feather," which follows a section on "Colored Hats": "A feather is trimmed, it is trimmed by the light and the bug and the post, it is trimmed by little leaning and by all sorts of mounted reserves and loud volumes. It is surely cohesive" (25). The focus shifts here from center to margin, from the hat to its trimmings, one of which is the feather. But of course a feather is also an instrument of writing that needs to be trimmed to be put to use, and which needs to be leaned a little to be brought into action. The result may then be "loud volumes," books that are predictable in their cohesiveness. Stein's experimental poetry, of course, is not.

Stein playfully drew upon the culturally constructed genderedness of knowledge in *Tender Buttons*, wielding discourses such as fashion, household management, and cooking—all of which granted women expertise—against scientific discourses and those of modernist writing connoted with masculine authority. In the process, she questioned not only authority in general, but also the effects hegemonic knowledge had on regulating identity categories and the use of language. Shattering the linguistic and rhetorical rules of discourses renders their effects unpredictable, subverting their normative power. This aesthetic as well as political strategy can be found throughout the text.

Tender Buttons consists of passages of differing lengths that carry short titles such as "A Piano," "A Chair," "Roastbeef," and "Sugar." Since most titles refer to food or objects, these shorter texts are sometimes referred to as "still lifes." The "still lifes" are organized into three sections or chapters: "Objects—Food—Rooms," putting food at the center of the text. As with fashion, food discourses and practices serve the production of a seemingly stable, homogenous, and hegemonic heterosexual gender order. Like fashion, food discourses endorsed and produced female experts such as the authors of domestic advice literature. Stein twists characteristic elements of this genre (one that helped to normalize proper womanhood and heterosexual relations) and creates a space to write about women's creative production and intimate relations with other women.[20]

There are numerous references to the language of advice literature in *Tender Buttons*. Sentences such as "Dirt and not copper makes a color darker" (13), "Sugar is not a vegetable" (9), or "Light blue and the same red with purple makes a change" (10) resonate not only with the linguistic structure of household manuals but also with their concern with women's tasks: cleaning, cooking, decorating, and fashion.[21] The specific discourse with its linguistic and stylistic peculiarities is adapted and dissolved, since the advice given is non-intelligible. This not only adds aesthetic dimensions to the text, but also resists the authority of instructions such as those found in advice literature, which seem harmless enough but participate in ordering gender, the nuclear family, and women's sexuality.

One example of the complex use of cookbook discourse in *Tender Buttons* is the passage "Roastbeef," which opens the "Food" section: "Please spice, please no name, place a whole weight, sink into a standard rising, raise a circle, choose a right around, make the resonance accounted and gather green any collar" (37). Here the text moves from "please" slowly into the imperative structure of advice literature and specifically the recipe (the reference to collard greens reinforces the connection to food). Imperative structures of words such as "spice," "place," and "gather" can be found throughout the "Food" section, creating further associations with recipe writing.[22] One of the effects of the recipe's imperative structure is that it lends normative authority to the text; it signals to the reader that an expert is talking and that his or her words demand to be followed. But the reader of "Roastbeef" is not told what to do. The emptiness of the instructions points at the construction of authority through language (it is the imperative that creates the expert) and calls it into question. Stein's "recipes" expose how the language of household manuals has normative effects. But these subversively altered "recipes" do not claim authority over the reader or the reading process, since the opaqueness obscures any potential instruction.

The subsequent paragraph abandons the imperative structure and leads to a form of infinitive construction often found in nineteenth-century cookbooks:

> To bury a slender chicken, to raise an old feather, to surround a garland and to bake a pole splinter, to suggest a repose and to settle simply, to surrender one another, to succeed saving simpler, to satisfy a singularity and not be blinder, to sugar nothing darker and to read redder, to have the color better,

to sort out dinner, to remain together, to surprise no sinner, to curve nothing sweeter, to continue thinner, to increase in resting recreation to design string not dimmer. (38)

Stein seems here to explore the poetic potential of cookbooks that merge effortlessly in their tables of contents such diverse issues and objects as these listed in a classic nineteenth-century cookbook: "Astral lamps, (management of,)" "Bed-feathers, (to wash,)" "Black silk sleeves, (to restore when faded,)" "Book-muslin dresses, (to wash,)" "China, (to pack,)" "Coat, (gentleman's—to fold,)" "Faded dresses, (to bleach,)" "Fruit stains, (to remove,)" "Grease, (to remove from a dress,)" "Hand soap, (to make,)" "Ink, (to make,)" "Ink spots, (to remove,)" "Lace, (to wash,)" "Lawn, (bishop's—to wash)" "Lamp oil, (to extract from a dress,)" "Marabout feathers, (to clean,)" "Moussaline de laine, (to wash,)" "Muslins, (smell—to do up,)" "New wood, (to remove its taste,)" "Pink dye," "Preparing rooms for summer," "Paint, (to remove from a coat,)" "Packing a large trunk," "Remedies for stings, &c," and "White-washing." Behind these activities, which Eliza Leslie lists among many others in the table of contents of her *Directions for Cookery* (1840), stands not only the endless drudgery of the housewife's everyday work; there is also something magical and enigmatic when shorn of its historical context. Why would somebody need to clean "Marabout feathers"? Who would want to taste new wood? The list creates its own poetics and meanings in accidental juxtapositions such as the ink that needs to be made, and the ink spot that needs to be removed. Narrative moments emerge, possibly piquing a later reader's curiosity (how did the lamp oil get on the dress? Where will the large trunk go?). The enumeration of activities and objects creates its own almost Borgesian logic. The only connection between the items lies in the daily repetition of women's practices. These poetic and structural effects of cookbook logic, contradicting scientific logic, can be found in *Tender Buttons* and its reflection on "A Carafe, That Is a Blind Glass," "Glazed Glitter," or "A Substance in a Cushion," (9)—to quote only from the first page of the book. In this text, the home and its intimacy create their own taxonomy that cannot be conquered by scientific definitions.

Infinitive constructions in cooking advice were commonly used as headings for instructions on basic techniques that can be generally applied. Like the linguistic function of the infinitive, these headings signify the unaltered, unconjugated techniques of cooking and home making. In *Directions for Cookery* one finds for instance "to roast beef," "to boil a salted or pickled tongue," and "to corn beef." But the techniques *Tender Buttons* evokes are very different: "to sort out dinner," "to suggest a repose," or "to remain together" may be better described as basic techniques of living together and making a relationship work, while "to surrender one another," "to satisfy a singularity," "to surprise no sinner," and "to curve nothing sweeter," may evoke erotic associations. "Roastbeef," which seems to begin with a sunset and a flashback to the previous night, presents sexually evocative language: "Lovely snipe and tender turn, excellent vapor and slender butter, all the splinter and the trunk, all the poisonous darkening drunk, all the joy in weak success, all the joyful tenderness, all the section and the tea, all the stouter symmetry" (35). More than the references to fluids and odors, the simple, happily galloping rhyme seems to catch the atmosphere of happiness. The "symmetry" of the passage takes up a prominent motif of "Roastbeef," the mischievously staged collapse of the binary opposition between difference and sameness that crescendos in a breathless variation of the word "kind": "The time when there are four choices and there are four choices in a difference, the time when there are four choices there is a kind and there is a kind. There is a kind. There is a kind" (36). The paragraph ends "The kindly way to feel separating is to have a space between. This shows a likeness" (37). While one of the themes of "Roastbeef" is the production of meaning, for which the distinction between difference and identity is crucial, the play on "kind" ("kindness," "being of one kind") and "likeness" may capture feelings of recognizing oneself in the other, as in falling in love, or as in renegotiating sexual difference. The bodies involved come "in kind cuts" but inhabit "thick and thin spaces" (34). They are no longer distinguished by differences in genitalia but by their shapes and textures.

The references to furniture, pieces of decor, and household objects such as spoons, curtains, doors, and tables create a room for this intimacy, a safe space, and a space that, with references to food preparation and discourses, is marked as feminine, borrowing from established gender ascriptions but fragmenting them. *Tender Buttons*, with its allusions to cookbook and recipe writing, advises with authority on the basic "techniques" for a successful intimate relationship between two women, but the opaqueness of the passage also protects it from pornographically or scientifically exploitative readings.

References of age and aging appear in "Food" repeatedly. In a few passages a voice seems to surface momentarily, the voice of an older speaker: "Anyway, to be older and ageder is not a surfeit nor a suction, it is not dated and careful, it is not dirty.... Why should ancient lambs be goats and young colts and never beef, why should they, they should because there is so much difference in age" ("Roastbeef," 36). In the earlier passage "In-Between" (24), a sentence says two "old ladies" live in a "perfectly unprecedented arrangement." The "old ladies" are juxtaposed with virgins ("A virgin, a whole virgin"). The slide from virgin to old ladies possibly hints simultaneously at the misperceived asexuality of older women and non-heterosexual practices. "Roastbeef" and "Mutton" begin the food section, reminding the reader of the nineteenth-century culinary preference for mature meat, and wittily referring to the pleasures shared by bodies that are no longer "colts." Stein seems to echo here the idea of the spinster as a position to inhabit and from which to speak. While lesbians were largely invisible and voiceless in American culture until the early twentieth century, the spinster was a well-known figure in the public imagination of the nineteenth century. Older, unmarried, and in Victorian ideology therefore marginalized, these women gained limited visibility and authority in their function as negative examples. At the same time, the spinster was an important character for the household manual of the nineteenth century. In the position of the narrator, she could credibly pronounce upon gender norms. But while doing so, the spinster herself was standing outside these norms, defeating the assumed true purpose of women to be wives and mothers, thereby proving that women could survive outside the nuclear family. Nonetheless, the spinster is positively connoted in these texts: she stands for women's knowledge and expertise. But in medical accounts on female homosexuality in the early twentieth century, the spinster was sometimes conflated with lesbian women or suffragettes.[23] Stein drew upon this notion in *Q. E. D.* when she described Sophie's body as a spinster's body. The spinster was therefore—in all its ambivalence—a culturally established and visible figure for women outside the heteronormative order.

Evidently, the traditional discourse of household manuals that affirms the heterosexual family is perforated and disturbed in *Tender Buttons,* but at the same time remains a visible structuring element expressed in the headlines and subheads and some of the text's grammatical structure.[24] Stein's text accumulates textual objects, food, and rooms to create a discursive home that can serve as an alternative to the home of normative discourses. Many of the objects in the text therefore come with a small difference: the buttons are tender, the glass of the carafe is blind, the cushion is not described, but the substance filling it is, and so forth. As Stein remarks, perhaps slightly menacingly, at the beginning of *Tender Buttons:* "The difference is spreading" (9). All these textual objects that are a little different create a home with a difference.[25] This is more than a mere play of thoughts. The household manuals of the nineteenth century were based on the idea that the home produces the identities of the people who live in it. Color, pictures, and furniture not only built character, they were believed to create men, women, Christians, white middle-class Americans. The nineteenth century generated the idea of masculine and feminine rooms. The gendered rooms were the floor plan for the heterosexual family home. Objects and their decoration were thought of in moral terms—a piece of furniture that was veneered, for instance, was dishonest, and fashionable geometric patterns were considered flimsy and not as durable or as elevating as patterns that mimicked nature such as leaves, flowers, garlands, and the like. Honest, durable, and natural furniture and decoration were considered to produce honest, durable, and natural people.[26] Gertrude Stein's differing objects therefore create people with a difference. The rooms become non-normative spaces that make room for non-normative identities. And her play on household instructions opens up space for the invention of new kinds of homes and families.

"LA CUISINE C'EST LA FEMME": THE ALICE B. TOKLAS COOK BOOK

In Gertrude Stein's *Everybody's Autobiography* (1937), the narrator tells an anecdote predicting that Alice Toklas will start her own career in 1934:

> We wondered what the career of Alice Toklas was going to be and when it was to begin and then it almost began she decided to write a cook book and if she did the career would begin and she will but she has not yet had time, naturally enough who can and of course this she would not let me do for her and with reason. (296)

It would take another twenty years and Gertrude Stein's death for Toklas to find the time to write *The Alice B. Toklas Cook Book*. It turned out to be an homage to Stein, not only in the memoirs she serves with her recipes, but also in her stylistic references to Stein's writings, especially *The Autobiography of Alice B. Toklas* (1933). The text goes beyond these references, the recipes, and the memoirs to merge and experiment with different genres. Toklas plays with recipes, instructions, and expectations to construct the image of two women living together for more than thirty-five years—reformulating notions of national as well as gender identity, re-creating concepts of family, marriage, and love. It is a text that, like *Tender Buttons,* resists and subverts the hetero-normativity of the cookbook genre. But it does not stop here: it also bends and queers the conventions of autobiographical writing that support the idea of a progressively developing subject who is thought to be autonomous, straight, and male.

"Cook-books have always intrigued and seduced me," (37) writes Toklas in her 1954 cookbook that became most famous for its recipe for "Haschich Fudge" (259), which does not do justice to the complexity and literary value of the text. While the title locates the book firmly within the field of cookbook writing, it may be most noticeable for its disruptions of the genre. The text provides the reader with recipes and places them into a narrative that claims to be autobiographical. The two modes, the autobiographical and the culinary, generate interruptions even as they enhance one another. The recipes create a reality effect that lends credibility to the narrative, while the recipes gain authority from their context.

The Alice B. Toklas Cook Book has received more recognition and attention from cooks than from scholars of modernist literature, autobiography, or queer studies. Despite its little culinary traps and often playfully irreverent treatment of recipes, most of the instructions are reliable and call for fresh ingredients of high quality, setting a slightly snobbish standard of cooking. More than once the narrator sneers at an American cuisine that relies increasingly on canned and pre-cooked food—a notion that met general approval by gourmets and amateur chefs and contributed to the book's success over the last sixty years.[27] "Can one be inspired by rows of prepared canned meals? Never. One must get nearer to creation to be able to create, even in the kitchen" (131). Cookbook writers regularly acknowledge their indebtedness to Toklas's inventive and whimsical handling of the genre.[28] Together with M. F. K. Fisher, Toklas is the unchallenged forerunner of the literary cookbook.

That the text has become part of the American cookbook canon is nonetheless surprising, insofar as the text undermines the genre in many ways. Chapters such as "Murder in the Kitchen," "Food to Which Aunt Pauline and Lady Godiva Led Us," or "Servants in France" organize the recipes in clusters that do not follow the traditional cookbook structure based on main ingredients (meat, fish, vegetable) or mealtimes (breakfast, lunch, tea, dinner). Toklas's structure puts the emphasis on the stories told, while the recipes seem to be sprinkled in unpredictably, functioning as *amuse-bouches* for what Toklas presents as her memories. Sometimes Toklas places recipes right in the middle of her narrative. Occasionally they conclude a chapter. Mostly she mixes them in, creating an amalgam of story and instructions. The recipes punctuate and supplement the stories told, and interrupt the illusion of coherence and linearity—the sense-making—of autobiographical writing.

The recipes—many of them, tellingly enough, for mutton and beef—often feature whimsical titles such as "Swimming Crawfish" (204), "A Hen with Golden Eggs" (109), "A Giant Squab in Pyjamas," (111) or "A Fine Fat Pullet" (149). In the section "Treasures" she gives a number of recipes—such as "Nora's Ice Cream" and "Alice's Cookies"—that recognize the authors of the recipes, but ends with "Nameless Cookies" (99), satirizing the practice. Some recipes are introduced wittily, such as the lobster recipe in the section "Food in the United States." "It is unnecessary to say," writes Toklas, "that the menu was entirely a French one, and therefore a recipe of one of its courses has no place here. The temptation however is too great. This is the way to prepare LOBSTER ARCHIDUC" (128). By presenting her recipes within a literary context, Toklas exceeds the rules of the genre, and she also makes the instructions part of the literary discourse, as in her recipe for "Lobster, Breast of Chicken and Black Truffle Salad" (216) which, she asserts, is good for reading but impossible to reproduce.

Beyond the recipes, food plays a prominent role not only to advance the plot and a steady Proustian stimulation of memories, but also to discuss the experience of war. Toklas, who had lived in Paris since 1907, experienced both World Wars in France. Her account of them adds severity to her otherwise chatty and often celebrity-studded narrative. The chapters on the two wars are not an account of political or military developments in France and the world, but strings of strictly personal anecdotes revolving around food and the craving for it, describing the hardship of wartime (as experienced by two middle-class Americans far from the front lines). World War II is the backdrop to a number of dinners made possible despite adversity thanks to creativity. The reader learns how difficult it has been to find eggs, butter, or meat during the occupation, which the two protagonists and their dog spent in the French countryside in the Bugey. Toklas does not reflect on the causes for war or its cruelty, but on the challenges of coping with shortages of servants and negotiating the black market. She departs from the conventions of war writing, especially that of the male modernists. The characters she describes in this chapter rarely suffer or starve. Instead, it seems as if all the Bugey held its breath and waited for the occupation to end. But while the text could be dismissed as an account of two privileged women ignorant of the suffering that war brings, it can be also understood as a statement against war in general.[29] The narrator's perspective describes, not without irony, a war on the home front, with its—often trivial—worries over food, the sense of helplessness, the need to cope with change, and the endless waiting for the end, thus making the account relatable to an American audience in the 1950s. She resists any notions of heroism. The lack of causes, reasons, or political analysis renders the war meaningless. Instead of a people aroused in patriotic frenzy, the French are depicted as paralyzed. War itself becomes banal, a constant source of deprivation, a reduction in quality of life even for those who are relatively safe and comfortable in Toklas's detached narration, leaving no room for romanticism, patriotism, or nostalgia. But the experience is not belittled since, as she states, "Wars change the way of life, habits, markets and so eventually cooking" (162). No other human-made event has the power to change not only borders and the fate of nations, but also the most mundane, quotidian activities of everybody involved. Nothing and nobody remains untouched, and the hope of the soldiers that they will return to their old lives after the war ends is doomed, since everything and everyone they left behind are lastingly altered by the war, too. War violently ends life as it used to be and its outcome is uncertain, allowing no hope for victory, since everybody involved necessarily loses.[30]

Food plays an important role in the maintenance of civilization and order in the chapter on World War II. The potential of resistance through food is emphasized in wordplays such as "piece-de-résistance," with which she labels her first illegally purchased food items (204). Instead of sticking to ration cards, the illegal trade in food, and eating as well as possible, become acts of rebellion against the occupation. Everything the French eat cannot be taken by the Germans.

The Germans are described as lacking both civilization and order, and therefore taste. Their lack of taste stands for all that differentiates the belligerent Germans from the civilized French and, by extension, the Americans they house. Their disregard for manners symbolizes for their lack of discipline and genteel refinement.

> The German soldiers were interested in butter. It appeared that many of them had never tasted it. Had not Hitler asked them if they wanted butter or guns and had they not given the right answer? One day, marketing for whatever unrationed food might still be for sale, a German soldier came into the shop. He pointed to a huge mound of butter and said, One kilo. One kilo, the clerk exclaimed. The German nodded his head impatiently. The butter was weighed and wrapped up. Unwrapping one end of the package the German

walked out of the shop. From the open door where I was standing I saw him bite off a piece of the butter. It evidently was not what he expected it to be for with a brusque movement he threw it violently over the garden wall of the house opposite. The story got about. People came to look at it. No one would touch it. (203)

The butter anecdote depicts Germans in a concise manner as barbaric, rapacious, and ignorant. The uneducated appetite and coarse greed of the German soldier become a metaphor for the imperialist ambitions of his government.

While in the chapter on World War II food serves as a signifier for a stable national identity, the text in other places features more complicated approaches to nationality, most significantly in the narrator herself and in the character of Gertrude Stein. In the beginning of *The Alice B. Toklas Cook Book* the narrator states that she "wrote the [cookbook] for America" (n. p.). Referring to "we" when addressing the audience, the narrator identifies herself as sharing the same culinary culture and heritage as her readers (4). Stein is later introduced as being homesick for American food (29). The narrator establishes herself thus as an American in Paris, sharing with her audience her experiences with French cooking, the peculiarities of the French, and their dining culture in a confident tone, often writing critically. American dishes, on the other hand, are praised as reliable and trustworthy. Toklas creates a tourist gaze, inviting the reader to take a journey through an exoticized French cuisine. This changes abruptly in the later chapter "Food in the United States in 1934 and 1935." Stein, who previously was described as an enthusiast of American food, is asked to return to the States for a lecture tour. Her fears and doubts about returning to her homeland converge in the question of whether the food will suit her:

> When during the summer of 1934 Gertrude Stein could not decide whether she did or not want to go to the United States, one of the things that troubled her was the question of the food she would be eating there. Would it be to her taste? A young man from the Bugey had lately returned from a brief visit to the United States and had reported that the food was more foreign to him than the people, their homes or the ways they lived in them. He said the food was good but very strange indeed—tinned vegetable cocktails and tinned fruit salads, for example. Surely, said I, you weren't required to eat them. You could have substituted other dishes. Not, said he, when you were a guest. (123)

Just as the narrator has reported about French food to an American audience, now a French informant is reporting to her and Stein about the state of

American cuisine. The bleak image the Frenchman draws does not in the end prevent Toklas and Stein from going to the States. But in *The Alice B. Toklas Cook Book* the narrator discloses that she and Stein are always relieved when they come upon French food during their trip, and Stein often escapes into a diet of eggs and oranges or similarly unprocessed foods to avoid American cooking. Toklas here changes perspective: while her narrator first chaperones the audience through strange French culinary culture, she now turns the tourist gaze upon the United States, discusses American idiosyncrasies as peculiar and exotic, and is critical of what Americans eat.

The inventory of American cuisine she presents in this chapter is as surprising as her choice of recipes: beside "Oysters Rockefeller" (130) and "Vanilla Cream Sauce" (125), the only dishes she deems worth mentioning are "Aioli" (124), "Bird's Nest Pudding" (129), and Mexican "Dulce" (133). In this way she represents the best of American cuisine to be its ethnic dishes, and defines American cuisine through its hybridity. Toklas reimagines an American national cuisine as transcending its national boundaries.

The shift of perspective in this chapter places the narrator between two national cuisines and cultures, which allows her to mediate and criticize both of them simultaneously. The expatriate's in-between expertise is not only positively connoted but is also established as a position of authority—it places her at the same time inside and outside both cultures. As she states in her preface: "Though born in America, I have lived so long in France that both countries seem to be mine" (n. p.). Her mediating position is further stressed with an entire chapter, "Little-Known French Dishes Suitable for American and British Kitchens," in which she explicitly refers to her double cultural knowledge. Here and in other places, the narrator understands national identity as unfixed and fluid, the expatriate having an in-between existence—neither fish nor fowl.[31]

Just as Toklas challenges the notion of a stable national identity, she also questions notions of binary gendered identity. The text seems to establish a version of the heterosexual economy and division of labor between the narrator and the character Gertrude Stein: the narrator tells us that she started to cook when she came to live with Stein because Stein wanted Toklas to prepare "American" dishes for her, and she complied. The narrator is presented as a caretaker serving Stein's wishes and needs, thus presenting a legible family structure for an American mainstream audience: the wife cooks for her beloved. Stein, on the other hand, is described as driving the car and repairing it, if necessary, and as being active in the public sphere as a lecturer and writer. This "gendered" division of labor is further supported by Toklas's notorious and widely reported entertaining of the wives of artists who came to the Rue de Fleurus to see Stein, since, as the story was told, Stein could not be bothered with talking to wives. This explicitly "gendered" assignment of activities and duties mirrors the economy of heterosexual marriages. Toklas in this way marks the relation between the narrator and the character Stein as one that is, so to speak, like a marriage, using the cultural inventory that she had at her disposal to describe a lifelong commitment of two people.

But *The Alice B. Toklas Cook Book* subverts the heteronormative notion of gendered labor not only in assigning each side of the divide to a woman, but also by parodying traditional notions of gender in mirroring them distortedly. The element of parody becomes apparent when the *Cook Book* is contrasted to other texts that feature lesbian relationships according to the gender binary, such as Fannie Flagg's *Fried Green Tomatoes at the Whistle-Stop Cafe* (1987), which employs a butch/femme plot that is more coherent than *The Cook Book*'s.[32] *Fried Green Tomatoes* tells of the love affair of tomboy Idgie and Southern belle Ruth. Following conventional romantic story lines, the couple meets under tragic circumstances, overcomes obstacles, builds a life together, parents a child, and is finally parted by death. The desire of the women for one another is subtly introduced in some memorable food scenes: in the beginnings of their courtship, for instance, Idgie reaches into a beehive to bring Ruth honey, thereby declaring her love (83–87).[33] Like *The Alice B. Toklas Cook Book, Fried Green Tomatoes* discreetly protects the female protagonists' space, not venturing into their sex life nor presenting confessions that would openly manifest their same-sex desire. The effect, as in *The Cook Book,* is that their relationship is "normalized." But Flagg, much more than Toklas, presents her protagonists as firmly "gendered." Idgie behaves in many regards as stereotypically masculine. She drinks, frequents prostitutes, and saves Ruth, a damsel in distress, from an abusive husband. Although traditional heteronormative ideology is untraditionally applied here to two women, the gender binary itself is barely challenged. While the "gendering" helps to establish the relationship as an erotic one, its simplistic binary organization is owed to the fairy tale–like function the love story has within the book. The Whistle Stop Café that the two women run is a heterotopian place in which not only a different South is possible (one in which love, tolerance, and justice prevail) but also where women can escape the discursive force of law and science (although not cancer).

In *The Cook Book,* gender roles are less determined and stable than in Flagg's text. Toklas introduces her narrator and the character Stein along the heteronormative gender divide, but she subverts these notions and comments on them. "We spoke of each other as the chauffeur and the cook," the narrator confides, reflecting ironically on how people thought of them (72). The text then discloses that Stein was not able to drive the car in reverse and "repaired" her car by coaxing men to help her, while the narrator claims that she hardly ever cooked (nor was she any good at cooking), since there were always servants who took over the kitchen work. While Toklas is introduced as the cook and Stein as the one cooked for, the stories told present the two protagonists mostly eating together in restaurants, friends' houses, on ships, in cafeterias, or in hotels. Middle-class status marked through eating out, and these eating-out scenes also transcend gender binaries, presenting two women eating and being cooked for and served. Here *The Cook Book* also breaks with the ideals of femininity that were usually represented in cookbooks. The restaurants or the friends' dining rooms serve as a neutral spaces in which binary gendered power relations are abolished (replaced by those marking class). The gender binary is constantly confused and complicated in *The Cook Book.*

The genius-and-wife plot Stein used semi-ironically in *The Autobiography of Alice B. Toklas*[34] is humorously undone in *The Cook Book.* The term "genius" appears only once in the text and is applied to a female cook (93). The Stein of this text, far from appearing as a genius, is depicted in a number of intimate episodes that show her away from the art scene, the Parisian salons, and the famous names of modernist literature. Stein appears as shy and full of lovable foibles, and while little is revealed about her thoughts and emotional makeup, the narrator's intimate knowledge of her makes a special claim of closeness. Stein, we learn, is afraid of spiders and when confronted with one will yell for help until Toklas, armed with a broom, comes to her rescue (278). In their garden work, Stein tends to the flowers, while the narrator weeds and grows vegetables (266). It is also revealed that Stein suffers from stage fright that she circumvents with long walks before lectures and a special diet to calm her upset stomach (127). The text claims ownership over the person rather than the genius, while defending its authority over its own "true" version of Gertrude Stein's life.

The narrator also redefines the assumption that the wife's role is merely to support the genius by conflating "genius" and "wife" when it comes to the production of art and power relations. The text follows cookbook conventions in celebrating the importance of cooking and kitchen work. While literature and art are rarely mentioned, and authors and painters appear chiefly in asides (often in relation to diets, or, as in the case of Picasso, because of their food preferences [30]), cooking is defined as a form of artistic expression:

> These dishes . . . are most of them a slow evolution in a new direction, which is the way great art is created—that is, everything about is ready for it, and one person having the vision does it, discarding what he finds unnecessary in the past. Even a way of cooking an egg can be arrived at in this way. Then that way becomes a classical way. It is a pleasure for us, perhaps for the egg. (139)[35]

In speaking of cooking rather than art, and of cooks rather than painters and poets, Toklas implicitly argues that her work (supervising the menu, shopping, and cooking) is of no less importance than Stein's or that of their guests. The genius-wife power relation breaks down when Toklas makes a claim to her own artistic production.

But *The Cook Book* not only denaturalizes gender in assigning heteronormative conventions to two women; it also hints at its constructedness when dwelling on the differences in the imagination of "woman" and "man" in France and the United States, displaying the cultural contingency of gender organization. Toklas locates this comparison in the kitchen. Unlike in the United States, she argues, in France men "play a very active part in everything that pertains to the kitchen" (3): "In France it is not unusual for some man in the family not only to be interested in the menu and the cooking of it but occasionally to supervise or even cook the dish" (15). Where Toklas explains that in France men cook and take an interest in food, she challenges the conservative gender ideology of the 1950s in the States that sought to send women back to the kitchen as their "natural" domain. But the narrator does not claim that the French are more progressive than Americans when it comes to gendered power relations. She states that when a man in the kitchen "raises the standard of cooking in the home, the mistress is spurred to greater effort by a constant gentle criticism. Women are not supposed in France to be *gourmets*" (15). Emphasizing national difference in gender organization, she acknowledges that cultures create particular forms of gender. Depicting herself as an expert on good food, a gourmet, but an average cook, the narrator diverges from both nations' ideals of femininity.

Instead of creating an image of domestic bliss, *The Cook Book* depicts its protagonists traveling, exploring the French countryside, visiting Spain or the United States. During their travels and the many dinners they partake in, the narrator always takes the time to point out which dishes have been cooked by women and praise them for their superior skills, thus reevaluating women's culinary work as a form of art. Sometimes, though, she does so in rather gender-conservative terms: "The cooks were women and the owner was a woman and it was managed by women. The cooking was beyond compare, neither fluffy nor emasculated, as women's cooking can be, but succulent and savoury" (129). Here Toklas affirms the popular notion of an inherent femininity that needs to express itself in cooking, along with the expectation that women's cooking tends toward frivolousness and lacks heft, affirming gender stereotypes of the early twentieth century.[36] The concept of gender in *The Cook Book* is thus ambivalent and contradictory.

The instability of power relations also becomes obvious in her report of the cooks working for her household over the years in a chapter she dedicates to the "Servants in France." Cookbooks and household manuals of the nineteenth and early twentieth centuries (but no longer in the 1950s, when Toklas published her book) often included extensive advice on how to hire and treat servants. Marion Harland's *Common Sense in the Household* (1872) discusses "the servant question" over twelve pages in between recipes for rhubarb pie and pudding, and pleads that they be well treated. "Aunt Babette," another cookbook author, compares servants with children: "Servants and children are great imitators, and the consequence will be they will do likewise. How pleasant is a home where kindness reigns! A good and appreciative servant will show her appreciation by serving to the best of her ability" (8).

These texts effortlessly reproduce the xenophobic, classist, and racist stereotypes of their times. Like older cookbooks, *The Alice B. Toklas Cook Book,* too, approaches the subject from an unreflective upper-middle-class perspective. Toklas describes the cooks she has hired over the years with humorous detail, often oblivious of the power relations involved but occasionally also disrupting them. She spends more time and space on the first cook she encountered in the Rue de Fleurus, Hélène, than on Picasso or Matisse, and more on feeding their prominent guests than on their work, thereby making visible the commonly invisible prerequisites of artistic production. But she talks about most of the cooks in the household in a paternalizing fashion and with ignorance, as for instance when she reports about her "unreliable but thoroughly enjoyable experiences with the Indo-Chinese" (186). Here she not only invokes the "childish joy" that their first "Indo-Chinese" employee, Trac, allegedly displayed when taught how to make desserts, but also informs the reader about his poor French, and that he lied, and was "secretive" and "restless" (187). References to his nationality are informed by classic prejudices. The "Indo-Chinese" cooks she writes about are Southeast Asian, but are often praised for their excellent "Chinese" cooking, and she thinks of the cooks themselves as "delightfully Chinese" (188). Like the late-nineteenth-century cookbooks that refer to servants with the generic term "Bridgets,"[37] class distinction is conflated with undifferentiated otherness.[38]

But Toklas also departs from the conventional treatment of servants in this genre: The servants she parades before the reader's eye are credited with special dishes and culinary inventions, and recipes given in this chapter are identified as theirs. The power relation between the narrator and the servants is not stable but often seems fragile and at times is reversed. The servants are beyond her control and seem to leave the household or return to it as they see fit. Of Hélène, we know that she was the one who "made all the practical decisions" in the Rue de Fleurus, which led a friend to comment that he hoped that Hélène "left a free choice of the Picassos to Gertrude Stein" (171). But the servants hold another kind of power over Stein and Toklas, since "We had certainly luck in finding good cooks, though they had their weaknesses in other ways. Gertrude Stein liked to remind me that if they did not have such faults, they would not be working for us" (173). This remark may refer to the reluctance servants might have felt to work for a lesbian couple. One anecdote about a nameless Austrian cook is explicit. The cook, who had worked for Americans before, stays for only three days in the household of Stein and Toklas: "She was a nice person and apparently pleased with her work and us. It had come to our being pleased when they were pleased with us. On the third morning she looked at me severely and said that we 'lived French' and that that was not what she had been led to suspect and she was leaving, which she did" (180).

As Anna Linzie avers, Toklas here comes closest to "coming out of the closet in writing" (178). This is of course only the case when one reads *The Cook Book* as a closeted text, a text that veils the "true" nature of the women's relationship, promoting what Catherine Stimpson dubbed "the lesbian lie": to maintain decorum, the author avoids explicitness about the lesbian relationship she is representing. This interpretation is based on the assumption that a same-sex relationship needs to be marked as such, since it departs from the "normal"—that it needs to confess itself—and, even more questionably, that this marking of homosexual identity needs to be performed in a fashion that follows today's standards and discourses.[39] But as Brian Loftus asks in

his "Speaking Silence: The Strategies and Structures of Queer Autobiography,"
"How can a text consolidate a subject on the grounds of sexuality when that
sexuality has no history to document, no proper cultural space and no symbolic categories?" (31). He describes the dilemma of the queer self in autobiography: "the available terms to describe these sexual positions simultaneously define and rearticulate heterosexuality." Otherwise the homosexual I,
"forced into the margins of a symbolic system that refuses it, . . . can only
impinge upon the heterosexualized center not as coherent 'I,' but only nega-
tively as a figure of excess or absence" (29). Instead of marking herself as "a
figure of excess or absence" Toklas introduces the marriage plot, employing
it to mark her relationship with Stein as sexual, but simultaneously denatu-
ralizing heterosexual marriage when using it as metaphor and rearticulating
it as a same-sex relationship. As Loftus phrases this strategy, it forces "the
normative term of heterosexuality to mean differently to the point that it
signifies the homosexual relation it should refuse" (41).

In writing *The Cook Book,* Toklas also unsettled heteronormativity in
employing the cookbook genre, a genre that traditionally promoted heterosexual relationships and constituted the cooking for another person as an act
of love and commitment. In detail the narrator describes how she started to
cook occasionally for Stein at Stein's request, and how she then tried to please
her with food. Food and eating were, of course, activities that were traditionally sexualized in Western art. While repeating the cookbook trope that all
housewives' striving should be concentrated on pleasing the husband, she
similarly challenges it with dry humor.[40]

Toklas disturbs the authority of the cookbook that excluded traditionally
non-heterosexual relationships and family life by reinterpreting and decon-
structing the role of the expert and by introducing recipes within an autobiographical narrative of two women eating together. She queers cookbook
writing by renouncing the normative power of the genre as well as by decon-
structing the ideals of femininity and heterosexuality conventionally represented in cookbooks. The autobiographical frame does not allow for generalization, and no advice is given in Toklas's cookbook on how to set the table
or clean the kitchen. Stressing the particular, the historical moment, the
personal memory, she resists the normative voice of the expert in cookbook
writing. Her reformulation of the "servant problem" as servants having problems working for a lesbian couple shows self-confidence as well as self-irony.
Not only does she avoid becoming transfixed in a homosexual identity when
rejecting a confessional mode; in her discussions and representations of

nationality and gender she shows the instability of any such identity construction.

After a longish report of life during World War II, the book ends not with Gertrude Stein's death, but reaches out in a nostalgic gesture to the gardens at Bilignin, where Toklas and Stein rented a summer house from 1929 onward. Here the description of lush berries and plentiful and diverse vegetables evokes the image of Toklas's personal Eden with two Eves. Far away from Paris and its turbulence, life in the gardens is defined by the hard work of planting and harvesting and the satisfaction of making things grow and live in nature. Recipes for simple dishes accompany the images of heavenly life. Toklas and Stein work in the garden side by side, even if Stein cares for the flowers and Toklas for the vegetables. This is a paradise built by both of them and lost because of Stein's death, which remains unspoken in the text.

The Cook Book communicates in manifold ways with Stein's writing, especially *The Autobiography of Alice B. Toklas,* by commenting on it, adjusting its images, and adapting it with gentle irony. *The Cook Book* is in many regards *The Autobiography*'s counterpart, not only in style but also in content: many of Toklas's anecdotes retell and confirm *The Autobiography*—if often with a twist, as described above, because in Toklas's version the cook becomes the genius.[41]

The Autobiography uses a number of strategies to challenge not only the genre but also the underlying assumptions in the constitution of subjectivity and authorship that conventions of autobiographical writing have promoted. For example, the assumed congruence of the author, narrator, and protagonist—the autobiographical pact that is important for the claimed authority and authenticity of the text—is subverted, when in the last sentences of the book Stein is revealed as the author of Toklas's "auto" biography (which, to make it even more complex, features Stein, not Toklas, as its main protagonist).[42] As Leigh Gilmore and others have argued, Stein thus creates an autobiographical subject position that is not inhibited by an independent, autonomous, male, straight I, but by a lesbian couple that is inseparably intertwined—"Gertrice/Altrude" (205).[43] Thus the text challenges not only the autobiographical I but also its normative function. *The Autobiography* also refuses to follow contemporary dominant definitions of lesbian identity. The text maneuvers within the narrow space of hegemonic discourses that define lesbians as deviant, as outlined by the sexologists' discourses, or as flamboyant, as in the reports of the Parisian salons à la Natalie Barney, or as melancholic, as in the literature of the 1920s. It refuses any explanation of the nature of the relationship between Toklas and Stein.[44] Nonetheless it is revealing in the end when author, narrator, protagonist, and also Stein and Toklas merge into each other, imploding not only the autobiographical pact but all notions of the binary I/you as well as the imagined autonomy of the Western subject.

The Cook Book, too, disturbs the conventions of autobiographical writing. Although it features a rough chronological structure, leading the reader from World War I to World War II, this timeline is perforated. The chronological narration is disturbed by flashbacks, for instance to the narrator's childhood, or chapters that present general notions on a certain topic within their own chronological structure (such as "Servants in France," a straightforward chronological narration that disrupts the broader time organization of the book). Any notion of linearity and development is confused, but two important elements keep the text together: the recipes and the relationship with Gertrude Stein. The autobiographical text covers roughly the years of the relationship between Stein and Toklas; little is revealed of the narrator's life before Stein, and nothing of her life after Stein's death. Cooking, eating, and Stein, or cooking for Stein and eating with Stein, are the thread through the narrator's life, the source of coherence and her way of making sense.

Both The Autobiography and The Cook Book challenge notions of authorship and authority.[45] Ideas of the author as an original and autonomous authority in the text are subverted in The Cook Book. In language and content the text explicitly refers to The Autobiography and other writings of Stein, and the recipes presented are usually credited to other cooks. Thus the text renounces ideas of uniqueness or originality. Authorship and authority are constantly deflected onto others. At the end of The Cook Book, Toklas also renounces "again" her authorship of The Autobiography. This time, no other ghost writer is introduced, but Toklas dryly ends her memory with the often-quoted statement: "As if a cook-book had anything to do with writing" (280). Toklas's exclamation has been read as a mere expression of modesty and self-deprecation, which does not do justice to the complex effect of the sentence nor to its prominent placement at the end of the text.[46] Like the ending of The Autobiography, the statement creates a moment of alienation. The sentence reminds readers that they have just digested a cookbook, something that is easily forgotten when reading The Cook Book because of its captivating narration. But if a cookbook cannot be "read" (since it is not "written"), what is The Cook Book? While being a cookbook, the autobiography changes the meaning of what a cookbook is. Not only does it subvert the conventions of both genres, it plays them against each other. *The Cook Book* destabilizes clear-cut borders between genres, the concepts of "high" and "low" art, and the gender implications that come with both.

WHAT LESBIANS EAT: IDENTITY, FOOD, AND SAME-SEX DESIRE

Alice Toklas utilized the conventions of the cookbook genre to speak of her commitment to Gertrude Stein, writing with and against a tradition that made food synonymous with a woman's love for her partner and family. Two generations of authors of cookbooks, memoirs, and autobiographical texts followed in her footsteps, using food imagery to negotiate women's love and same-sex desire or to indicate sexual awakening or sexual difference, sometimes explicitly referencing Toklas as an inspiration.[47]

A small corpus of cookbooks has come on the American market over the last few decades addressing lesbian cooks.[48] These texts write against the normative depictions of hegemonic performances of femininity as well as women's sexuality that are commonly found in cookbooks. Cookbooks addressing a lesbian audience make the demands the genre traditionally placed on women visible, and dispute them. Food, the kitchen, and cooking as spaces and practices of gender conformity and signifiers of a normative organization of sexuality have also played an important role in memoirs and autobiographies concerned with sexual identity, marking moments of sexual awakening and/or resistance against social expectations toward women. Like the cookbooks and (more recently) cooking blogs, they write against the normative gender notions traditionally presented in cooking advice. This reflects a disenchantment, growing since the 1960s, with the expectation that women find fulfillment in the kitchen, and the assumption that kitchen labor is women's work—a major impact of feminist thought. But even more specifically it challenges the well-established heteronormative underpinning of kitchen labor. Besides writing against a firmly established tradition, the texts have little in common and employ different strategies: leaving, despising, or endorsing the kitchen, food, or cooking. By no means is every text that challenges the gendered conventions of cooking advice purely liberating. Since many of the texts address an imaginary lesbian cook, they have to answer the question: who is that? In the process of voicing a culinary identity, texts produce new normative imperatives and complex exclusionary mechanisms that demand further scrutiny.

In autobiographical texts, food has become a vehicle to explore non-hegemonic sexual subjectivities, but also to express the complexity of same-sex desire and relationships. Audre Lorde's autobiography (which she marks as fictional by calling it a "biomythography") *Zami: A New Spelling of My Name* (1982) describes how the narrator's sexual awakening as well as her understanding of sexual difference came together in the act of cooking. The day the narrator starts menstruating (thus symbolically acquiring the body of a woman), she is in the kitchen, using her mother's mortar, a connection to her mythic West Indian heritage that she has known only from the stories her mother tells. "The mortar was of a foreign fragrant wood, too dark for cherry and too red for walnut. To my child eyes, the outside was carved in an intricate and most enticing manner. . . . I loved to finger the hard roundness of the carved fruit" (71). In the mortar's sensuality, food, sexuality, and the foreign imaginary home conflate. On this special occasion it marks her initiation as woman, and her understanding that she is different:

> As I continued to pound the spice, a vital connection seemed to establish itself between the muscles of my fingers curved tightly around the smooth pestle in its insistent downward motion, and the molten core of my body whose source emanated from a new ripe fullness just beneath the pit of my stomach. That invisible thread, taut and sensitive as a clitoris exposed, stretched through my curled fingers up my round brown arm into the moist reality of my armpits, whose warm sharp odor with a strange overlay mixed with the ripe garlic smells from the mortar and the general sweat-heavy aromas of high summer. (78)

The autoerotic scene is disturbed when the mother enters the kitchen and tells her daughter that she is using the mortar wrongly, and demonstrates to her the "right usage":

> "Now you do, so!" She brought the pestle down inside the bowl of the mortar with dispatch, crushing the last of the garlic. I heard the thump of wood brought down heavily upon wood, and I felt the harsh impact throughout my body, as if something had broken inside of me. Thump, thump, went the pestle purposefully, up and down in the old familiar way. (80)

The "purposefulness" and "the old familiar" "thump, thump" of the "right" way to use the pestle is thus superimposed on her own sensual experimentation with the mortar. After learning that "in my mother's kitchen there was only one right way to do anything" and that her using the mortar, as well as the sensual awakening connected to it, must be somehow wrong, she never uses the mortar again (80). The first experience of her sexuality marks her as deviant, in need of correction, foreshadowing her actual coming out, but to her readers she is coming out at this moment, not from the closet, but from the kitchen.[49]

As the kitchen is the place in which normative femininity and hetero-sexual desire are produced, it can also become the place in which non-normative femininities become apparent, and alternate desires manifested. Countless culinary memoirs over the past few decades, many of them including recipes that invite readers to participate in the narrative on a gustatory level, use the *topos* of food as a structuring element, a thread to guide the text through lives that are necessarily messy and nonlinear, and as a means to make sense of the past and the self. Traci Marie Kelley has defined a culinary autobiography as a text in which "functions of cooking, history, and story-telling blur" and "the recipes provide verisimilitude for the stories, and the stories explain the food."[50] Often food is used as the means to explore iden-tity, as in *Miriam's Kitchen* (1997), in which Elizabeth Ehrlich discovers her Jewish heritage by learning how to cook kosher, or in Vertamae Smart-Grosvenor's *Vibration Cooking: Or, The Travel Notes of a Geechee Girl* (1986), another text inspired by *The Alice B. Toklas Cook Book,* in which the author seeks her own place between black nationalism and global citizenship.[51] As Anne Goldman states, culinary memoirs with a focus on ethnic identity often discuss homesickness, alienation, and the question of home and cul-tural belonging.[52] Rafia Zafar says of *Vibration Cooking* and culinary auto-biographical texts by African American authors in general that they also serve to write against racist and sexist stereotypes.[53] Culinary memoirs and autobiographical cookbooks that explore female same-sex desire tend to dis-cuss family, community, and same-sex desire (and, recently, marriage) as well as questions of gender. But even these broad categorizations are oftentimes exceeded, especially in recent texts, showing that there is no such thing as a homogeneous lesbian community or identity, and that the question of whether there is such a thing as a lesbian identity alone is always already complicated. Food serves as an organizing tool in many such explorations, as autobiographical storytelling conventions increasingly allow for more frag-mented recordings of lives.

Bode Noonan's *Red Beans and Rice: Recipes for Lesbian Health and Wisdom* (1986), an autobiographical cookbook that weaves memories into its recipes, radically undermines the parameters of cookbook writing.[54] It bears only a faint resemblance to what readers of cookbooks have learned to recognize as elemental to the genre: There are no lists of ingredients, no imperatives, no instructions, no claim to authority. Each of the only five recipes in the book is presented as its own chapter written in essayistic prose. Only those who read the whole chapter can assemble the dish. The instructions given are vague, encouraging the cook to produce her own dish rather than simply follow the author's instructions. Meandering between unconventional wisdom, general advice, autobiography, and food memories, Noonan tells us how to make egg salad, red beans and rice, bread and spinach casserole, potato salad, and fruit juice. All five recipes are comfort foods, she lets her reader know, for the bruised and battered.

Written in the 1980s, the text is conscious of the problems that come with identity politics. It tries to emphasize diversity and individuality while simultaneously imagining a community based on sexual identity for political and emotional support. This does not have to be a contradiction, as the author explains in her chapter on potato salad:

> Potatoes, I thought. Potatoes are a lot like Lesbians. They're all the same and they're all different. You have New potatoes, Russett potatoes. Red potatoes, brown potatoes. Boiled potatoes, fried potatoes. Baked potatoes, peeled potatoes. But all potatoes are composed of carbohydrates and water.... Some of us play softball.... Some of us wear three piece suits and do our daily work in courtrooms where we defend against what we see as unjust. Some of us don't do a damn thing at all. Some of us aren't even gay. Some of us are men. Men? What am I saying? (46–47)

While Noonan obviously tries to avoid an essentialist definition of what constitutes the lesbian subject, she still grasps for a way to define what it means to be a lesbian, what constitutes the community's water and carbohydrates. In this process, she severs lesbian identity entirely from sexual acts and rearranges it around the experience of exclusion and marginalization, but specifies this experience as different from the experience of racism and sexism insofar as it has at its core the pain of being rejected and disowned not only by society but, even worse, by your own family and childhood friends—an experience, she argues, that is central to lesbian identity. Hence the emphasis on comfort food in the text. It is familiar childhood food that in a Proustian manner brings back with its flavors the distant memory of unconditional love and acceptance. Giving the readers the knowledge to prepare these dishes gives them the possibility to care for themselves and create their own families, the author argues.

Noonan also discusses lesbian identity in terms of gender performance. She describes how her mother labored unenthusiastically over her much-acknowledged signature potato salad, despising the process of preparing it but doing it anyway, complying with social expectations. Cooking disciplined her mother into gender-appropriate behavior. She contrasts this description with one of her former lovers, who made her less-than-perfect potato salad with great enthusiasm, intensively enjoying every minute of it. The difference, Noonan suggests, is that cooking can be a liberating and creative act for women who reject the notion that their femaleness condemns them to the kitchen and have rich lives otherwise. The mother cannot escape from the kitchen because her self-esteem depends on the acknowledgment she gains for her flawless performance of hegemonic femininity. The lesbian lover, in contrast, makes up her own gender performance, picking what pleases her instead of what pleases society. Here, as in other places, *Red Beans and Rice* engages in romanticized notions of lesbian identity. Identity for Noonan is not only centered on the experience of rejection but also described as an alternative, more liberated, and perhaps more enlightened form of feminine gender performance. The lesbian subjectivities Noonan constructs in the text thus waver between victimization and empowerment.

Julia Ehrhardt, analyzing the use of food imagery in literary writing by Chicana lesbians, argues that the poets she focuses on, such as Alicia Gaspar de Alba and Angela Arellano, use "cooking as a vital source of female identity and pride" (94). While leaving the kitchen and food preparation intact as places of women's power, the poets rewrite the implicit heteronormative assumptions by infusing cooking practices with sexual allusions. Ehrhardt shows that the texts thus negotiate femininity, ethnicity, and sexuality through the use of food imagery. Embracing cooking, and the kitchen as a traditionally all-female space, the authors endorse a distinctive culinary heritage to mark ethnic identity and to set themselves apart from the American mainstream. But as cooking is also a possible site of limitation and mandatory hegemonic gender performance, lesbian authors have also written against the kitchen as a place of disempowerment.

In Paula Martinac's "Fast, Free Delivery," for example, home cooking is associated with the heterosexually organized lifestyles of conformist suburbs that have no space for lesbians. Martinac's text appears in Arlene Voski Avakian's *Through the Kitchen Window: Women Explore the Intimate*

Meanings of Food and Cooking (1997), a collection of texts exploring women's complicated relations with food. Many of the texts are accompanied by recipes, inviting readers to share the foods the authors talk about, thus making it a culinary autobiography of its own kind. The texts frame and explain the recipes, making sense of them by providing context. While the borders between the autobiographical and the literary are fluid in many of these texts, the context claims them as discussions of the authors' coming to terms with questions of identity as they crystallize around food. Four of the texts explicitly negotiate questions of same-sex desire and experience. In Martinac's story, escaping the kitchen is what eventually sets her narrator free. Fast, free food delivery is here associated with urban, successful, and sexually liberated lifestyles that she encounters first with a friend, who is "an active participant in the lesbian and gay community," and lives, it seems, from delivered foods alone (163). In the story the narrator moves from living and cooking for herself to her own fast, free delivery lifestyle in Manhattan. As this coincides with her becoming an acknowledged writer and entering a long-term relationship with a woman, freedom from kitchen work here is the path that brings her into her own.

Martinac describes "take-out as the realm of the possible" and thus as a way to realize one's own potential (164). The narrator rents an apartment in a neighborhood with easy access to falafel, northern Italian food, and a kosher vegetarian Indian restaurant. The multiethnic resources at her disposal, tokens of cosmopolitanism, serve uncritically as signifiers of an urban lifestyle that is pitted against the homogeneity of the suburbs, specifically the suburbs of Pittsburgh, where she was raised. The contrast with the life she left behind is stark. She associates the lower-middle-class background of her family with fast-food joints, the only takeout that her family could afford when she was a child. For her, this also epitomizes the heteronormative expectations she was raised with: after meeting a school friend and his wife at the salad bar of a fast-food restaurant, the narrator wonders: "If I had never left Pittsburgh . . . would I have been eating there with my husband?" (167).

"Fast, Free Delivery" seems to credit same-sex desire with class mobility, as intolerance toward her sexual orientation has propelled the narrator to leave her family and familiar surroundings and explore the world in search of other possibilities. In the story, her new class status is marked not only by being able to afford a Manhattan apartment and regular takeout, but also by occasionally cooking a meal together with her lover "from scratch" (167). But this is not a return to the narrator's suburban past, as it is pitted against the processed foods of her Pittsburgh childhood. In Martinac's story, this enlightened cooking from scratch is also different, as it happens occasionally and is a woman's choice rather than her duty. Cooking together with her partner instead of for her partner serves as a sign of a healthy, mutually nourishing relationship. This praise for fast, free delivery is accompanied by a recipe for "A Simple Chicken Marinade for Saturday Night" (168), inviting readers to participate in this form of happy, liberating, relationship-building cooking.

Manhattan in "Fast, Free Delivery" is more than a setting. Providing easy access to many foods, it also forces its inhabitants to come out of their apartments, which are the size of a "Swanson's frozen dinner box" and do not facilitate dinners or heteronormative families (167). "Manhattan kitchens are more like aisles than rooms" and will not "accommodate a proper dinner table" (while suburban kitchens are designed for "family use") (163, 167). Manhattan, where women hold hands in public, is a "city where anything is possible" (167). And so Martinac's move to Manhattan becomes "the final departure from my family and my class background" (164). The endless culinary and sexual possibilities are unequivocally liberating. Martinac's class mobility is identical with her ability to buy food whose sophistication is represented by its ethnic diversity. Food cooked or purchased becomes the way she demonstrably leaves behind her blue-collar Catholic origins to establish a new sexual and class identity.

Class background is similarly important in another story in *Through the Kitchen Window:* Sally Bellerose's one-and-a-half-page short story "Gravy." The author provides a vignette of an uncomfortable family meal in which the narrator's lesbianism and vegetarianism conflate—both equally foreign to and unwelcomed by her family. The meal is ruled by the mother's unspoken verdict that difficult topics cannot be brought up over dinner (or at all, it seems)—a rule that the narrator and her father frequently choose to break. Eventually the mother insists on eating dinner in front of the TV to avoid all conversation.

The narrator's lover was invited to join the family for dinner, but declined, so the daughter's vegetarianism becomes the topical stand-in for her same-sex relationship since "My father believes that all lesbians are vegetarians" (40). The mother's lack of understanding toward her daughter's food (and, implicitly, sexual) preference becomes evident when she prepares "vegetarian stew" with "two-inch chunks of beef in it," which she picks out after cooking so that her daughter will eat the dish (40). The narrator eats her portion without complaining, but with bitter feelings. When she and her father trade tastes of the gravy from one another's plates, the father proclaims: "you got unnatural gravy." The daughter, after tasting his gravy, retorts: "Hormones... Antibiotics, Pesticides" (41). While father and daughter have found an uncomfortable way to communicate with one another, even if only to criticize the other's choices, the mother's silence and withdrawal are insurmountable. Bellerose, like Martinac, shows the return to one's birth family and home as moments of alienation and rejection, reminding the reader of Bode Noonan's claim that this experience can be central to lesbian identity.

But for the alienation the narrator experiences with her family, she retaliates by describing with distance and slight irony the less-sophisticated "plastic pickle tongs that [the mother] got free at a Tupperware party," the father's disdain for broccoli, and the TV game shows (*Wheel of Fortune* and *Jeopardy*) that the parents like to watch (40). All of which, apparently, are no longer parts of the narrator's world, nothing to which she would wish to return, even if invited. As the vignette does not reveal the details of the narrator's current lifestyle, it is not possible to assess from what position she is viewing her parents' lives, but it seems as if she, like Martinac's narrator, also feels some relief at being liberated from a world that has become too narrow and oppressive for her.

"Gravy" is one of the few stories in the collection not accompanied by a recipe. The heaviness of the dinner scene described does not invite the celebration of cooking or eating. Shared meals, as opportunities to build community or maintain relationships, are here a painful liability in which parents and children mutually disown each other.

Martha Ayres's recipe for "Shish Kebab" comes with a story that credits her lover, Arlene, as the author of the dish. Arlene brings the leg of lamb, reflecting her Armenian heritage, to the narrator's family reunion, in which she will be introduced to the extended family. In this "coming-out reunion," as the narrator dubs it, she expects her family to be less than accepting of Arlene as well as her offering of the "foreign" shish kebab. This is exemplified in the mother's resistance to serve the unfamiliar food, which she see as only another indicator of her daughter's otherness. The marinated lamb "further accentuated our difference" (159) as "Shish-ka-bob and jello are at the opposite ends of the food spectrum" (158–59). The mother fears that the lamb will draw even more attention to her daughter's same-sex relationship, and therefore fiercely opposes it. The narrator is torn between appeasing the mother (by not serving the lamb) and thereby hurting Arlene, who intends the lamb to be a present. In the end the narrator does not sacrifice Arlene or her lamb for family peace and has it served at the picnic, where "some relatives loved the shish-ka-bob and others passed it over for fried chicken," as presumably some of the relatives were accepting of their relationship and some not (159).

While the three texts above concentrate on the negotiation, via food imagery, of sexual identity with the family into which one is born, Dorothy Allison's "A Lesbian Appetite," also in *Through the Kitchen Window*, discusses the families one builds.[55] The short story employs a similar autobiographical mode as the others, but incorporates dream sequences. It opens with a description of Southern foods the narrator craves while living in the North: greens and pork fat, biscuits, beans. This "diet of poor Southerners" she claims as her culinary identity, her fingerprint, the food that reminds her of "who I was": "Poor white trash. . . . I eat shit food and I am not worthy" (277, 278). She then juxtaposes it with the dishes her lovers have brought into her life: "Red beans and rice," "refried beans on warm tortillas," "lamb cooked with olive oil and lemon slices" (276). "Food is more than sustenance; it is history," the narrator asserts; "I remember women by what we ate together" (277). The one woman she met who did not like to eat "didn't last long," as the narrator "couldn't think what to do with her when the sex was finished" (277). The women that the narrator describes are sketched by their food choices. She has deli food in Georgia with Mona and her mother, spiced with disappointment, since the narrator had hoped for a Southern spread. She engages in an erotic food fight with Lee, who likes healthy food, in the kitchen while cooking eggplant. Unfortunately, the feminist activist Lee and her diet of vegetables, tofu, and water with lemon make the narrator sick. She falls for Southern barbecue and the woman who promises it to her, Marty (290).

Despite the claim the narrator posits at the beginning of the story that the women in her life also brought their food to hers, the story is at its core an homage to Southern cooking and the author's roots. Athletic Jay, who is into kinky sex, lets the narrator feed her Southern food to satisfy her more homey appetites. Sad Virginia the narrator seduces with the promise of a Southern meal. Comfort food expresses the narrator's quest for home in her relationships, a place she feels safe and accepted. Lee's healthy vegetarian food stands for the lack of nourishment she finds in their relationship, as the narrator craves meat, standing for substance and home in the text. In "'Lesbian Appetites': Food, Sexuality and Community in Feminist Autobiography," Antje Lindenmeyer summarizes the ideological struggles within lesbian communities over meat eating as a generational fight between "the worthy vegetarian, chickpea- or tofu-consuming radical-feminists and the young, daring, taboo-breaking, meat-eating sex radicals" (479). But in Allison's story, the difference between the narrator and Lee seems to be based on class. As Lee wins the struggles over what they eat and cook, the narrator's sense of unworthiness grows.

Only in the final paragraph does the narrator find some peace. She describes a dream in which the women in her life, lovers and family, come together for a big feast and bring the food that stands for each of them. This dream of a community of women of different classes, backgrounds, and flavors as well as sexual orientations overcomes all differences. The idea of such an idealized family satiates the narrator fully: "For the first time in my life I am not hungry" (295).

In the recipes and stories of *Through the Kitchen Window,* food plays a crucial role when it comes to marking lesbian identity while mostly avoiding stereotypical depictions. It serves to discuss the indifference and hostility that women in same-sex relationships can face, including from their parents and relatives. Food can be a marker of love, as in "The Parable of the Lamb" and "A Lesbian Appetite," or it can signify withheld love, as in "Gravy." In "Fast, Free Delivery," paying someone to cook can be a gesture of freedom. In "A Lesbian Appetite" as well as in "Fast, Free Delivery" it can become the means to build one's own family. While using the firmly established image of food as a proxy for love and sexuality and grappling with the complexity of class privilege around the consumption of ethnic food, all these texts transform conventions as commonly presented in cooking advice by inscribing non-normative experiences into American food and literature.

Amy Scholder's compilation of recipes *Cookin' with Honey: What Literary Lesbians Eat* (1996), like *Through the Kitchen Window,* presents recipes framed by short accounts by their authors on how they fit into their lives. Unlike in the previous texts, the title of the book insinuates that there is a difference not only in how lesbians live, but also in how they eat. The contributors of the recipes, mostly professional writers, accompany their dishes with vignettes that describe their relation to the recipe. Some discuss their lives as writers, some discuss their loves, and some their regional and ethnic backgrounds, showing a diversity of approaches to making sense of life with the help of food.[56] The recipes span from "Tequila Cranberry Salsa" to "Hoecakes" and "Bavarian Bread Dumplings" (18, 37, 150). The answer to the question of what lesbians eat therefore seems to be: anything. The text makes it apparent that food choices are mainly informed by class, ethnicity, and regional background, and even in the small sample group the text represents, these are manifold.

The autobiographical mode that remains with personal experience to circumvent generalization is not the only strategy in the pursuit of describing lesbian identities without reverting to stereotypical expectations. In 1998, Ffiona Morgan published *The Lesbian Erotic Cookbook: Cuisine Extraordinaire to Caress and Fondle the Palate*.[57] The cookbook features recipes such as "Raging Hormone Rice," "Get Down Crepes," "Road to Ecstasy Applesauce Bread," and "Peel My Clothes Off Fried Rice," and these are only some of the tamer titles. Attaching sexual excitement to the recipes marks their difference from other cookbooks and claims them as an expression of sexual and same-sex desire. Beyond the racy titles, the recipes themselves are not different from those in other cookbooks; they feature lists of commonly available ingredients and detailed instructions, and produce dishes not different from those in other cookbooks. Most challenging to the rules of the genre is that the recipes are embedded in suggestive short stories and photos that present as erotic a diversity of female bodies in various states of dress or undress, displaying voluptuous, slender, aging, muscular, sagging, pierced, soft, and flabby bodies with firm, spotless, or wrinkled skin. The text thus defies the mainstream vision of female attractiveness. Clearly in love with female muscle and endorsing body fat, the cookbook defines the lesbian body as less regulated by hegemonic beauty standards and erotic in its individuality. The cookbook, fully functional as a manual, resists the embodiment of normative gender performances and the incorporation of heteronormative narratives. The recipes are meant to nourish diverse bodies. Food is presented lustfully, and eating is shown as pleasure-inducing.

While *The Lesbian Erotic Cookbook* queers ideas of the female nude, it presents as erotic only abled bodies. While variety and individuality are important in the depictions of queer female bodies in this text, they are not free of normative assumptions. Most of the depicted women wear their hair short and no makeup, but compromise with hegemonic beauty ideals in mostly displaying hairless bodies and faces. The text stretches and bends ideas of ideal femininity but it also uses familiar images from a culturally sanctioned reservoir of depictions of women's sexuality, such as voluptuous flowers and luscious fruits and curvy statues of fertility goddesses. The cookbook thus reiterates well-worn notions of women's bodies as soft, swollen, delicious, and sweet-smelling, showing how impossible it is to entirely escape from cultural stereotypes.

The staging of the erotic, too, utilizes conventional imagery, such as the display of fragmented naked bodies emphasizing similar body parts that would be presented in the context of the heterosexual erotic, most prominently breasts. But the text does not offer only conventional productions of the erotic; it also gives space to alternatives. Biceps, for instance, are staged as sexually attractive female body parts. Juxtaposed with breasts, they mediate between hardness and softness, concepts that have traditionally been misused to distinguish between the sexes. Tucked among the depictions of breasts, bellies, and bottoms is a photo of hands, body parts commonly neglected in heterosexual pornographic depictions. Showing hands within this sexualized framework acknowledges their importance for the erotic experience.

Perhaps most notable are the many depictions of women eating and feeding each other. As Susan Bordo has argued, representations of women eating have almost entirely vanished from public discourse as a radical consequence of the cultural dictum that men eat and women cook.[58] In these images of women feeding each other, the symbolic connection between feeding and loving is left intact, but reappropriated without its heteronormative implication. There is a long tradition in American culture that values a woman's restraint of her appetite as a positively connoted sign of control over her sexual desires and other ambitions, and thereby her acceptance of male primacy. *The Lesbian Erotic Cookbook* presents women's lustful eating as desirable and the lesbian subject as guiltlessly giving in to all her cravings—also, of course, a romanticized notion of queer subjectivity.

The Butch Cookbook, too, redefines and negotiates gender identities. Published in 2008 by Lee Lynch, Nel Ward, and Sue Hardesty, it is a compilation of recipes sent in by cooks who self-identify as butch.[59] Compiled cookbooks have traditionally been used to create a sense of community. At the same time, they defy the notion of a central, authoritative voice, since all contributors share in defining the community to which they belong. *The Butch Cookbook* utilizes both of these aspects to deal with the problems that come with the term "butch" (a term that has been called "overtheorized," "underdetermined," and "infinitely elastic").[60] The cookbook struggles hard to achieve a complex and inclusive description of butch identity. It also exploits a number of common stereotypes, often impishly, with great humor and self-deprecation. The illustrations in the book feature, quite out of context, trucks and motorcycles to accompany the recipes. One of the contributors advises: "Use a food processor—what's a butch without power tools?" To no surprise many illustrations present real power tools in the kitchen. Some recipes call for beer, either as an ingredient or as "emotional" support for the butch who has to face the hazards of the kitchen (102, 115). Many recipes feature sexual or romantic allusions, such as this one that instructs the readers on how to cook for a new girlfriend:

Tips for First Dinner Cooked by Butch for New Girlfriend

Take a deep breath and remember this is the only meal you'll have to cook.

Go to deli and pick up something green, something red or orange, and something pre-cooked.

Check to make sure she doesn't buy at the same deli.

Check to see if the microwave is working.

Serve deli stuff in dishes borrowed from gay guys next door.

If you're lucky, the guys will jump at the chance to cater the meal for you. Take their offer without question. They'll disappear at the last moment and give you all the credit.

Hide all the deli cartons before she arrives. (87)

The recipe employs three stereotypes at once: butch lesbians who cannot cook and do not enjoy it, femme girlfriends who will take over the cooking of future meals, as well as gay neighbors who are experts in the kitchen and possess the right china.

The cookbook also provides (clearly jokingly) a test to distinguish a butch from a femme. It asks you to look at your nails. If you curl your fingers inward you are butch, while the femme looks at the back of her hand (as if in the act of checking her nail polish). The test claims that butchness is not only about attitude, but also about queer embodiment, a form of resistance against the hegemonic production of the female body that is less critically adapted by the femme. The text suggests that butchness undermines the disciplinary mechanisms that render the female body as dainty, incapacitated, fragile, and decorative. The butch body needs specific nourishment, and this, not surprisingly, excludes some of the items that are connoted as feminine in society. For instance, the text claims a butch eats vegetables only if her femme makes her. The salad section is called "Rabbit Food" (13).

The hyper-butchness that is displayed throughout the text is, of course, constantly undermined by the fact that the text is a cookbook. The editors jokingly admit that when they started to collect recipes they expected "30 recipes for boxed mac and cheese" (i), but learned to their surprise "that butches can cook" (iii). Because cookbooks have a long tradition of being associated with hegemonic feminine gender performance, the context of the cookbook implicitly subverts the performance of butchness as a renegade gender identity. Again the text and its authors deal with the dilemma playfully. To neutralize the cookbook's gender norm–affirming potential, the contributors and editors mainly use three strategies. Firstly, the butch cooks for sexual gratification. Recipes feature titles such as "Green Beans for Butches Hoping for Sex on the First Date" (55). The drink section of the cookbook is called "Love Potions," and the breakfast section "The Morning After" (157, 163). Echoing strategies in cookbooks for men described earlier, wowing women is a sufficiently butch endeavor to limit the damage cooking may be doing to the cook's dissident gender identity. Secondly, many of the contributors explain in detail why they took up cooking in the first place: a partner got sick and the butch took over the household chores; it serves as a creative outlet to balance a more menial day job; or, in a more unusual explanation, the author was in a Zen cloister and was ordered to cook to further her spiritual enlightenment. All these explanations make it obvious that the butch does not cook because it comes naturally (as is implied for women within the heterosexual economy) but because of very specific circumstances that make the act an individual choice or the result of necessity.

A third strategy is the contribution of specifically butch recipes. These are recipes that are centered on the idea of speed, simplicity, and convenience. For instance, the recipe for "Mostly Peas" asks for only three ingredients: a can of V8 juice, 1/2 cup frozen peas, and Tabasco sauce to taste. No fussing around in the kitchen is required here, only a microwave and a spoon. Only a few of the recipes produce food from scratch. Recipes for pancakes, pies, and cakes usually start with boxed mixes. One recipe suggests bagged salad as a side dish and advises the reader to take the salad out of the bag before serving it (184). The butch recipe stages a lack of competence and unfamiliarity with the kitchen, rejecting the expertise and authority culture has traditionally assigned to women there, thus disassociating itself from hegemonic ideas of what constitutes an ideal woman.

At first glance, these strategies may seem to echo the rationalizations and defense mechanisms familiar from generations of cookbooks for men. But whereas male cooks sought to protect themselves from the effeminizing potential of kitchen work, butch cooks assert a positive identity as an alternative to the weakness inherent in society's prescription of a single kind of acceptable femininity linked to food. Importantly, these simple definitions and descriptions of butchness are complicated on every page of the text. Contradictions are invited and not silenced in an attempt to homogenize butch identity. The cookbook, for example, features complex and sophisticated recipes too, as well as apparently not-so-butch recipes for lemon chiffon pie, mushroom risotto, and mango compote.

The generalization of butchness the text presents is balanced by short texts that accompany the dishes in which the contributors explain what the recipes and butchness mean to them. Under the title "Butch Bio," blacksmiths, community organizers, writers, and stay-at-home-butches write. One such is Barb Bayenhof, who chose to devote her life to feeding her partner for the better of eleven years. Truck driver Bevin Allison calls herself a "domestic butch" (159). Melissa Freet describes herself as a cross between Martha Stewart and MacGyver, and Marythegood writes: "Can handle sheetrock and split wood, but my pie crust will melt in your mouth" (99). Elisabeth claims: "I tend to consider myself both butch and femme at the same time" (7), and Carolyn Gage explains: "I am one of these dykes who feels like a femme around some lesbians, but like a butch around other lesbians who are femmier than me" (6). These bios show how butches cross the gender dichotomy back and forth in their daily lives, experiencing gender performance as a spectrum rather than a clear-cut binary.

Despite its at times stereotypical representation of butchness, the text in the end presents "butch" as an umbrella term for a great variety of gender performances that do not—or do not entirely—conform to ideas of hegemonic femininity and that are directed at an audience of women who cook for other women. Thus the definition of butchness oscillates in the text between gender and sexual subjectivities and produces an infinite number of potentialities.[61]

While *The Lesbian Erotic Cookbook* and *The Butch Cookbook* explicitly address a lesbian audience, other culinary memoirs by self-identifying lesbian authors published in recent years engage broader audiences. Unlike *The Alice B. Toklas Cook Book,* published half a century earlier, their tone is confidential and casual. More earnest in their intent to tell stories, they are less likely to engage in artistic experimentation. In a further contrast, they tend toward the confessional. They recount, often in painful detail, the downsides of relationships, love turned stale, breakups, and the disappointed hope for romance. But like in *The Alice B. Toklas Cook Book,* food commonly serves as a stand-in to discuss sexuality and desire.

Candace Walsh's *Licking the Spoon: A Memoir of Food, Family, and Identity* (2012) is not simply a coming-of-age story, nor is it a coming-out story, although it has both elements. Organized loosely around the dinners the narrator cooked and ate, the memoir tells how she overcame a problematic childhood, sexual abuse, and eating disorders and describes her path from slightly abusive heterosexual relationships to same-sex ones in her late thirties. The story of surmounting every obstacle and the climax and "happy ending" make the memoir resemble a fairy tale, culminating in the wedding of Walsh and her partner Laura after a political quest for equal marriage rights in the state of New York. Foreshadowing techniques, and seemingly random details that in hindsight turn out to be clues waiting to be neatly tied together, give Walsh's final relationship and wedding with Laura a fated quality. Her career and motherhood play a marginal role in the memoir, which instead centers on her relationship with her parents, her own body, and her changing partners. Walsh narrates her relationships, without giving any sexual details, through food imagery. The book's prologue presents the culinary bookends of Walsh's first marriage: she describes a risotto she made the first time she cooked for her future husband, Will. The juxtaposed cooking scene that takes place nine years later describes how she prepares a "multicourse dinner for six," one of whom is the person Walsh had just fallen in love with, whose name she initially gives only as "C." Only in the course of the story will it be revealed that C. is a woman. Although Walsh will not have a sexual relationship with Celine, whom she tries to woo that evening with her culinary prowess, the food she prepares signals her sexual awakening. Her sexual tastes, revived after her marriage has dulled, help create mushroom chestnut soup, lamb chops braised with onions, potatoes with thyme, and a bittersweet chocolate tart with a walnut crust (xii–xiii). While Celine cannot be cooked into a relationship, Walsh reports that "she gave me lots in return: With each bite, she closed her eyes and sighed or very faintly moaned with pleasure" (258). Walsh cooking for Celine, and Celine receiving pleasure from the food, is the most erotic the relationship will get, using food as a substitute for sexual satisfaction, employing a well-worn cultural convention.

Walsh's marriage to Will started promisingly with the risotto, but has become stale and an unsafe place because of his regular bursts of anger. The failure of her marriage Walsh also discusses in terms of food: "Even cooking for Will had become joyless. What made it worse was that he insisted that I do it. If I didn't, his low blood sugar made him even more likely to lose his temper.... So I made uninspired food—dinners of the defeated.... My depleted cooking jones went along with my depleted libido" (217). Walsh announces her emotional alienation from her husband and the beginning of their separation by declaring to him, "I'm not cooking anymore" (248). Freeing herself from the act of cooking is her declaration of independence and determination to leave her joyless marriage. Also announced by food imagery, her first sexual relationship with a woman after her separation from Will is doomed from the beginning to end unhappily: Maxine is a dogmatic eater (who eats "steamed acorn squash sprinkled with spirulina" for breakfast, following ayurvedic advice), and on top of that, she is a mediocre cook (265). Early on Walsh cheats on Maxine culinarily by sneaking out for a burger, foreshadowing that this relationship will not last (265). The text thus avoids simple ascriptions: same-sex desire is not necessarily always delicious. Each lover, each relationship, has its individual textures and flavors. As Walsh describes people through the food they eat, she records and makes sense of her own complicated and conflicting emotions by the foods she eats and cooks with each of them.

Walsh narrates her life from relationship to relationship. The longer sexual relationships she had before Laura were with men. But she gives ample space to the cravings she had for women before her marriage. Although none of them ever went beyond a crush, she is thus creating a coherent history for her same-sex desire. She inscribes her desire for women as a constant in her life, one that created an alternative possibility next to her problematic heterosexual relations. Trying to make sense of her sexual pasts, she says:

> I loved sex with women way more than sex with men.... That's not to say that I looked back and saw my sexual history with men as a disappointment. I pursued, wooed, loved, and savored men.... If you spend your whole life eating pork chops and applesauce with sauerkraut, you have no idea how much you prefer pork served with a mole of cacao nibs, six kinds of chilies, cinnamon, anise, cloves, coriander, ground almonds, pumpkin seeds, and garlic... until you try it. (271)

Thus she makes sense of her sexual past in a way that illustrates that her same-sex desire was inherently always there but needed to be kissed awake. Illustrating with food imagery the evolution of her sexual desires, it is not her coming out that is central to the story. The novel culminates in her marriage to her partner of four years, Laura, reflecting the concerted political campaigns for marriage equality of LGBT activism of the past twenty years. Her coming out is not entirely smooth or drama free, but mostly she feels supported by her inner circle. It is more decisive for the narrator to have her relationship socially recognized and protected by law. For this she becomes politically active by collecting signatures and sending letters to undecided New York senators who are about to vote on the Marriage Equality Act. When same-sex marriage is legalized in 2011, she is able to celebrate her wedding, and while this, too, does not go entirely as planned, it is a happy event crowned by a wedding cake that the narrator baked herself. Unlike the catered wedding cake for her first wedding, which was too sweet, it is perfect. This indicates the sense of control the narrator has gained in the process of working through her childhood traumas, and through living her same-sex desire, but also taking fate politically into her own hands and making her marriage possible. Just in time for the wedding, the narrator is also able to resolve her lifelong eating disorder, to overcome the memory of sexual abuse she suffered at the hands of a relative, and to find a modus vivendi with her father, for whose support and recognition she has been struggling in vain her entire life. The wedding therefore serves as closure, not only to the book, but also to the narrator's alienation from her family and her body.

The memoir comes with recipes that invite the reader to participate in Walsh's journey. The recipes, such as "Bacon-Wrapped Eggs with Polenta," are not fictional; they come with ingredient lists and instructions that, if followed, result in real dishes (313–14). They are introduced with a few sentences that relate to the events in the memoir: "As Easter approaches every year, Laura and I look forward to making these delicious baked eggs, mentioned in Chapter 27" (313). The recipes, together with their introductions, serve as apparent evidence for the truthfulness of the memoir, creating an autobiographical pact of sorts, suggesting that not only the dinners actually happened, but the conversations and emotions surrounding them, too.[62] By converting culinary experiences into the textual form of the recipe, Walsh urges her reader to literally incorporate her narrative, combining kitchen and text into an emancipatory, sensory act of self-definition.

Gabrielle Hamilton's *Blood, Bones & Butter: The Inadvertent Education of a Reluctant Chef* (2011), like many of the culinary memoirs written by professionals in the food industry, provides no recipes. The story follows the narrator from one kitchen to the next, trailing the "reluctant chef" from her start as a freelance catering cook to becoming the celebrity chef and owner of the acclaimed New York restaurant Prune. Instead of boosting credibility through recipes, she offers an "Author's Note" in which she discloses the changes she made to the story, and assures her readers that "Otherwise, this book is a true account of my experiences as I remember them" (293).

Hamilton spends the first third of the book establishing herself as a Bourdain-esque badass persona, narrating her decision to drop out of college (after her third attempt she will graduate and later receive an MFA) as well as her use of drugs and illegal financial ploys, ripping off her employers during her early years in New York. Her same-sex relationships are mentioned, but in passing. More important for the narrative are her relationships to the other cooks who have shaped her career or her identity as a chef. Most prominently, she discusses her alienation from middle-class lifestyles (75–77). Raised in the bohemian surroundings of a burned-out sugar mill in rural Pennsylvania by a former dancer and a set designer, working most of her life in kitchens, traveling extensively in Europe, and becoming the owner of a successful restaurant, Hamilton struggles with her possible class privilege throughout the text. She repeatedly calls herself a "dishwasher" and feels excluded in college from an intellectual culture she experiences as elitist and unnecessarily theoretical. As food connoisseurship is a marker of class ambition, most recently incarnated in foodie culture, Hamilton frequently lashes out against amateur food aficionados: "Everyone thinks cooking is 'fun.' Everyone who doesn't do it professionally thinks it's fun" (77). About the emerging hipster food culture in Brooklyn she writes in no uncertain terms, "I would rather starve and kill my children—Medea-like—than eat the truffle oil omelette with chorizo 'foam' and piquillo peppers" (260). As the text shows Hamilton's own move from the ambitious food of catered weddings to a love of the simple and the well-made, she loathes all food snobbery and prefers those who have a pragmatic palate. About her mentor Misty, she writes with admiration: "I loved that she gave her kids homegrown vegetables and big glasses of sugary processed Kool-Aid right alongside. That is my favorite kind of integrated person. Some of each thing and not too much of any one" (79).

Like Walsh, Hamilton explains her interest in good food and cooking as coming from her ethnic heritage, since she learned to cook from her French mother. (Walsh describes her own heritage as Irish and Eastern European, and begins her memoir by narrating the lives and cuisines of her grandparents.) Both texts romanticize foreign, and in particular European, foodways as more "authentic," simpler, more honest. Hamilton describes her encounter with a zucchini blossom vendor in Italy as "my ideal kind of man. Missing most of his teeth, with his zipper gaping open," and expresses regret that these vendors who grow their own produce and sell it, just scraping by and in no position to pay for dental work, are about to go extinct (240). She sees them being replaced by a new generation, represented by a young man selling produce who wears "a T-shirt emblazoned with a currently hip rock band and a huge pair of counterfeit Gucci sunglasses with white, diamond-crusted frames. His teeth are gleaming, his ass is packed into stonewashed jeans. His hands are clean. He didn't grow it, pick it, water it, or even pack it" (241). In contrast to the picturesque zucchini vendor, whom she would like to conserve, the man at the produce stand can afford healthy teeth and pants that close. She finds him too Americanized and craves the nostalgic other-ness the zucchini vendor represents (241). For all her class consciousness, Hamilton's enchantment with the cuisines she encounters on her travels has an idealizing undertone that is oblivious to the realities of economic hardship.

Licking the Spoon presents a clear linear development, narrating a life that culminates in the political and personal achievement of the celebration of a happy wedding. *Blood, Bones & Butter,* in contrast, emphasizes the acciden-tal and the fragmented. While initially the narrative follows Hamilton's career, it seems a success story only by accident. As a catering cook who never worked in a restaurant, Hamilton claims, she never thought of opening a restaurant herself, but this she does when she is fortuitously offered a suitable space. Creating the menu for Prune, she draws on the many different food experiences she has had in her life, including two years of traveling, mostly through Europe. As Hamilton seems to stumble into the restaurant business, she also stumbles in her thirties into a joyless marriage to Michele, an Italian man. Hamilton, who has defined herself as a lesbian earlier in the text, starts an affair with him seemingly accidentally while she is still living with her long-term girlfriend, "whom I had come to think of as a great love of my life" (166). The marriage with Michele is reported in strikingly bitter terms. Hamilton recognizes in hindsight that she got a culinary warning when she started dating Michele: As part of his courtship, he brings her ravioli he made for her that are "tender and translucent and beautiful" but, as it turns out, indigestible: "[we] had to spit them out immediately, they were so incredibly salty" (253). After a three-year affair, Hamilton agrees to marry Michele, ini-tially to give him access to a green card. Michele, the narrator thinks, married her for love. But by the time of their honeymoon in Paris, the arrangement has become complicated. He withdraws, and Hamilton is "curious about how devastated I felt" (170). What follows are seven years of marriage that the narrator describes as mostly loveless, despite the two children they have together. They move in together only after the second child is born, functioning mostly as parents only.

As Hamilton describes, it is Michele's Italian background that gives her the greatest pleasure in her marriage. Spending most of her summers in Italy with his family, Hamilton, estranged from her own mother, falls in love with her mother-in-law, Alda, and with Italian food and Italian culture. In her first summers, Hamilton does not speak Italian and communicates with the women in the family by cooking together. These summers, she believes, are what keeps the marriage together. But at the end of the book and during the fifth summer they spend in Italy, she has become increasingly disillusioned. She still cannot communicate with her mother-in-law (while her Italian has gotten better, Alda's hearing has gotten worse). And although she cooks for the family, she still does not feel part of it, and is disenchanted with the idea of spending all her summers in the same place (272, 286, 288). What she liked about Italy in the first place, the weight of tradition and family, no longer lures her, and she feels her Americanness (defined as cheerfulness and a "can-do" mentality) taking over (263). The things she found enchanting about Italian culture start to annoy her, such as the slight chaos and decay of the villa in which they spend their summers:

> I need to take all the shit off this table—this beautiful old granite-topped table—and put it where it belongs. I need to be a wicked American, a total Italian failure and put the ironing in the laundry room and the cookies in the cookie tin and the scrap paper in the scrap paper drawer and the diaper cream in the diaper bag and the keys in the key pouch in [Alda's] purse and the batteries for the camera into the camera so that here on the kitchen table we can just shell black-eyed peas. (252)

Her falling out of love is all-compassing and concerns not only Michele, but his family and culture, too. Distancing herself from Italian culture, her descriptions become increasingly critical: she questions, in good colonialist tradition, the cleanliness, health, and work ethic of the culture in which she is a guest. The final scene of the book describes how she cleans up the summer villa's garden, clearing out branches, with the kind intention of giving Alda a view of the ocean. This she does despite the request of Michele, who explains that it would be an inappropriately proprietary gesture that the other members of the family would understand as a form of disrespect. Eventually she decides that her instincts are right and proceeds with her project. Her

Americanness finally wins out. Alda's enjoyment of the new view, the narrator feels, justifies her actions (285–90).

The book ends by announcing a possible divorce. Unlike Walsh, the food Hamilton cooks does not reflect her emotions, or the state of her relationship. Hamilton insists on quality food in all situations of life. But she reveals moments of intimacy (or the lack thereof) in small food vignettes. She loves Michele when he takes care of her with offerings of food. Unlike the inauspicious, salty ravioli from the beginning, the moments when he brings her beer on ice, or finds her a mortadella sandwich when she is hungry, appear as the happiest and most intimate moments in their relationship (265, 260–61). When he rejects her food offerings, she is at her most bitter. When Michele does not acknowledge the narrator in what she most identifies herself as, being a cook, he rebuffs her most effectively.

In contrast to how I have summarized Hamilton's story here, the second part of the book does not move in a linear mode. The author loops and flashes back to narrate her relationship, representing how the marriage runs in circles and goes nowhere. The fragmentation of the story line heightens the coincidental structure that Hamilton gives her narrative: "The Inadvertent Education" that this "Reluctant Chef" receives describes life as a combination of unexpected chances and opportunities she must cope with, but it accords her little control. Hamilton does nothing in her text to reconcile her moving from her relationships with women to her marriage to a man, which seems as coincidental as her opening of a restaurant. Her girlfriend initially tolerates her affair with Michele. Neither she nor Hamilton believes that a liaison with a man could pose a threat to their own relationship (161). Prune's staff, many of whom Hamilton describes as being in same-sex relationships, are supportive of her marriage to Michele and attend their wedding excitedly (159–60). If there were any costs to her, or if she had any doubts about moving from same-sex relations to a heterosexual relationship, Hamilton chooses not to tell. Unlike Walsh, who gives her same-sex identity a linear evolution in hindsight, Hamilton's sexual identity is fluid and unpredictable and seemingly does not require exploration or explanation.

In the 2010s, the availability of cooking advice directed at lesbians has somewhat increased, thanks to culinary blogs and the easy accessibility of print on demand. At the same time, the urgency with which sexual identity is discussed in these texts has lessened. Topics that were common tropes—coming out, struggles with parents, family, and childhood friends after coming out, as well as coming to terms with one's own difference—take less space in memoirs and in cooking advice. In general, the tone of cooking advice directed at lesbians has also become more serious and less playful. The self-published *Lesbians Have to Eat, Too! (Stories and Memoir)* (2011) by Jenice Armstead, for instance, reflects the author's loving relationship with her extended family and rarely discusses her understanding of her sexual self. Despite the forward title, Armstead focuses in her recipes on health and exercise as well as how to have a spiritual and happy life rather than on same-sex experiences: "Food is a vessel of 'Life Energy' which not only provides nutrients for a body, but also provides creative ability for the soul and gives the mind opportunities for growth. . . . Food is a facet of the process of creation" (18). Armstead, who comes from a military family and herself has served in the U.S. Navy, recollects her past as only loving, supporting, and happy. The text lacks the erotic allusions, the anxiety and pain that coming out can cause, and any sense of abandonment, social pressure, or even references to specifically lesbian lifestyles.

Similarly unconcerned with questions queer texts have traditionally asked are many of the new cooking blogs and vlogs that have emerged in the past few years. As social media allows the splintering of cooking-advice audiences, creating ever more specific niches while diminishing obstacles to publication, a growing number of food blogs and Internet cooking shows addressing a lesbian audience have appeared.[63] It is no longer the discussion of same-sex identities that is at the forefront of many of these blogs, but the food cooked and sampled. One such is *Queer Vegan Food,* a popular blog by Sarah Brown that has run since 2011. Brown states in the "About" section of her site that the central concern of her blog is living vegan, as "A vegan diet helps improve personal health and the health of the planet. Articles on this site are written with the goal of promoting freedom and joy for all human- and non-human beings."[64] "Queer" is used not only to describe "people of all sexual orientations" but also to endorse recipes that do not try to imitate the "non-Vegan food world." (As an example, she offers "chocolate-covered kelp noodles.") Queerness or LGBT issues are not usually discussed, save when Brown makes it a point that vegan cuisine is genuinely queer, but beneficial to everybody.[65]

Similarly subjected to the culinary rather than the sexual are such blogs as *Butch in the Kitchen* or *Two Lesbians Eating Out (Lesbian Foodie Couple and Amateur Food Critics),* which despite their provocative titles are little concerned with discussing their sexualities, or sexuality in general, and concentrate on what they consider "good" food, mainly along the guidelines of foodie culture: an educated mix of ethnic dishes, artisan products, high-end American regional cuisines and comfort foods, health food, and locally sourced, fair-trade, and environmentally responsible foods. On the one hand, this may be an indicator of the successful mainstreaming of formerly marginalized sexual identities, as well as a liberation from limiting notions of identity. On the other, it shows an often-uncritical endorsement of middle-class privilege and entitlement of the kind that can be found in many other foodie blogs. The (unnamed) author of *Butch in the Kitchen,* launched in January 2011, describes herself as "an easygoing, nerdy, and sometimes a silly dorky butch who has a partner who puts up with me" ("About"). The recipes for "Lemon Vinaigrette" or "Shrimp Sambuca with Wild Rice and Asparagus" are presented with little narrative, mostly concentrating on the process of production, save a rare aside such as "Serving Suggestions for Butches" in the entry for "Easy Cherry Cobbler." The text here implies that butches may be in need of such suggestions, and it sexualizes the act of cooking by including some feeding: "as a sexy gesture spoonfeed your femme then give her a soft kiss between bites" ("Easy Cherry Cobbler").

Two Lesbians Eating Out features reviews of restaurants, products (such as "Coconut Balsamic Vinegar"), and dishes that resonate for the most part with foodie ideals. Giving recipes for "Individual Potato Gratin with Parsley Chiffonade" or "Bacon Hearts," as well as defining the purpose of this blog as reviewing "restaurants ranging from the 'holes in the wall' to the 5-star dining locations," illustrates the definition Josée Johnston and Shyon Bauman developed to describe foodie culture: an erosion of highbrow and lowbrow tastes and an aestheticized approach to food that is based on knowledge and connoisseurship.[66] Foodie culture has in some ways replaced gourmet culture, positing that it is less snobbish, but although it is more inclusive of lowbrow dishes and locations, it still promotes a "status-based exclusion and cultural distinction."[67] Engaging in foodie culture takes time, knowledge, skill, and money. While often politically engaged, it typically promotes individual action via consumer choices (such as buying local or fair-trade products) over structural fixes (such as organizing to oppose corn subsidies), although these choices do not need to be mutually exclusive.

The "status-based" interest dominant in many of the lesbian blogs may explain why the YouTube spoof cooking show *Cooking with Lesbians* by Unsolicited Project feels compelled to push back against it. Each episode opens with the line "Welcome to *Cooking with Lesbians,* a cooking show for lesbians with a lesbian," perhaps ridiculing the appreciation of authenticity within contemporary culinary discourse in which food is often regarded as best when prepared by a cook who is a cultural insider. The host (who gives herself a different name in each show) parodies the exaggeratedly chipper tone of female-hosted TV cooking shows (generously salted with swear words) and their assumptions of ideal femininity (happy, high-pitched, confidential). In contrast to food shows that demand that their viewers present perfectly cooked, visually appealing dishes that meet everybody's taste, the show presents very basic dishes with great fanfare and cooked with exaggerated sloppiness. The subtle sexualization of cooking shows, demanding that the female cook be not only caring but sexy too, is constantly queered with juicy insider jokes ("These lesbian tacos were so easy, I should have call them bisexual tacos" ["Lesbian Turkey Tacos"]), and plenty of sexual innuendo. Presenting the ingredients for "First Date Couscous," the host advises, "the best kind of tomato is one that feels firm, just like your girlfriend's breast," and claims about the extra-virgin olive oil that it is "the only thing virgin in the entire place."[68] Canola oil is "lube" and lettuce becomes "lettuce fuck later."[69] The "Lying Cheating Lasagna" episode, which deals with breaking the news of an escapade to one's girlfriend, suggests frozen lasagna as the main course (since nobody will enjoy the meal anyway), and gives recipes for some morale-boosting drinks instead.[70]

Rather than being critical only of mainstream food culture, the show lashes out against insider phenomena such as vegan lesbians. Recognizing that veganism has become a common political food choice among lesbians, the host warns the viewer that the new date probably is a vegan, but that the cook who wants to woo is best advised to ignore it: the host first uses chicken broth and then decides to dump the entire chicken in the dish, too. The show thus takes aim at any food dogma, and perhaps not only at a middle-class obsession with food choices, but also at the dominance of middle-class lifestyles in representations of same-sex experiences. Without offering a counter-narrative, the satire seems to undermine the idea that middle-class values as expressed in this context via food are representative for all lesbians, or for most.

HOW TO COOK WITH LESBIANS

The diverse body of texts discussed above written by authors in same-sex relationships, self-identified lesbians, or written explicitly for a lesbian audience reveal a number of different strategies to contradict a common trope in American culture that associates food with heterosexuality. One of the few issues all the texts have in common is that they write against concepts of dominant femininity and the obligatory conflation of ideal femininity and heterosexuality as conventionally asserted by cooking advice.

Nineteenth-century cookbooks emerged as a genre that constructed and circulated complementary gender roles and heteronormative family ideals that had far-reaching implications for cooking advice in the twentieth and even into the twenty-first century. But, taking a closer look for instance at the Beecher sisters' *The American Woman's Home,* these discourses were neither homogenous nor unambivalent, but rather contradictory and open to challenge. Still, they reflected strict gender ideologies, defining ideal femininity along the lines of domestic work and a tight heterosexual order that firmly defined a woman's place. Even if, in the process, they made women's labor visible and sought to elevate it, they endorsed if not invented the idea that women cook out of love, and that they do it for the people they love most, their husbands and children.

Texts in the twentieth and twenty-first centuries used the firmly established trope that conflated cooking and love, but to their own ends, reinscribing non-normative experiences of desire, love, sexuality, and family into the practices of cooking and eating. While the texts discussed above are diverse in many ways (impact, intended audience, political vision, et cetera), they share a critical stand toward the implications established by cooking advice about the gender and sexuality of the domestic cook, and the authority cookbooks claimed over their readers.

In *Tender Buttons,* Gertrude Stein used the linguistic peculiarities of cookbook writing but stripped them of their normative power. Alice Toklas merged the memoir with cookbook writing using the cultural inventory of her time, cooking for the loved one, to narrate her relationship with Stein in the gender-conservative and homophobic 1950s. Both texts resisted and subverted the heteronormativity that cookbooks so often promoted and produced, but Toklas left the central idea of shared food as a marker of family intact in order to give her relationship with Stein legible contours.

Second-wave feminism has since the 1960s has challenged the notion that the kitchen is a woman's place to be. But cooking at the end of the twentieth century was still a powerful part of gendered expectations as well as constructed as a site of feminine power. Some of the texts discussed used the kitchen as a place to come to terms with social expectations of gender and sexuality. Some sought liberation from the kitchen, whereas others embraced the kitchen as a place in which identity could be newly defined.

Inserting the lesbian cook altered—or queered, if you will—the conventions of cookbook writing, most notably perhaps in *The Alice B. Toklas Cook Book* and *Red Beans and Rice*. *The Alice B. Toklas Cook Book,* in its juxtaposition of memoirs and recipes, pushed the limits of both genres, the cookbook and the autobiography, to reinscribe the experience of a same-sex relationship. *Red Beans and Rice* dissolved the formal rules of cookbook writing to create an amalgam of comfort and support for those who do not find their lives reflected in traditional cookbooks. Most texts presented new ways to think about women cooking, depicting it as a means to care for themselves rather than others, or left older images intact in which women's cooking was shown to build families and communities but without the pressure of cultural expectation.

The mostly chronological organization of the previous chapter did not intend to make an argument for a linear development of the texts, nor of the lesbian cook. One can easily argue that Stein's *Tender Buttons* is more radical in its aesthetic form and political implications than most cooking blogs today. The definition of a concise sexual identity has become less burning of an issue in recent texts than in the 1980s, but this is true for *The Alice B. Toklas Cook Book* from the 1950s, too. Authors have found a diversity of standpoints to write against a tradition that excluded them. Some employ explicit sexual references; some do not discuss sexuality at all. Some center on the families they are born into; some on the families they build. Some are explicitly political; some are deliberately not. Thus emerged a heterogeneous body of texts producing liberating but also new normative effects. Culinary texts addressing a lesbian audience approach food, sexuality, and identity in different ways that refuse to adhere to the recipes for identity established by normative structures. Stein was right: the difference is spreading, but in unpredictable and unlimited ways.

Digestif

POWER, RESISTANCE, AND FOOD

FOOD IS POWER. Food discourses help to determine a person's station in life and decide their access to cultural capital, and therewith access to financial, educational, and other resources that influence people's careers, health, and overall quality of life. Food expert discourses and their reflections in literature, art, and the media negotiate not only what we eat, but what we are. The images, narrative strategies, and concepts they produce help to shape the ideas and images a culture has about masculinity and femininity; sexual, racial, and class identity; and about the "self" and the "other," all of which we literally incorporate when we eat. Food-expert discourses tell us how to eat, when, what, why, and with whom. They tell us how to raise food, where to buy it, how to prepare it or have it prepared, how to design our kitchens, which equipment to use, how to spice, how to serve food, how to talk about it, how to reduce or increase calorie intake, how to hold a fork, or how to eat an ear of corn. By complying with these discourses we take our place in the world as gendered, racialized, and sexualized people with access to the privileges and disadvantages that come with our subject position. In not complying with expert discourses, we take our place in the world, too, more likely at its fringes. Food, the way we prepare it, and how we eat it mark our age, our religion, our national belonging, even our marital status, and many other characteristics that produce what we have come to recognize as our selves. Food practices and discourses are not simply part of our daily experiences; in the end they help make us. Foodways, therefore, hold power over our lives.

Food expert discourses are multilayered and complex. Published food advice has been dominated by white middle-class authors, promoting gender-conservative and heterosexual norms, for most of the history of the United States. It reflected values that come with class and racial privilege, helped to legitimize those privileges by propagating middle-class and white food habits as the (only) right way to eat, and naturalized the worldviews reflected in them as normal or desirable. These values were by no means homogenous at any given time and continuously shifted in meaning.

Because of the ideological power it holds, food advice is disputed, and inspires lively dissent. Its often only thinly veiled ideological implications wield disciplinary effects over the individual or entire populations and provoke the formulation of alternatives, be they a republican dismissal of table manners and rich tastes associated with European tradition, manly cooking as a reaction against the forces of modernization and scientification of bodies and foodways, or cooking advice that does not yield to a heteronormative agenda. These alternatives, even if promising greater inclusion or equality, carry their own normative and disciplinary force, and propose a national cuisine based on slave or cheap immigrant labor, educate us on how real men eat, or define lesbian identity as the experience of suffering at the hands of intimates.

Food discourses are never unanimous. As each chapter has shown, even expert discourses can be discordant and ambiguous. Expert discourses in their contradictions produce ambivalences that allow renegade readings, thus offering potential for resistance in unexpected places such as detective novels, memoirs, or vlogs. Those produce their own inconsistencies, open to further controversy.

Looking at resistance and power in food advice, it becomes apparent that the implied binary opposition is deceptive. All three parts of this book deal with examples of resistance, that, when scrutinized, were examples of the establishment of disciplinary power as well. Republican cuisines were an attempt to formulate an American cuisine that was independent from European paradigms and more inclusive, democratic, and egalitarian. The resulting model cuisines excluded indigenous, African, African American, Mexican, and other traditions; stabilized New England's culinary primacy; and established middle-class values as benchmarks of citizenship. Texts protesting these omissions created their own exclusions and hierarchies. White middle-class women claimed authority over the genre as a way to participate in building the nation, arguing that food preparation is a woman's expertise, but depicted immigrant and African American women as unskilled and in need of supervision. Cooking advice for men explicitly intended to empower white middle-class men in the kitchen, a space that held limited prestige, and over which men lost some authority in the course of the nineteenth and twentieth centuries. Men in these texts are depicted as robbed and cheated out of their natural entitlement. While these texts engaged in resistance on many levels against the authority of mainstream food advice, they stabilized in one more way the notion of male primacy. Cooking advice for lesbians resisted the heteronormativity of traditional cooking advice, but occasionally uncritically embraced national bias, class privilege, or beauty norms, or created romanticized, stereotypical, and exclusive definitions of lesbian identity. Power and resistance therefore are better thought of as oscillating effects in food discourses that are themselves in constant flux.

Foodways are crossroads of power and resistance; or, if we no longer think of these as opposites, they are webs of power and resistance. Food discourses are constantly changing; as different ideas and practices struggle for dominance, hegemonic discourses adapt in the process. For example, cookbooks in the nineteenth century gradually became more inclusive of regional difference, absorbing the resistance against New England's dominance into a more encompassing image of the nation. Formerly elite practices, such as fine dining during the early nineteenth century, reappeared at a different time with a different agenda, such as gourmet cooking in the middle of the twentieth century. Any analysis can thus represent only a snapshot of a temporary, locally and historically contingent, cultural moment.

The newspaper and magazine articles, cookbooks, novels, memoirs, films, artworks, household manuals, and v/blogs analyzed here show that expert food discourses are located within a certain cultural context, which they influence and by which they are shaped. Food discourses reflected in literature, art, and media often serve to record changes in the cultural construction of gender, nationality, and sexuality. Joel Barlow's "The Hasty Pudding" showed a new national self-confidence by embracing corn as a staple representing American foodways and virtue. *In Our Time* and *The Maltese Falcon* suggested that men who cook represent a gender organization in which masculinity and femininity are thought of as opposites. Culinary memoirs such as *Blood, Bones & Butter* reflected a more fluid way to think about sexual identity in the early twenty-first century. Paying attention to the use of food imagery in texts can thus reveal an entire cultural panorama in a nutshell, contextualizing narratives and giving them a cultural location.

Cookbooks follow the most varied political agendas. Cookbooks for men may seem at first glance to shake up the gendered order, but on closer analysis turn out to reinforce traditional gender norms. Cookbooks for women sometimes provided the financial support the authors needed to be the

breadwinners of their families, even though the genre traditionally reinforced the idea that women were homemakers. Cookbooks long held up
heterosexual family models as the unquestioned ideal, but became a venue for
authors to express same-sex desire. Cookbooks commented—often critically—on many cultural paradigms, including those of nation, education,
nutrition, and gender. All of this defies the idea that cookbooks are mere
instructional manuals. They may hold a humble status in the world of literary
studies, but they present narrative strategies, plots, stories and characters,
manifestos and memoirs. They can be read as literary, cultural, and historical
texts, rich repositories of meaning too often left unexplored.

This investigation of the workings of culinary cultural power in the past
has permitted a clearer understanding of certain historical moments. It also
points toward insights into the contemporary era, and what might still be on
the menu of an agenda for further research.

In this investigation, taste has appeared as a powerful tool of distinction,
not only when it comes to class but also in the making of gender and national
identity. Early American authors strategically pitted bland republican tastes
against rich tastes connoted with Europeanness and aristocracy. Taste, the
right taste, can be a political tool and an element of nation building. It is not
farfetched to think that this republican taste, with its suspicion of everything
foreign, unknown, and complex, also held racial connotations. Cooking
advice for men often refers to taste in the pursuit of stabilizing gender difference. Arguing that men and women crave different foods, gender difference
is referred back to the biological body. As women's taste (dainty, artificial,
uninspired, bloodless, fat-reduced) is described as inferior to manly tastes
(hearty, honest, meaty, pleasurable, genius), it also establishes a clear hierarchy. Cooking advice for lesbians may not have established a universal
binary of heterosexual and homosexual tastes, but some of the texts use taste
for the sake of empowerment, adopting styles with normative claims to superiority (vegetarian/vegan, from-scratch, pragmatic, ethnic difference–
embracing tastes versus meat-eating, processed, overly ambitious tastes).
Economies of taste emerge as a valuable entry point for scholars to investigate
the power structures of texts and eating practices.

"'For All Grades of Life': The Making of a Republican Cuisine" discussed
how authors, turning a blind eye on their standpoint privileged by class and
race, created an American cuisine that reflected values that regarded as legitimate citizens only those who complied with their advice. That food advice
and citizenship are still powerfully intertwined is demonstrated by recent

discussion of the "obesity epidemic." Headlines such as "Many Fronts in the Obesity War," "America's Weight Loss," "Battling the Obesity Crisis," and "Obesity in America: What's Driving the Epidemic" have become familiar over the last dozen years, indicating that food consumption again has become a point of public interest and a topic of national focus.[1] "Obesity remains a daunting problem that demands more effort—from Americans and their government," wrote the *Washington Post* in 2014, invoking a biopolitical effort around obesity whose ideological underpinning is seldom questioned, although it should be.[2]

Studies of obesity often use race as an indicator, rather than income or environmental factors. They thereby implicitly suggest that obesity is a racial problem, not one connected to economic inequality and the inadequacies it produces in the realm of medicine (such as in health insurance and the provision of available health care services) or the built environment (sports facilities for children, fresh produce available within walking distance, et cetera).[3] As in nineteenth-century cookbooks, articles on obesity today typically point to individual responsibility, even if the focus has changed. While in nineteenth-century cookbooks abstinence from pleasure was the measure of self-control, today it is abstinence from calories, fat, and sugar. Excessive or unhealthy eating is commonly identified as the culprit for surplus weight, which falls under the responsibility of the individual, and those who do not comply appear less in control, less rational, and, when it comes to child obesity, less caring toward their children, all of which are already problematic assumptions, but even more so when racialized.[4] Only a few authors think of obesity as the result of lack of exercise possibilities, which, unlike overeating, can be solved only through communal effort (by providing safe and clean playgrounds, sports facilities, sidewalks, and so on). The few studies that consider location, such as the difference in obesity rates in urban versus suburban or rural settings, present data that suggest that unequal access to nutrition-rich foods may play a role when thinking about obesity, also an issue that exceeds individual responsibility.[5] If articles explore the origins of obesity, they occasionally blame women (from the middle class, one assumes) for entering the workforce and no longer cooking family dinners on a regular basis, but do not go further to examine why the gendered division of labor is so slow to change.[6]

Recent scholarship, sometimes bundled together under the label "Fat Studies," has started to explore the ideological layout of campaigns against obesity.[7] Historical analysis adds the insight that health concerns, when it comes to food, are firmly established as markers of class and citizenship in American culture. The politics of obesity therefore follow a familiar pattern of education and reform of the individual rather than, say, reassigning subsidies from meat, dairy, and corn to vegetable crops. Understanding these struggles on the right way to eat within their historical context and as part of an American political discourse that transmitted a set of values and has distinctive ideological underpinnings may help lead to new political strategies, or at least studies that are less exclusionary, seeking to empower all Americans to enjoy the same freedom and opportunity in the essential act of eating as the American narrative claims constitutes the nation itself.

"'Wolf in Chef's Clothing': Manly Cooking and Negotiations of Ideal Masculinity" showed that cooking advice for men seems at first glance to promote the erosion of the gendered division of labor, and therefore to posit a challenge to gender binaries in general. But a closer look revealed that these texts tried with various strategies to stabilize the cultural differences between men and women. Most of them claimed that men's cooking is fundamentally different from women's, and proof of men's fundamental difference from—and superiority over—women.

Cooking advice for men today mostly operates along the same lines. Men's magazines still assume that men cook differently from women.[8] Men now host a large number of TV shows on the Food Network and the Cooking Channel. But representations of masculinity are often still surprisingly conservative when one considers that contemporary foodie culture has opened up new venues to include men in culinary discourses. From Ted Allen to Bobby Flay, male culinary celebrities are often presented in the traditional role of manly cooks, such as barbecuers, artistic chefs, or famous professionals. Women, too, are usually depicted in traditionally gendered ways. For instance, women hosts are dressed in stereotypically feminine and sexually appealing outfits, while male hosts wear professional chefs' garb. Women hosts prepare family meals. Men cook for "the guys," or a date, or a party, or to entertain themselves.

The genderedness of the shows also materializes in their unsubtle staging. Guy Fieri's show *Guy's Big Bite,* for example, is set on a stage that seems to be a contemporary incarnation of the *Playboy* penthouse: a worry-free playground for the bachelor, firmly secured by markers of heterosexuality translated into the twenty-first century. Viewers see a loft-like apartment with an open kitchen in the front. In the background are a backlit bar, a pinball machine, a billiard table, and a drum set. Left of the kitchen, a giant TV screen perpetually shows car races and scenes from other manly sports or video games. Staged like this, cooking is narrated as another leisurely activity or manly hobby, just like playing pool or watching a race. Fieri is staged as a professional chef who cooks guy food in his leisure time for friends or himself rather than for a family, and because he likes to, not because he has to. All of this is in striking contrast to another signature show on the *Food Network: 30-Minute Meals* with Rachael Ray, who, in her colorful, 1950s-inspired kitchen presents family dishes, supposedly helping mothers to put delicious meals on the table every day. Cooking shows continue to perpetuate the notion of an inherent gender difference between men's and women's cooking, in which women are responsible for the daily feeding of their families, and men are specialty, leisure, and event cooks.[9]

But the twenty-first century has also brought ruptures and departures from traditional narratives of manly cooking. One of these is the evolution of "dad's cooking" in recent years. Websites and blogs such as *Dad Cooks Dinner, Cooking for Dads, My Daddy Cooks, What's Dad Cooking,* and *Cook Like a Dad* promise "Recipes and Resources for Dads" and show, firstly, that men cooking for their families is a phenomenon that has arrived in the American popular imaginary. Secondly, the idea of a man cooking for his family is still so special that it warrants dedicated websites and cookbooks. And finally, these sites reinforce the conviction that dad's cooking is fundamentally different from mom's cooking. In line with the tradition of manly cooking discourses, many of these texts offer recipes that are meat heavy, require grilling, or make use of alcohol—an unexpected choice for food intended for children.[10]

Independently of the question of whether "dad's cooking" represents a substantial break from the strategies described above, it invites an analysis of class and race. "Real Men Cook," an African American initiative that has organized charity cookouts on Father's Day in major American cities since 1990, presents a parallel interest in culinary fatherhood to what has taken hold in white middle-class culture, but at the same time it is different in the values it embraces, the assumptions it makes, and the concepts of fatherhood and masculinity upon which it is based. During these events, thousands of men volunteer to cook their signature dishes for their communities; the money from ticket sales is donated to nonprofit organizations.[11] But as founder Karega Kofi Moyo writes in the introduction to his cookbook *Real Men Cook* (2005), the aim of the initiative is not only to raise money, but also to correct images of men, especially black men, in mainstream media, where they are often depicted as "criminals, drug addicts, absentee fathers, and jailbirds" while "women and children are given the roles of perpetual victims" (vii). The cookbook as well as the cookouts therefore explicitly intend to change ideas of masculinity, and specifically black masculinity, by creating a public space in which African American men can be caretakers, fathers, and nourishers to their communities and families, and be recognized as such.

Foodie culture is another phenomenon that warrants further investigation into its genderedness. Scholars have shown that the alleged classlessness of foodie culture, with its endorsement of high and humble dishes and restaurants, is questionable.[12] Others have pointed out that the interest in ethnic and foreign cuisines may be an appropriation rather than an appreciation of other cultures.[13] I believe that foodie culture also promises a gender neutrality it cannot fulfill. Recent work on "New Domesticity" that investigates women's renewed endorsement of practices such as cooking, baking, and so on is a first step, but it concentrates on the production of femininity.[14] Men's engagement in foodie culture, on the other hand, is still under-researched.

"'The Difference Is Spreading': Recipes for Lesbian Living" showed that food plays an important role when it comes to establishing not only the paradigm of heterosexual relationships but also that of same-sex desire. There is a long tradition of linking food to sexuality as elemental sensual experiences, and the preparation and consumption of food as culturally determined to demarcate heterosexual performance. The advent of texts authored by self-identified lesbian authors has opened up a new genre rich with potential for new approaches to the study of sexuality. And, as some of the examples have shown, there is a tendency in these culinary texts to think of sexual subjectivities as fluid rather than fixed, which may lead further scholarship to rethink homosexuality and heterosexuality as necessary opposites, as some of the texts discuss how sexual identity changes over one's lifetime.[15]

Since food discourses have played an important role in the representation and production of binary gender difference, it seems only logical that this informs the study of these discourses, too. In this study, for instance, gender is mostly referred to in binaries. But this reflects and perpetuates thinking of gender difference as an opposite. As transgender issues slowly enter mainstream culture, they affect the culinary, and thus hopefully complicate such a theoretical framework. When Chris Trapani, owner of the Urban Cowboy Southern Fusion food truck in Austin, Texas, appeared on the Food Network's *Chopped,* he decided to make his transgenderedness visible to the audience by showing pictures of himself as a child, as a girl. In the episode, his story stands next to the story of a chef whose husband is serving in Afghanistan, and another who hopes to invest their prize money in a trip to Israel, causes that can expect to find widespread support in the American population, thus asserting that Trapani's may find support, too.[16] But beyond the fact that transgender issues found an entryway into the culinary mainstream, the story, with its references to the "cowboy" food Trapani cooks, also complicates assumptions about the biological roots of male appetites that still prevail. Trapani's performance of culinary manliness juxtaposed with his childhood images makes simple gender assignments no longer possible. This also changes the interpretation of such acts. The analysis of cooking advice written by transgendered authors is similarly promising for rethinking the analysis of culinary texts. As demonstrated above, cookbooks can serve to mainstream marginalized experiences, and make them more palatable to a general audience through the food they offer with the memories. In *Cooking in Heels* (2012), Ceyenne Doroshow describes her family life as a child: "it was my brother, the football jock, my mom and dad, both educated and working, and me, the little tranny child" (11). In the text, the kitchen becomes the only place in which she can live her femininity as a child. After her parents divorced, "cooking became a way to survive in that house" (12). Her father tolerates her cooking for him and her brother:

> But he still let me know every day that he was mad about me being in the kitchen. In one way, the kitchen was like my heaven. It was my little island where my brother didn't go, where my father was conflicted about going. But it was also the place where I got my beatings, because my dad really hated the young lady I was becoming. (13)

In describing growing up transgendered, Doroshow goes through the experiences many transgendered people still have in the United States: being kicked out of school, living in shelters, enduring assaults, taking drugs, not finding a job, turning to sex work, and finally, after being convicted for it, suffering through a prison sentence. As the culinary memoirs by Walsh and Hamilton invited readers to think about sexual identities in less static and more fluid terms, Doroshow's text asks for a more open understanding of gender that reaches beyond binaries, employing for her purposes a genre that traditionally upheld a most rigid organization of gender.

This study has offered perhaps more than only a taste of power. It has shown that delving into food advice and reflections of food in art and popular culture can be a fruitful pursuit for the study of the construction of subject positions in American culture and history. It revealed the ways in which they are created and contested. But on a broader level it also argued for an understanding of power and resistance as deeply mutually informed categories that cannot be disentangled. Whether looking at cookbooks; the use of recipes in novels, short stories, or poems; or food in film, food discourses are engaged in the making of what we are. Exploring them can thus teach us about how we come into existence as subjects. Laura Esquivel says: "Everyone's past is locked up in their recipes. . . . The kitchen is where we deal with the elements of the universe. It is where we come to understand our past and ourselves."[17] The kitchen and the texts it has inspired are a storehouse of cultural capital that historically has not been shared equally among Americans. It is perhaps no coincidence that we live in an era of both sharpening economic inequality and increasing obsession with food. The explosion of culinary discourses warrants critical engagement, if history can teach us anything. The "emergence" of ever-new superfoods, re-signifying long-known foods such as quinoa, kale, or blueberries, as well as the search for the latest little-known cuisine, best prepared in an "authentic" restaurant in another part of town or as fusion food in food trucks that tweet their locations, are all trends that carry their own ideological implications. They should not only be enjoyed, but thoughtfully digested.

NOTES

INTRODUCTION

1. The argument that you are what you eat was made twenty-five years later by another philosopher, Ludwig Feuerbach: "Der Mensch ist, was er isst" (the human being is what he eats). He was arguing strictly materially (in the way that Brillat-Savarin is often wrongly understood) that the human body is not less important than the human spirit, and that philosophy needs to redirect its interest from metaphysics to questions of human nature. Ludwig Feuerbach, *Die Naturwissenschaft und die Revolution* (1850). See also Priscilla Parkhurst Ferguson, *Accounting for Taste: The Triumph of French Cuisine* (Chicago: University of Chicago Press, 2004), 1–2.

2. The term "foodways" is often used in the fields of anthropology and folklore studies to designate the cultural dimension of food (as opposed to the scientific study of food and nutrition). It will be used here to refer to the sum of discourses and practices that emerge around food.

3. Lisa Heldke, *Exotic Appetites: Ruminations of a Food Adventurer* (New York: Routledge, 2003), 1–60.

4. See Sherrie Inness's chapter "Bachelor Bait: Men's Cookbooks and the Male Cooking Mystique" in her *American Women and Culinary Cuisine* (Iowa City: University of Iowa Press, 2001), 17–36; Camille Bégin, "'Partaking of Choice Poultry Cooked a la Southern Style': Taste and Race in the New Deal Sensory Economy," *Radical History Review* 110 (Spring 2011): 127–53; Melissa Salazar, "Public Schools, Private Foods: Mexicano Memories of Culture and Conflict in American School Cafeterias," *Food and Foodways* 15, nos. 3–4 (2007): 153–81; Maya D. Guendelman, Sapna Cheryan, and Benoît Monin, "Fitting In but Getting Fat: Identity Threat and Dietary Choices Among U.S. Immigrant Groups," *Psychological Science* 22, no. 7 (2011): 959–67.

5. Hasia R. Diner, *Hungering for America: Italian, Irish, and Jewish Foodways in the Act of Migration* (Cambridge, MA: Harvard University Press, 2001), 49–50.

6. An example of a critical stance against Foucault from a feminist perspective is the work of Nancy Hartsock. See for instance Nancy C. M. Hartsock, "Postmodernism and Political Change: Issues for Feminist Theories," in *Feminist Interpretations*

of Michel Foucault, ed. Susan J. Hekman (University Park: Pennsylvania State University Press, 1996), 39–55. See also Susan Bordo, "Feminism, Foucault, and the Politics of the Body," in *Up Against Foucault: Explorations of Some Tensions Between Foucault and Feminism,* ed. Caroline Ramazanoglu (London: Routledge, 1993), 179–202. For a thorough discussion of different feminist positions, see Margaret A. McLaren, *Feminism, Foucault, and Embodied Subjectivity* (Albany: State University of New York Press, 2002).

7. See Garrett Stewart, *Dear Reader: The Conscripted Audience in Nineteenth-Century British Fiction* (Baltimore: Johns Hopkins University Press, 1996).

8. Chief among them are Warren Belasco, Amy Bentley, Anne Bower, Hasia Diner, Betty Fussell, Donna Gabaccia, Lisa Heldke, Karen Hess, Harvey Levenstein, Lucy Long, Mark McWilliams, Fabio Parasecoli, Krishnendu Ray, Waverly Root and Richard de Rochemont, Kyla Wazana Tompkins, Helen Veit, Psyche Williams-Forson, and Doris Witt, to name only a few whose work on food and American culture helped shape this book.

9. I have been especially influenced by the work of Susan Bordo, Anne Goldman, Sherrie Inness, Mary Drake McFeely, Laura Shapiro, Susan Strasser, Janet Theophano, and Nicole Tonkovich. Their publications and many other useful studies appear in the endnotes and the bibliography.

10. Pioneering work in this field has been done by Sherrie Inness and Jessamyn Neuhaus, who present historical analyses on cookbooks for men in the twentieth century. See Sherrie Inness, "Bachelor Bait," 17–36; and Jessamyn Neuhaus, *Manly Meals and Mom's Home Cooking: Cookbooks and Gender in Modern America* (Baltimore: Johns Hopkins University Press, 2003).

11. Jack Goody, *Food and Love: A Cultural History of East and West* (London: Verso, 1998); Elspeth Probyn, *Carnal Appetites: FoodSexIdentities* (London: Routledge, 2000); Julia C. Ehrhardt, "Towards Queering Food Studies: Foodways, Heteronormativity, and Hungry Women in Chicana Lesbian Writing," *Food and Foodways* 14, no. 2 (July 2006): 91–109.

CHAPTER ONE

1. Kariann Akemi Yokota, *Unbecoming British: How Revolutionary America Became a Postcolonial Nation* (New York: Oxford University Press, 2011), Kindle ed., 10.

2. For more on marginalization through foodways in general, see Roger Abraham, "Equal Opportunity Eating: A Structural Excursus on Things of the Mouth," in Linda Keller Brown and Kay Mussell, eds., *Ethnic and Regional Foodways in the United States: The Performance of Group Identity* (Knoxville: University of Tennessee Press, 1984), 19–36.

3. See Helen Zoe Veit's discussion of citizenship and food regulation in *Modern Food, Moral Food: Self-Control, Science, and the Rise of Modern Eating in the Early Twentieth Century* (Chapel Hill: University of North Carolina Press, 2013), 36.

4. Robert E. Shalhope, "Republicanism and Early American Historiography," *William and Mary Quarterly* 29, no. 1 (1972): 334–56, quoted at 335.

5. See for instance Frances Milton Trollope's discussion of American dinners in *Domestic Manners of the Americans* (New York: Penguin, 1997 [1832]), 129ff.

6. For this and a longer discussion of travel writing and American food, see Mark McWilliams, *Food and the Novel in the Nineteenth-Century America* (Lanham, MD: Altamira, 2012), 18–23. See also Waverly Root and Richard de Rochemont, *Eating in America* (New York: Ecco Press, 1981), 119–26.

7. James McWilliams, *A Revolution in Eating: How the Quest for Food Shaped America* (New York: Columbia University Press, 2005), 319–21. See also "Personal Habits: Dining, Dinking, Tobacco Chewing, and Gun Use" in Kenneth Rose, *Unspeakable Awfulness: America Through the Eyes of European Travelers, 1865–1900* (New York: Routledge, 2014), 131–50.

8. Mark McWilliams defines republican simplicity this way: "Drawing on an ideal agrarianism that combined Jefferson's sense of natural aristocracy with a kind of frontier egalitarianism, proponents of republican simplicity reinterpreted the necessities of often harsh colonial life as a model for a new society that rejected the luxuries and hypocrisies of the Old World." Mark McWilliams, *Food and the Novel in the Nineteenth-Century America,* 6.

9. Robert E. Shalhope, "Republicanism and Early American Historiography," 335.

10. See also Mark McWilliams, *Food and the Novel in the Nineteenth-Century America,* 8.

11. Trudy Eden, *The Early American Table: Food and Society in the New World* (DeKalb: Northern Illinois University Press, 2010), 3.

12. That this is a phenomenon not exclusive to Europe or the New World is evident in Betty Fussell's *The Story of Corn,* where she discusses the Ottoman Empire's disdain for corn (New York: Alfred Knopf, 1992), 19.

13. See for instance Keith Stavely and Kathleen Fitzgerald, "This Beautiful Noble Eare: Corn," in *America's Founding Food: The Story of New England Cooking* (Chapel Hill: University of North Carolina Press, 2004), 4–48.

14. See Margaret Visser, *Much Depends on Dinner* (New York: Grove Press, 1986), 40. She and Betty Fussell show that corn dishes became fashionable in some parts of Europe at different times, for different reasons (for instance, during the nineteenth century, in a wave of nostalgia for the rural). Betty Fussell, *The Story of Corn,* 245.

15. See Betty Fussell, *The Story of Corn,* 19–20.

16. Oscar George Theodore Sonneck, *Report on "The Star-Spangled Banner," "Hail Columbia," "America," and "Yankee Doodle"* (Washington, DC: Government Printing Office, 1909; New York: Dover Publications, 1972), 131.

17. Ibid., 133.

18. Ibid., 134.

19. On the importance of the taxation of food items in the American Revolution, see for instance Waverly Root and Richard de Rochemont, *Eating in America,* 89–90.

20. See Charlotte Silver, *Charlotte au Chocolat: Memories of a Restaurant Girlhood* (New York: Riverhead Books, 2012).

21. According to Waldo Lincoln's bibliography of culinary texts, *American Cookery Books 1742–1860* (Worcester, MA: American Antiquarian Society, 1954), 12–15, "The Hasty Pudding" (written in 1793) was first published in 1796, the same year in which the first cookbook written by an American author, Amelia Simmons, was published. Judging from the many reprints in the following years, the text was a great success.

22. See Theodore Grieder, "'The Hasty Pudding': A Study in American Neoclassicism," *Bulletin. British Association for American Studies* 11 (1965): 35–42, at 36; and Leo Lemay, "Contexts and Themes of 'The Hasty Pudding,'" *Early American Literature* 17, no. 1 (1982): 3–23, at 3–4.

23. Initially Barlow served as an agent of the Scioto Land Company, selling land in Ohio, before the company was dissolved amid charges of fraud. Maldwyn Allen Jones, *American Immigration* (Chicago: University of Chicago Press, 1992), 59.

24. Edmund Burke, who earlier had supported American independence, warned that the French Revolution would lead to anarchy and atheism. He criticized the concept of "natural" rights, promoted peaceful reform over violent change, and argued that the goals of the revolutionaries were too abstract to be successful. *Reflections on the Revolution in France* (London, New York: Macmillan & Company, 1890 [1790]).

25. Betty Fussell calls Savoy "the heart of French cornmeal cooking" in *The Story of Corn,* 235. Praising the regional food of Savoy certainly endeared Barlow to the hearts of the people whose political support he was seeking.

26. On the concept of natural rights at this time, see for instance David M. Ricci, *Good Citizenship in America* (New York: Cambridge University Press, 2004), 63.

27. Frances Pohl and others have shown that Native American as well as Greek and Roman deities were often used to legitimize American republicanism and nationhood. Pohl writes that during the Continental Congress, nations such as the Iroquois were named as models for successful democracies. *Framing America: A Social History of American Art* (New York: Thames & Hudson, 2008), 92.

28. Rafia Zafar, "The Proof of the Pudding: Of Haggis, Hasty Pudding, and Transatlantic Influence," *Early American Literature* 31, no. 2 (1996): 133–49, 135.

29. Ibid., 137. Rafia Zafar reads this form of cultural cannibalism in the light of Werner Sollors's concept of "pseudo-ancestry." In *Beyond Ethnicity: Consent and Descent in American Culture* (New York: Oxford University Press, 1986), Sollors argues that postrevolutionary Americans had to rethink claims of native peoples and nations to land and resources. While this led to violent policies and campaigns, narratively it was accompanied by stories that romanticized Native Americans as noble and sage. The stories served as memento mori that empires are transient, making the extinction of entire nations during the European settlement seem predestined. European Americans were depicted as rightful, divinely ordained stewards of the continent, thus legitimizing expansion.

30. Robert Arner reads this passage differently, claiming that it expresses anti-European sentiment. "The Smooth and Emblematic Song: Joel Barlow's 'The Hasty Pudding,'" *Early American Literature* 7, no. 1 (1972): 76–91.

31. It was printed in (to name only a few) *The New York Magazine* (January 1796), *The Massachusetts Magazine* (March 1796), *The Pastime* (December 1807), and *The American Farmer* (April 1822).

32. Quoted in Andy Smith, "In Praise of Maize: the Rise and Fall of Corny Poetry," in *Food in the Arts: Proceedings of the Oxford Symposium on Food and Cooking 1998*, ed. Harlan Walker (Oxford: Oxford Symposium, 1999), 199.

33. Epicuri De Grege, "Cookery," *The Emporium of Arts & Sciences* (April 1, 1814): 456.

34. See the preface by Mary Tolford Wilson in Amelia Simmons, *American Cookery*, first ed., xi. All in-text citations refer to the first edition.

35. See Karen Hess, "Preface," in Amelia Simmons, *American Cookery*, second ed., ix–xv.

36. See also Kristin Hoganson, *Consumers' Imperium: The Global Production of American Domesticity, 1865–1920* (Chapel Hill: University of North Carolina Press, 2007), 105. On metonymical strategies of culinary nation building, see Arjun Appadurai, "How to Make a National Cuisine: Cookbooks in Contemporary India," *Comparative Studies in Society and History* 30, no. 1 (January 1988): 3–24, at 19.

37. Karen Hess has disputed the idea that Amelia Simmons was a New Englander and locates her in the Hudson Valley using a number of clues in the text, such as references to Dutch culinary traditions, the use of pearlash (produced in Albany), and the places where the text was printed. Karen Hess, "Preface," xi. The text is so dominated by New England culinary traditions, however, that in 1808 a plagiarized version of Simmons's book appeared under the title *The New England Cookery*. Waldo Lincoln, *American Cookery Books 1742–1860*, 19.

38. Amelia Simmons, *American Cookery*, second ed., 5–7.

39. Amelia Simmons, *American Cookery*, second ed., 43, 44, 47, 38. See also Nancy Siegel on the patriotic naming of dishes in the early nineteenth century: "Cooking Up American Politics," *Gastronomica* 8, no. 3 (Summer 2008): 58–61.

40. Sidney Mintz, *Sweetness and Power: The Place of Sugar in Modern History* (New York: Viking, 1985), 188; Waverly Root and Richard de Rochemont, *Eating in America*, 90.

41. See for instance "Observations on Flour and Bread," *Niles' Weekly Register* 12, no. 11 (May 10, 1817): 164.

42. See Annie V. F. Storr, "Raphaelle Peale's Strawberries, Nuts, &c: A Riddle of Enlightened Science," *Art Institute of Chicago Museum Studies* 21, no. 1 (1995): 27; and Nicolai Cikovsky Jr., "Democratic Illusions," in *Raphaelle Peale Still Lifes* (Washington, DC: National Gallery of Art, 1988), 54.

43. Not fashionable enough to make a living from it, though. As Wolfgang Born and others have noted, Peale remained poor until the end of his life. Wolfgang Born, *Still-Life Painting in America* (New York: Oxford University Press, 1947), 12.

44. See Norman Bryson, *Looking at the Overlooked: Four Essays on Still Life Painting,* (Cambridge, MA: Harvard University Press, 1990), 8; and Nicolai Cikovsky Jr., "Democratic Illusions," 34.

45. William Gerdts, *Painters of the Humble Truth: Masterpieces of American Still Life, 1801–1939* (Columbia, MO: Philbrook Art Center with the University of Missouri Press, 1981), 34.

46. On trompe l'oeil still lifes, see for instance David Lubin, *Picturing a Nation: Art and Social Change in Nineteenth-Century America* (New Haven, CT: Yale University Press, 1994), 275.

47. "Still-Life: Raphaelle Peale, American, 1774–1825," National Gallery of Art website, http://www.nga.gov/feature/artnation/still_life/peale_4.shtm.

48. Frances Pohl, *Framing America,* 185–94.

49. Alexander Nemerov, *The Body of Raphaelle Peale: Still Life and Selfhood, 1812–1824* (Berkeley and Los Angeles: University of California Press, 2001), 2–3.

50. In other early still lifes Peale uses redware, for instance in *Still Life with Dried Fish (A Herring)* (1815), oil on wood panel, anonymous collection.

51. *Blackberries* (1813), oil on wood panel, Fine Arts Museums of San Francisco; *Cheese and Three Crackers* (1813), oil on wood panel, Schwarz Gallery, Philadelphia; *Melons and Morning Glories* (1813), oil on canvas, Smithsonian American Art Museum, Washington, DC.

52. See also Annie V. F. Storr, "Raphaelle Peale's Strawberries," 25, in which she claims that Peale's paintings often present a "puzzling aspect" that can only be understood with the "fluent knowledge of classical culture and Enlightenment science that was a mark of distinction and privilege, and the pride of learned social circles in America."

53. Waverly Root and Richard de Rochemont, *Eating in America,* 150–55.

54. Susan Williams, *Savory Suppers and Fashionable Feasts: Dining in Victorian America* (Knoxville: University of Tennessee Press, 1996), 2.

55. Waverly Root and Richard de Rochemont, *Eating in America,* 167.

56. Susan Williams, *Savory Suppers,* 63.

57. Carolyn L. Karcher, *The First Woman in the Republic: A Cultural Biography of Lydia Maria Child* (Durham, NC: Duke University Press, 1994), 131.

58. Ibid., 131.

59. Ibid., 128.

60. Ibid., 130.

61. For a more detailed discussion of "separate spheres," see Barbara Welter's classic essay "The Cult of True Womanhood: 1820–1860," *American Quarterly* 18, no. 2 (Summer 1966), 151–74. The concept has been criticized and complicated by historians since the 1960s. For an overview, see Linda Kerber, "Separate Spheres, Female Worlds, Woman's Place: The Rhetoric of Women's History," *Journal of American History* 75, no. 1 (June 1988): 9–31. For a recent discussion, see Cathy Davidson and Jessamyn Hatcher, eds., *No More Separate Spheres!* (Durham, NC: Duke University Press, 2002). While historians have pointed out that in everyday life the spheres were less separate than nineteenth-century authors suggest, the

concept was a powerful ideological construct that guided political and cultural discussion on gender ideals.

62. Carolyn L. Karcher, *The First Woman in the Republic*, 133.

63. Barbara Welter offers Child's *The Frugal Housewife* as an example for a text promoting "true womanhood," as it depicted domestic virtues as beneficial and suggested that women should bear their lot. Barbara Welter, "The Cult of True Womanhood: 1820–1860," 169.

64. For instance his *Lemons and Sugar,* which also seems to be a recipe for lemonade, shows three lemons, a small carafe of water, and a sugar container with a spoon, inviting the viewer to mix the ingredients and sweeten to taste. For use of lemons in *The Frugal Housewife,* see pages 20 and 115.

65. Lydia Maria Child, "Letter to Mrs. S. B. Shaw 1873," *Letters of Lydia Maria Child* (Boston: Houghton, Mifflin & Co, 1882), 218–19; Carolyn L. Karcher, *The First Woman in the Republic,* 88.

66. Trudy Eden, *The Early American Table,* 14–20.

67. See Gayle Fischer, *Pantaloons and Power: A Nineteenth-Century Dress Reform in the United States* (Kent, OH: Kent State University Press, 2001), 10–14.

68. See also Gilbert Seldes, "Open Your Mouth and Shut Your Eyes," *North American Review* 225 (1928): 428–34, at 428: "Graham taught that health is the necessary result of obedience and disease of disobedience to physical laws, from which we deduce that we have only to discover the moral discipline of nature and subject ourselves to it in order to be always well."

69. On this point see also Kyla Wazana Tompkins, *Racial Indigestion: Eating Bodies in the Nineteenth Century* (New York: New York University Press, 2012), 85.

70. "For some reason all imported spices were found injurious to the human frame and imported sweets as well." Gilbert Seldes, "Open Your Mouth and Shut Your Eyes," 428. See also Kyla Wazana Tompkins, *Racial Indigestion,* 81.

71. Karen Hess, "Commentaries on Mary Randolph's *The Virginia House-wife,*" in Mary Randolph, *The Virginia House-wife* (Columbia, SC: University of South Carolina Press, 1984 [1824]), ix–xlv, at ix.

72. Carol Fisher, *The American Cookbook: A History* (Jefferson, NC: McFarland & Company, 2006), 19.

73. Betty Fussell, *The Story of Corn,* 233.

74. Nancy Hewitt, "Taking the True Woman Hostage," *Journal of Women's History* 14, no. 1 (Spring 2002): 159. See her argument that "true womanhood" is still a compelling category of analysis today.

75. Mark McWilliams, *Food and the Novel in the Nineteenth-Century America,* 15.

76. Carol Fisher, *The American Cookbook,* 22.

77. Kyla Wazana Tompkins, *Racial Indigestion,* 47.

78. Kariann Akemi Yokota, *Unbecoming British,* 17.

79. Quoted in Waverly Root and Richard de Rochemont, *Eating in America,* 113.

80. For excellent readings of the two authors, see Kyla Wazana Tompkins, *Racial Indigestion,* 61–62, in which she discusses how Sarah Josepha Hale's version of republican cuisine was imbued with imperial desires and fantasies of racial

superiority; and Amy Kaplan's reading of Catherine Beecher's ambiguous concept of the domestic in "Manifest Domesticity," in *The Anarchy of Empire in the Making of U. S. Culture* (Cambridge, MA: Harvard University Press, 2002), 23–50.

CHAPTER TWO

1. See for instance Jessamyn Neuhaus, *Manly Meals and Mom's Home Cooking: Cookbooks and Gender in Modern America* (Baltimore: Johns Hopkins University Press, 2003), 73–75.

2. See Molly O'Neill, ed., *American Food Writing: An Anthology with Classic Recipes* (New York: Library of America, 2007), 5, 6–11, 53–59, 61–65, 69–71, 73–74. See also Marie Kimball, *Thomas Jefferson's Cookbook* (Richmond, VA: Garrett and Massie, 1938), and for the recipes from Benjamin Franklin's papers, see *Benjamin Franklin on the Art of Eating* (Princeton, NJ: American Philosophical Society, 1968).

3. On female authorship of cookbooks, see Anne Willan, *The Cookbook Library: Four Centuries of the Cooks, Writers, and Recipes That Made the Modern Cookbook* (Berkeley and Los Angeles: University of California Press, 2012), 129, 131, 136, 143, 148, 193–94, 204ff; and Stephen Mennell, *All Manners of Food: Eating and Taste in England and France from the Middle Ages to the Present* (Champaign: University of Illinois Press, 1996), 201–14.

4. See Mary Barile, *Cookbooks Worth Collecting* (King of Prussia, PA: Wallace-Homestead Book Co., 1993), 30.

5. See Sandra Sherman, *Invention of the Modern Cookbook* (Westport, CT: Greenwood Press, 2010), xxiv.

6. For the early history of cookbooks in the United States, see Charlotte Biester, "Milestones in American Cooking Literature," *Journal of the American Dietetic Association* 31, no. 12 (1955): 1214–17; "The Story in the American Cookbook," *Journal of the American Dietetic Association* 29, no. 10 (1953): 988–92; L. Patrick Coyle, *Cooks' Books: An Affectionate Guide to the Literature of Food and Cooking* (New York: Facts on File Publications, 1985), 1–26; Mary Anna DuSablon, *America's Collectible Cookbooks* (Athens: Ohio University Press, 1994), 1–8; Carol Fisher, *The American Cookbook: A History* (Jefferson, NC: McFarland & Company, 2006), 6–16; Waldo Lincoln, *American Cookery Books, 1742–1860* (Worcester, MA: American Antiquarian Society, 1954), 7–27; Anne Moore, "The Cook's Oracle: Cookbooks at the American Antiquarian Society," *Journal of Gastronomy* 5, no. 3 (Winter 1989/1990): 19–31; Eric Quale, *Old Cook Books: An Illustrated History* (New York: E. P. Dutton, 1978), 131–47; and E. Neige Todhunter, "Seven Centuries of Cookbooks," *Nutrition Today* 27, no. 1 (January–February 1992): 8–12.

7. See also Jessamyn Neuhaus, *Manly Meals and Mom's Home Cooking,* 12.

8. Ibid., 13–14.

9. See Susan Strasser, *Never Done: A History of American Housework* (New York: Pantheon, 1982), 164. On class implications, see Glenna Matthews, *Just a*

Housewife: The Rise and Fall of Domesticity in America, 1830–1963 (New York: Oxford University Press, 1987), 32.

10. A feeble attempt to reclaim the domestic for male expertise, and to reinstate an older household management model in which the patriarch led the household in all questions, were mid-century country books. Like earlier British texts written by aristocrats that educated their readers on how to run estates, these books discussed gardening and interior design, raising and purchasing food, as well as hosting parties in suburban settings. Women's domestic talents were often relegated to the pursuit of practicality and economy, while men demonstrated their superior taste when they ventured into the domestic. See Maura D'Amore, "Suburban Men at the Table: Culinary Aesthetics in the Mid-Century Country Book," in Monika Elbert and Marie Drews, eds., *Culinary Aesthetics and Practices in Nineteenth-Century American Literature* (New York: Palgrave Macmillan, 2009), 22. This is an early example of how "taste" served not only the distinction of class status, but also that of gender. Men's tastes, in these texts, are naturally superior to women's, and therefore women's authority is questioned whenever the context calls for refinement.

11. Waldo Lincoln, *American Cookery Books, 1742–1860*, 19–31.

12. See Graham Russell Hodges, "Editor's Introduction," in Robert Roberts, *The House Servant's Directory, or a Monitor for Private Families: Comprising Hints on the Arrangement and Performance of Servants' Work* (New York: Charles S. Francis, 1827), 33.

13. Robert Roberts, *The House Servant's Directory*, 54.

14. Graham Russell Hodges, "Editor's Introduction," 15.

15. Immigrant women ran boarding houses in ethnic neighborhoods for income. Immigrants of both sexes opened restaurants reflecting the changing makeup of the labor force in cities and provided essential spaces for building diasporic community, typically through grueling hours of unrecognized toil. African American women, as Psyche Williams-Forson has shown, were able to gain limited financial independence by selling food, for instance to travelers on trains, but also without being recognized as entrepreneurs or having access to better-paying restaurant jobs. Psyche Williams-Forson, *Building Houses Out of Chicken Legs: Black Women, Food and Power* (Chapel Hill: University of North Carolina Press, 2006), 13–14, 21–37. Still, when the demand for professionally trained cooks and kitchen help rose after the Civil War, employers looked for men to hire, attracting immigrants and men from modest backgrounds to the profession. See especially Krishnendu Ray's work, including "Ethnic Succession and the New American Restaurant Cuisine," in *The Restaurants Book: Ethnographies of Where We Eat,* eds. David Beriss and David Sutton (Oxford: Berg, 2007), 97–114; "Exotic Restaurants and Expatriate Home Cooking: Indian Restaurants in Manhattan," in *The Globalization of Food,* eds. David Inglis and Debra Gimlin (Oxford: Berg, 2009), 213–26; and "Nation and Cuisine: The Evidence from American Newspapers ca. 1830–2003," *Food & Foodways* 16, no. 4 (August 2008): 259–97.

16. Harvey A. Levenstein, *Revolution at the Table: The Transformation of the American Diet* (New York: Oxford University Press, 1988), 11–12.

17. See Pierre Blot, *Handbook of Practical Cookery for Ladies and Professional Cooks. Containing the Whole Science and Art of Preparing Human Food* (New York: D. Appleton and Co., 1868); and James M. Sanderson, *The Complete Cook* (Philadelphia: Lea and Blanchard, 1846).

18. When upper-class families started to hire men trained in restaurants for their domestic kitchens, the press heatedly debated the virtues of male versus female cooks in private households, often making random claims about the gender implications of cooking. In an 1872 article, for instance, Pierre Blot stated that women could not be pastry chefs since they were unable by nature to produce complicated cakes. He allowed that they made better broth and were experts in roasting meats, since these dishes required patience, not artistry. The article concluded that male cooks are better for restaurants and elegant private kitchens, but women cooks are more "economical" for "small families and persons of limited means." Pierre Blot, "Female vs. Male Cooks," *The Galaxy. A Magazine of Entertaining Reading* 13 (May 1872): 720. The superiority of male cooking skills was heatedly disputed by female authors. An 1893 article in *Harper's Bazaar,* for instance, stated that there is no "root of truth" in the idea that male cooks are better than female ones, and that the only difference was that professional training was not available to women. "Cooks and Cooks," *Harper's Bazaar* 26 (May 27, 1883): 418.

19. Howard P. Chudacoff, *The Age of the Bachelor: Creating an American Subculture* (Princeton, NJ: Princeton University Press, 1999), 5–7, 16–17, 47–74, 75.

20. See for instance "Bachelors Do Their Own Cooking," *Lawrence Daily Journal*, May 21, 1891, 1.

21. Eve Kosofsky Sedgwick, *Between Men: English Literature and Male Homosocial Desire* (New York: Columbia University Press, 1985).

22. As an example of a typical cookbook, see Mary Newton Foote Henderson, *Practical Cooking and Dinner Giving* (New York: Harper & Brothers, 1877); or, for a specialty cookbook on camp cooking, see *Camp Cookery: How to Live in Camp* (Boston: Graves, Locke and Co., 1878) by the best-selling cookbook author Maria Parloa.

23. See also Mrs. Henry Ward Beecher's recommendations on barbecue in "How to Prepare a Barbecue," *Harper's Bazaar* 14, no. 17 (April 23, 1881): 269.

24. See Horace Park, *The Sportsman's Hand Book* (Cincinnati: Robert Clark & Co., 1886), 77; and Charles Hallock, *Camp Life in Florida* (New York: Forest and Stream Publishing Co., 1876), 32, 39, 179.

25. See Barry Stratton, *The Hunter's Handbook Containing a Description of All Articles Required in Camp with Hints on Provisions and Stores and Receipts for Camp Cooking* (Boston: Lee and Shepard, 1885), 39; and Howard Henderson, *Practical Hints on Camping* (Chicago: Jansen, McClurg and Co., 1882), 57–58.

26. Michael S. Kimmel, "Consuming Manhood: The Feminization of American Culture and the Recreation of the American Male Body, 1832–1920," *Michigan Quarterly Review* 33, no. 1 (Winter 1994): 7–36, especially 17–18.

27. Christopher E. Forth, *Masculinity in the Modern West: Gender, Civilization and the Body* (New York: Palgrave Macmillan, 2008), 159–60.

28. See Michael S. Kimmel, "Consuming Manhood," 54; and Katharina Vester, "Regime Change: Gender, Class, and the Invention of Dieting in Post-Bellum America," *Journal of Social History* 44, no. 1 (2010): 39–70, especially 44.

29. "The Diet of Brain-Workers," *Hours at Home: A Popular Monthly of Instruction and Recreation* (September 1869): 421–26.

30. See also Theodore Roosevelt, *The Wilderness Hunter* (New York: G. P. Putnam's Sons, 1909), 141, 159, 184, 292–93.

31. For publications for girls, see Anna Worthington Coale, *Summer in the Girls' Camp* (New York: The Century Co., 1919); and Hortense Gardner Gregg, *Camping for Girls* (Norway, ME: Advertiser Book Print, 1907). Examples of cooking instructions for boys can be found in Belmore Browne, "Ups and Downs of Cooking," in Franklin K. Mathiews, ed., *The Boy Scouts Year Book* (New York: D. Appleton Co., 1921), 122–26.

32. See for instance publications such as *The Rotarian* or *Popular Science Monthly*. Good examples are Charles Coleman Stoddard, "When You Live in a Duffle-Bag: An Autumn Vacation in the Woods," *Popular Science Monthly* 95, no. 4 (October 1919): 87–89.

33. A. Hyatt Verrill, *The Book of Camping* (New York: Alfred A. Knopf, 1917), 137. See also Steward H. Clyatt, *Campfire Cookery* (Cincinnati: W. B. Carpenter Co., 1921).

34. The narrator suggests keeping up decorum while eating: "Get a cheap yet 'homey' set of knives, forks and spoons for the table service, and take along a packet of paper napkins, so as to eat your meals like a human being" (139).

35. Michael Kimmel, *Manhood in America* (New York: Free Press, 1986), 87.

36. On cooking cultures in the 1920s and the cultural changes they facilitated, see Jessamyn Neuhaus, *Manly Meals and Mom's Home Cooking*, 57–72; Mary Drake McFeely, *Can She Bake a Cherry Pie? American Women and the Kitchen in the Twentieth Century* (Boston: University of Massachusetts Press, 2000), 34–50; and Laura Shapiro, *Perfection Salad: Women and Cooking at the Turn of the Century* (New York: Farrar, Straus and Giroux, 1986), 3–10, 71–105.

37. David Strauss, *Setting the Table for Julia Child: Gourmet Dining in America, 1934–1961* (Baltimore: Johns Hopkins University Press, 2011), 11.

38. See Ernest Hemingway, "Soldier's Home," in Ernest Hemingway, *In Our Time* (New York: Scribner, 1925), 69–77.

39. See also Sandra Gilbert's reading of this scene in *The Culinary Imagination: From Myth to Modernity* (New York: W. W. Norton & Company, 2014), 118–20.

40. At no point does the text suggest that women are part of the camping expedition. "Camping Out" was originally published in the *Toronto Star* on June 26, 1920. See http://grammar.about.com/od/classicessays/a/campinghemingway_2.htm.

41. Carroll Mac Sheridan, *The Stag Cook Book: Written for Men by Men* (New York: George H. Doran Co., 1922).

42. For a thorough comparison of the differences in recipes directed to men versus women, see Jessamyn Neuhaus, "Is Meatloaf for Men? Gender and Meatloaf

Recipes, 1920–1960," in Sherrie A. Inness, ed., *Cooking Lessons: The Politics of Gender and Food* (Lanham, MD: Rowman and Littlefield, 2001), 87–110.

43. For recipes as feminine discourse, see Susan J. Leonardi, "Recipes for Reading: Pasta Salad, Lobster à la Riseholme, Key Lime Pie," in Mary Anne Schofield, ed., *Cooking by the Book: Food in Literature and Culture* (Bowling Green, KY: Bowling Green State University Popular Press, 1989), 126–37.

44. See Jessamyn Neuhaus, *Manly Meals and Mom's Home Cooking*, 73.

45. See Christopher Breu, "Going Blood-Simple in Poisonville: Hard-Boiled Masculinity in Dashiell Hammett's Red Harvest," *Men and Masculinities* 7, no. 1 (2004): 52–76.

46. Bill Osgerby, "A Pedigree of the Consuming Male: Masculinity, Consumption and the American 'Leisure Class,'" in *Masculinity and Men's Lifestyle Magazines,* ed. Bethan Benwell (Oxford: Blackwell Publishing, 2003), 57–86, at 67.

47. Christopher Breu argues that it was "moving from the older discourse of manliness to a newer celebration of an active, exteriorized, and more violent conception of masculinity, one that was associated more readily with working-class men. Manhood was no longer a moral quality but a physical attribute; it was to be proven on the playing field, in the bar, in the bedroom, in the streets, and on the factory floor." Christopher Breu, *Hardboiled Masculinities* (Minneapolis: University of Minnesota Press, 2005), 6.

48. See Roy Hoopes and Lynne Barrett, eds., *James M. Cain Cookbook: Guide to Home Singing, Physical Fitness, and Animals, Especially Cats* (Pittsburgh: Carnegie-Mellon University Press, 1988), 5–6.

49. David Strauss, *Setting the Table for Julia Child*, 7.

50. See John MacPherson, *The Mystery Chef's Own Cook Book* (Garden City, NY: Garden City Pub. Co., 1943), vii.

51. Consumption was conceived as "passive, producing nothing, and easily overwhelming women's susceptible disposition," writes Jesse Berrett in "Feeding the Organization Man: Diet and Masculinity in Postwar America," *Journal of Social History* 30, no. 4 (1997): 805–26, at 811.

52. Bill Osgerby, "A Pedigree of the Consuming Male," 67.

53. Stuart Howe, "Dining Without Pain," *Esquire* (March 1934): 112.

54. For an account of the crossing-over of ethnic foods into mainstream culinary culture, see "Crossing the Boundaries of Taste" in Donna Gabaccia, *We Are What We Eat: Ethnic Food and the Making of Americans* (Cambridge, MA: Harvard University Press, 1998), 93–121.

55. John Burdick, "Food, Eating and the Quest for the Authentic Exotic Other," American Studies Lecture Series, American University, Washington, DC, November 25, 2013. See also the critical perspective of Lisa Heldke in *Exotic Appetites: Ruminations of a Food Adventurer* (New York: Routledge, 2003); and Lucy M. Long, "Culinary Tourism: A Folkloristic Perspective on Eating and Otherness," and Barbara G. Shortridge, "Ethnic Heritage Food," in Lucy M. Long, ed., *Culinary Tourism* (Lexington: University Press of Kentucky, 2004), 20–50 and 268–96.

56. David Strauss, *Setting the Table for Julia Child,* 207.

57. See Carrie Pitzulo, *Bachelors and Bunnies: The Sexual Politics of Playboy* (Chicago: University of Chicago Press, 2011), 82; and Barbara Ehrenreich, *The Hearts of Men: American Dreams and the Flight from Commitment* (New York: Anchor Books, 1983), 14.

58. On class performance in *Playboy,* see also Joanne Hollows, "The Bachelor Dinner: Masculinity, Class and Cooking in *Playboy*, 1953–1961," *Continuum: Journal of Media & Cultural Studies* 16, no. 2 (2002): 143–55.

59. See Carrie Pitzulo, *Bachelors and Bunnies,* 80.

60. Quoted in Bill Osgerby, *Playboys in Paradise: Masculinity, Youth and Leisure-Style in Modern America* (New York: Bloomsbury Academic, 2001), 130.

61. Carrie Pitzulo, *Bachelors and Bunnies,* 85.

62. Bill Osgerby, *Playboys in Paradise,* 131.

63. Quoted in Steven Watts, *Mr. Playboy: Hugh Hefner and the American Dream* (Hoboken, NJ: Wiley, 2008), 71.

64. Ibid.

65. This was for performative purposes. Practical utility won out in appealing to what readers needed: In the *Graham Kerr Cookbook,* Kerr not only gives accurate measurements, but gives them in three different systems: U.S., imperial, and metric.

66. Psyche Williams-Forson, *Building Houses Out of Chicken Legs,* 181. An earlier example is Paul Laurence Dunbar's late-nineteenth-century dialect poem "Possum." Here he lauds a meal of possum baked in its skin, a cooking technique he identifies as an African American method not used by the "ign'ant white man," "dem foolish people / Th'owin"way de fines' pa't." In Molly O'Neill, *American Food Writing,* 132. The pleasure the eater of a dish of possum experiences resembles Barlow's depiction of the pleasure an eater experiences over a bowl of corn mush. But the stanzas also evoke Barlow's pro-revolutionary message when Dunbar encourages pride in African American traditions and separates them from white ones, which he dismisses, thus turning the tables: "White folk t'ink dey know 'bout eatin', / An' I reckon dat dey do / Sometimes git a little idee / Of a middlin' dish er two;" "But dey ain't a t'ing dey knows of / Dat I reckon cain't be beat / When we set down at de table / To a unskun possum's meat!" The subtle move from "I" to "we" in the final stanza suggests a coming together around a shared heritage, which may create a momentum that cannot be defeated.

67. See also Andrew Warnes, *Hunger Overcome? Food and Resistance in Twentieth-Century African American Literature* (Athens: University of Georgia Press, 2004), 5.

68. See bell hooks, *Yearning: Race, Gender, and Cultural Politics* (Boston: South End Press, 1990), 42.

69. See Andrew Warnes, *Hunger Overcome?,* 5.

70. Of course, the eating of the entire animal is something that can be encountered in poor people's cuisines around the world, including poor white Southern cuisine.

71. Vertamae Smart-Grosvenor, *Vibration Cooking: Or, The Travel Notes of a Geechee Girl* (New York: Ballantine Books, 1986), 131–32.

72. Doris Witt, *Black Hunger: Soul Food and America* (Minneapolis: University of Minnesota Press, 2004), 104–7; Jessica B. Harris, *High on the Hog: A Culinary Journey from Africa to America* (New York: Bloomsbury, 2011), 211.

73. See Robin Balthrope, "Food as Representative of Ethnicity and Culture in George Tillman Jr.'s *Soul Food,* Maria Ripoll's *Tortilla Soup,* and Tim Reid's *Once Upon a Time When We Were Colored,*" in *Reel Food: Essays on Food and Film,* ed. Anne Bower (New York: Routledge, 2004), 101–16. See also Psyche Williams-Forson's reading of *Soul Food,* in which she criticizes the unhealthiness of the presented food practices, in *Building Houses Out of Chicken Legs,* 186–98.

74. Barbequing has not gone out of fashion, however. See for instance David Joachim, *A Man, A Can, A Grill* (Emmaus, PA: Rodale Press, 2003).

75. https://www.youtube.com/watch?v = 7Xc5wIpUenQ.

76. "The Conversation: Epic Meal Time," *ABC News,* January 14, 2011, on the web at http://abcnews.go.com/Entertainment/conversation-epic-meal-time /story?id=12615307.

77. See for instance Emily Schuman's "Cupcake and Cashmere" (cupcakesand-cashmere.com), Stefanie Pollack's "The Cupcake Project" (cupcakeproject.com), Michael Tonsmeire's "The Mad Fermantationist" (themadfermentationist.com), or Jason Rodriguez's "Brew Science" (sciencebrewer.com).

CHAPTER THREE

* For an earlier version of the section "Tender Mutton," see Katharina Vester, "Tender Mutton: Recipes, Sexual Identity and Spinster Resistance in Gertrude Stein," in *Another Language: Poetic Experiments in Britain and North America,* eds. Kornelia Freitag and Katharina Vester (Berlin: Lit Verlag, 2008), 289–300. Some of these analyses of lesbian cookbooks have also appeared in Katharina Vester, "Queer Appetites, Butch Cooking: Recipes for Lesbian Subjectivities," in *Queers in American Popular Culture*, ed. Jim Elledge (Santa Barbara, CA: Praeger, 2010), 11–21.

1. Antje Lindenmeyer, "'Lesbian Appetites': Food, Sexuality and Community in Feminist Autobiography," *Sexualities* 9, no. 4 (2006): 470–85.

2. See for instance Amy Bentley, *Eating for Victory: Food Rationing and the Politics of Domesticity* (Urbana: University of Illinois Press, 1998); Sarah A. Leavitt, *From Catharine Beecher to Martha Stewart: A Cultural History of Domestic Advice* (Chapel Hill: University of North Carolina Press, 2002); Jessamyn Neuhaus, *Manly Meals and Mom's Home Cooking: Cookbooks and Gender in Modern America* (Baltimore: Johns Hopkins University Press, 2003); and Erika Endrijonas, "Processed Foods from Scratch: Cooking for a Family in the 1950s," in *Kitchen Culture in America: Popular Representations of Food, Gender, and Race,* ed. Sherrie Inness (Philadelphia: University of Pennsylvania Press, 2001), 157–74.

3. Irma von Starkloff Rombauer, *The Joy of Cooking* (St. Louis, MO: A. C. Clayton Co., 1931). For further discussion, see Sherrie A. Inness, *Dinner Roles: American Women and Culinary Culture* (Iowa City: University of Iowa Press, 2001).

4. Marion Harland, *Common Sense in the Household: A Manual of Practical Housewifery* (New York: C. Scribner & Co., 1872), 14.

5. Susan J. Leonardi, "Recipes for Reading: Pasta Salad, Lobster à la Riseholme, Key Lime Pie," in *Cooking by the Book: Food in Literature and Culture,* ed. Mary Anne Schofield (Bowling Green, KY: Bowling Green State University Popular Press, 1989), 126–37, quoted at 134.

6. See the earlier discussion of Eliza Leslie and Lydia Maria Child in "Domestic Virtue and Citizenship in the Work of Lydia Maria Child" and "Cooking Contest: Regional, Transnational, and Class-Based Cuisines in the Antebellum United States."

7. The contradiction of the career woman who claims to be a household expert is sometimes acknowledged in cookbooks. See for example Marion Harland's *Common Sense in the Household,* in which she scolds: "Ninety-nine out of a hundred cook-books are written by people who never kept house" (18). Harland establishes herself, in contrast, as a "true" expert, a woman who kept house herself, by sharing a number of anecdotes that depict her as a housewife.

8. Mary Anna DuSablon, *America's Collectible Cookbooks* (Athens: Ohio University Press, 1994), 19.

9. Ibid., 20.

10. See the chapter "Going to Housekeeping: Creating a Frugal and Honest Home" in Sarah A. Leavitt, *From Catherine Beecher to Martha Stewart: A Cultural History of Domestic Advice* (Chapel Hill: University of North Carolina Press, 2002), 8–39.

11. See Rudi Bleys, *The Geography of Perversion: Male-to-Male Sexual Behavior Outside the West and the Ethnographic Imagination, 1750–1918* (New York: New York University Press, 1995).

12. An early example would be the German novel *Sind es Frauen? Roman über das Dritte Geschlecht* by Aimée Duc (Berlin: Eckstein, 1901). The two women protagonists, overcoming a number of obstacles, find each other in the end, and, as far as the reader knows, live happily ever after. The novel directly criticizes hegemonic scientific discourses. For a thorough interpretation, see Claudia Breger, "Feminine Masculinities: Literary and Scientific Representations of 'Female Inversion' at the Turn of the 20th Century," *Journal of the History of Sexuality* 14, nos. 1–2 (2005): 76–106.

13. See also Karla Jay, "The Outsider Among the Expatriates: Djuna Barnes' Satire on the Ladies of the *Almanack,*" in *Silence and Power: A Reevaluation of Djuna Barnes,* ed. Mary Lynn Broe (Carbondale, IL: SIU Press, 1991), 184–206.

14. Shari Benstock, *Women of the Left Bank: Paris 1900–1940* (Austin: University of Texas Press, 1986), 11–58.

15. Djuna Barnes paints a more desperate picture of the invert's melancholy in her novel *Nightwood* (London: Faber and Faber, 1936). Here the medical expert, in the character of Dr. O'Connor, appears as an understanding friend and wise voice before he drowns himself in alcohol. Other texts, such as *The Well of Loneliness* (1928) by the English novelist Radclyffe Hall, seem to endorse scientific discourses

on female homosexuality. Here, key sexology texts play an explicit role. Read by the protagonist Stephen Gordon (an Englishwoman given a boy's name at birth), they help her to establish a coherent identity and understanding of herself. As in the popular scientific texts of the time, homosexuality in the novel is described as "inversion" and a number of physical traits serve as indicators. Hall uses scientific discourse to educate her audience and also to make an appeal for greater acceptance of homosexuals by society. But in accordance with the assumed melancholy that comes with inversion, the story ends with the protagonist choosing loneliness as a response to the rejection she encounters at every turn. The melancholy of the invert, Hall argues, is not inborn but inflicted by society's prejudices.

16. The novel was written in 1903 but published after her death. See Gertrude Stein, *Fernhurst, Q. E. D., and Other Early Writings* (New York: Liveright, 1971).

17. Q. E. D., from the Latin phrase *quod erat demonstrandum* or "hence proved," sometimes appears after the demonstration of a successful experiment or mathematical proof. Earlier correspondence with Stein's sister-in-law shows her interest in scientific explanations of same-sex desire. For the exchange with Sarah Stein, see Jonathan Katz, *Gay/Lesbian Almanac* (New York: Harper & Row, 1983), 254–56.

18. Jaime Hovey argues that change is taking place in the realm of national identity when Adele finds herself suddenly at the margins of society, but the newly emerging view does not define Adele as a lesbian. Jaime Hovey, "Sapphic Primitivism in Gertrude Stein's Q. E. D.," *MFS Modern Fiction Studies* 42, no. 3 (1996): 547–68.

19. In the three-part novel *Three Lives* that also contains "Melanctha" (a story presumably inspired by the earlier *Q. E. D.*), scientific discourse is more openly criticized. Gertrude Stein, *Three Lives; Stories of the Good Anna, Melanctha, and the Gentle Lena* (New York: The Grafton Press, 1909). As Jaime Hovey argues, the exploration of same-sex desire in *Q. E. D.* and "Melanctha" produces another body of knowledge, contrary to and critical of scientific discourse ("Sapphic Primitivism" 556).

20. It has been suggested, for instance by Pamela Hadas, that *Tender Buttons* can be read as reflecting Alice Toklas moving into Stein's apartment and Leo Stein (Gertrude's brother) moving out. Pamela Hadas, "Spreading the Difference: One Way to Read Gertrude Stein's Tender Buttons," *Twentieth Century Literature* 24, no. 1 (1978): 57–75. Kathryn Kent in *Making Girls Into Women* (Durham, NC: Duke University Press, 2003) suggests that the references to advice literature represent the influence Toklas had on Stein and her genuine voice coming through in Stein's poetry. As Leigh Gilmore observes of Stein's *Autobiography of Alice B. Toklas,* biographical explanations "miniaturize" Stein's writings. Leigh Gilmore, *Autobiographics: A Feminist Theory of Women's Self-Representation* (Ithaca, NY: Cornell University Press, 1994), 199.

21. On the references to cookbook writing in *Tender Buttons,* see also Marguerite Murphy, "'Familiar Strangers': The Household Words of Gertrude Stein's Tender Buttons," *Contemporary Literature* 32 (1991): 383–402.

22. See also ibid.

23. See for instance the *N. Y. Times Book Review* from 1913, quoted in Jonathan Katz, *Gay/Lesbian Almanac,* 341.

24. This thought is developed in Franziska Gygax, *Gender and Genre in Gertrude Stein* (Westport, CT: Greenwood Press, 1998), 22ff.

25. Marguerite Murphy suggests that *Tender Buttons* creates an alternative home for a homosexual family. See "'Familiar Strangers,'" 383–402.

26. See Sarah Leavitt, *From Catherine Beecher to Martha Stewart,* 35–37.

27. James Beard offered this tribute: "Alice was one of the really great cooks of all time." James Beard, "Alice Toklas, 89, Is Dead in Paris," *New York Times,* March 8, 1967.

28. For instance Vertamae Smart-Grosvenor, who names *The Alice B. Toklas Cook Book* as an inspiration for her *Vibration Cooking.* See Doris Witt, "'My Kitchen Was the World': Vertamae Smart Grosvenor's Geechee Diaspora," in *Kitchen Culture in America,* 229.

29. On the question of how Gertrude Stein and Alice Toklas were able to survive the occupation as Jewish women, see for instance Janet Malcolm, "Gertrude Stein's War: The Years in Occupied France," *The New Yorker* (June 2, 2003): 58–82.

30. Gertrude Stein's writing on World War I, for instance in *The Autobiography of Alice B. Toklas,* seems similarly detached and was criticized for it. For a discussion of the different points of criticism, see Anna Linzie's *The True Story of Alice B. Toklas: A Study of Three Autobiographies* (Iowa City: University of Iowa Press, 2006), 160–61. For a more positive reading of Stein's war writings, see Maria Diedrich, "'A Book in Translation About Eggs and Butter': Gertrude Stein's World War II," in *Women and War: The Changing Status of American Women from the 1930s to the 1950s,* eds. Maria Diedrich and Dorothea Fischer-Hornung (New York: Berg, 1990), 87–106. She argues that Stein's focus on everyday life in wartime is a rejection of patriarchal "rationality, linearity, and hierarchical order" (92). Phoebe Stein Davis claims that in *Mrs. Reynolds* the "juxtaposition of national threat and domesticity . . . leads readers to see that the feminine, associated primarily in the novel with the domestic, is central to war, not secondary to it" (581). Stein refuses, she argues, "to portray the domestic sphere as the comforting constant during times of war" (582). Davis concludes that because of this strategy, "'home' can no longer be defined as a geographical space 'away' from war" (582). Phoebe Stein Davis, "'Even Cake Gets to Have Another Meaning': History, Narrative, and 'Daily Living' in Gertrude Stein's World War II Writings," *MFS Modern Fiction Studies* 44, no. 3 (1998): 568–607. Anna Linzie finds that Toklas's writing on war disrupts the "distinctions between private and public spheres, domesticity and warfare" (163).

31. Anna Linzie argues in *The True Story of Alice B. Toklas* that Toklas, in her narration as well as in her recipes, creates an amalgam of American and French cooking, a hybrid cuisine, fitting her narrator's identity (157).

32. Fannie Flagg, *Fried Green Tomatoes at the Whistle-Stop Café* (New York: Random House, 1987). While *Fried Green Tomatoes* did not feature recipes, food is so central to the story that Flagg published a cookbook, *Fannie Flagg's Original Whistle Stop Café Cookbook* (New York: Ballantine Books, 1995).

33. Laura Lindenfeld, in her analysis of the film *Fried Green Tomatoes,* reads this scene not as sexual metaphor, but as Idgie's breaking with her masculine role in nurturing Ruth (228). Laura Lindenfeld, "Women Who Eat Too Much: Femininity and Food in *Fried Green Tomatoes,*" in *From Betty Crocker to Feminist Food Studies: Critical Perspectives on Women and Food,* eds. Arlene Voski Avakian and Barbara Haber (Liverpool, England: Liverpool University Press, 2005), 221–45. I see it differently. Not only is this a desexualization of the scene, but ritualized feeding is part of courting in Western society. A man who pays for his date's dinner is not displaying his feminine side. The film *Fried Green Tomatoes* was not only a surprise box-office success, it also drew some academic attention. On the topic and representation of cannibalism in the film, see Jeff Berglund, "'The Secret's in the Sauce': Dismembering Normativity in *Fried Green Tomatoes,*" *Camera Obscura* 14, no. 3 (September 1999): 124–59. The filmmakers decided to depict the relationship between the two women far more ambivalently and as less explicitly homosexual so that it would suit a mainstream audience. On this aspect see Naomi R. Rockler, "A Wall on the Lesbian Continuum: Polysemy and *Fried Green Tomatoes,*" *Women's Studies in Communication* 24, no. 1 (2001): 90–102.

34. See Leigh Gilmore, *Autobiographics,* 211ff. Brian Loftus claims that Stein actually reverses the genius and wife plot in *The Autobiograpy of Alice B. Toklas* by having the wife talk. Brian Loftus, "Speaking Silence: The Strategies and Structures of Queer Autobiography," *College Literature* 24, no. 1 (February 1997): 28–44.

35. Anna Linzie, in *The True Story of Alice B. Toklas,* points out the reference of this passage to some of the thoughts in Stein's "Composition as Explanation" (168).

36. See also the analyses in the previous part, "Wolf in Chef's Clothing."

37. See for instance Marion Harland, *Common Sense in the Household,* 13.

38. *The Cook Book* invites a "queered" reading of itself to destabilize the power relations inscribed here. Monique Truong presented such a postcolonial rewriting of Toklas's text in her *Book of Salt* (Boston: Houghton Mifflin Harcourt, 2003). Truong retells the setting in the Rue de Fleurus from the perspective of the Vietnamese cook Bình, who lived for five years with Stein and Toklas. Whereas Toklas remarks on Bình's broken French in *The Cook Book,* Truong draws a direct connection between Bình's French and Stein's modernist poetry. Truong destabilizes the power relations between the servant and "his Mesdames" (1) and lets the text vibrate with disappointed assumptions of sexual, racial, and gendered identity.

39. As Julia Watson states, "in autobiography, only homosexuals have sexuality." "Unspeakable Differences: The Politics of Gender in Lesbian and Heterosexual Women's Autobiographies," in *De-Colonizing the Subject: The Politics of Gender in Women's Autobiography,* eds. Sidonie Smith and Julia Watson (Minneapolis: University of Minnesota Press, 1992), 139–68, quoted at 140.

40. See for instance the beginning of chapter 3, in which she reports that she prepared a turkey dressing with mushrooms, chestnuts, and oysters, since Stein could not decide which ingredient she preferred. The recipe for this concoction is not included, although the narrator claims it was a success (29).

41. It has been pointed out before that *The Autobiography of Alice B. Toklas* and *The Alice B. Toklas Cook Book* relate to each other in narrative voice and style, but

this has been taken as proof that Stein was able to reproduce Toklas's language accurately. I would argue that Toklas constructs a deliberate reference to Stein's *The Autobiography*. Her later (self-authored) autobiography, *What Is Remembered* (New York: Holt, Rinehart and Winston, 1963), is considerably different in language.

42. See Stephen Scobie, "'I Is Another': Autobiography and the Appropriation of Voice," in *American Modernism Across the Arts,* eds. Jay Bochner and Justin D. Edwards (New York: Peter Lang, 1999), 124–36, especially 126–27.

43. Sandra Gilbert and Susan Gubar argue in *No Man's Land: The Place of the Woman Writer in the Twentieth Century* (New Haven, CT: Yale University Press, 1988) that this merging of Toklas and Stein runs through Stein's oeuvre (241–42). Against an overly positive reading, they warn that Toklas's voice is "appropriated" by Stein (251).

44. On the explicit sexual references in Stein's writing when it comes to Toklas and eating, see ibid., 243.

45. On Toklas's text as culinary autobiography, see Traci Marie Kelly, "'If I Were a Voodoo Priestess': Women's Culinary Autobiographies," in *Kitchen Culture in America*, 251–69.

46. For instance by M. F. K. Fisher, who wrote the foreword to the 1984 edition (xiv). This reading stands in stark contrast to the narrator's presented self-confidence in cooking as artistic expression.

47. See for instance Amy Scholder, "Don't Try This at Home," in *Cookin' with Honey: What Literary Lesbians Eat,* ed. Amy Scholder (Ithaca, NY: Firebrand Books, 1996), 9–11.

48. For an early example not discussed here, see Lou Rand Hogan, *The Gay Cookbook* (New York: Bell Publishing Company, Inc., 1965).

49. The experience of racism in *Zami* is connected to food, too. When the protagonist travels by train to Washington, DC, she is not allowed into the dining car because she is black. For a discussion of fruit imagery in the text as an expression of sexuality as well as ethnicity, see Antje Lindenmeyer, "'Lesbian Appetites.'"

50. Traci Marie Kelly, "'If I Were a Voodoo Priestess,'" 253.

51. Doris Witt, "'My Kitchen Was the World,'" 229.

52. Anne E. Goldman, *Take My Word: Autobiographical Innovations of Ethnic American Working Women* (Berkeley and Los Angeles: University of California Press, 1996).

53. Rafia Zafar, "The Signifying Dish: Autobiography and History in Two Black Women's Cookbooks," *Feminist Studies* 25, no. 11 (Summer 1999): 449–69, quoted at 449–50.

54. Bode Noonan, *Red Beans and Rice: Recipes for Lesbian Health and Wisdom* (Trumansburg, NY: Crossing Press, 1986).

55. The short story initially had been published in 1988, in Dorothy Allison's collection of stories *Trash: Stories and Poems* (Ann Arbor, MI: Firebrand Books, 1988), 151–62.

56. See for instance "Thanksgiving Feast, Chinatown Style" by Kitty Tsui, 49–55, or Terry Wolverton, "Crumbs," 78–84, in *Cookin' with Honey.*

57. Ffiona Morgan, *The Lesbian Erotic Cookbook: Cuisine Extraordinaire to Caress and Fondle the Palate* (Novato, CA: Daughters of the Moon, 1998).

58. Susan Bordo, *Unbearable Weight: Feminism, Western Culture, and the Body* (Berkeley and Los Angeles: University of California Press, 1993), 119.

59. Sue Hardesty, Lee Lynch, and Nel Ward, eds., *The Butch Cookbook* (Newport, OR: Teal Ribbon Publications, 2008).

60. Sherrie A. Inness, *The Lesbian Menace: Ideology, Identity, and the Representation of Lesbian Life* (Amherst: University of Massachusetts Press, 1997), 81.

61. For another example of diversity, see Baking Butches, a website where women can post images of themselves baking. The site's introduction invites "Butch, Dyke, Trans, Genderqueer, Inbetween, Boi, Sissyboi, Tomboy, Wotever . . . it does not matter about your identity, we still want your pictures. Baking Butches is inclusive of EVERYTHING." Accessed September 20, 2014, BakingButches.tumblr.com.

62. On the use of recipes in culinary autobiographies as a means to establish "truth," see Traci Marie Kelly, "'If I Were a Voodoo Priestess,'" 265.

63. On the fast-growing emergence of food blogs, see Signe Rousseau, *Food and Social Media: You Are What You Tweet* (Lanham, MD: Rowman & Littlefield, 2012), 6–7.

64. Accessed September 29, 2014, queerveganfood.com/about/.

65. Sarah E. Brown, "Reflections on Being a Queer Food Blogger," October 14, 2012, accessed September 29, 2014, http://queerveganfood.com/2012/10/14/reflections-on-being-a-queer-food-blogger/.

66. Josée Johnston and Shyon Baumann, *Foodies and Distinction in the Gourmet Foodscape* (New York: Routledge, 2010), 59.

67. Ibid., 3.

68. Unsolicited Project, "First Date Couscous," *Cooking with Lesbians,* February 19, 2014, https://www.youtube.com/watch?v=4qqh5za2t3Q.

69. Unsolicited Project, "Lesbian Turkey Tacos," *Cooking with Lesbians,* August 6, 2014, https://www.youtube.com/watch?v=E0BH9s8lSh4.

70. Unsolicited Project, "Lying Cheating Lasagna," *Cooking with Lesbians,* May 7, 2014, https://www.youtube.com/watch?v=gKnTK44FHm8.

DIGESTIF: POWER, RESISTANCE, AND FOOD

1. Jane Brody, "Many Fronts in the Obesity War," *New York Times,* May 21, 2013, 4; "America's Weight Loss" editorial, *Washington Post,* August 20, 2013, A14; "Obesity in America: What's Driving the Epidemic?" *Harvard Health Publications: Harvard Men's Health Watch* (February 2012).

2. "The Fat Trap," *Washington Post,* March 4, 2014, B1.

3. See for instance Susan Levine, "Study Finds Racial Divide in the District," *Washington Post,* November 6, 2007, B1; and Yolanda Young, "'Big Is Beautiful': Not All Good News," *USA Today,* December 30, 2010, 11A.

4. In her article "Many Parents Can't See Child's Obesity," Sandra Boodman writes that African American parents are even more worried about child obesity than white parents. *Washington Post*, January 8, 2008, HE2. Charlotte Biltekoff states: "The campaign against obesity generated stigma that severely compromised the life chances of those it purported to help." Charlotte Biltekoff, *Eating Right in America: The Cultural Politics of Food and Health* (Durham, NC: Duke University Press, 2013) 111.

5. See Lenny Bernstein, "Outside the Superstar Spotlight, Minorities Struggle with Obesity," *Washington Post*, September 15, 2009, HE3.

6. Jane Brody, "Many Fronts in the Obesity War."

7. See for instance Charlotte Biltekoff, "The Terror Within: Obesity in Post 9/11 U.S. Life," *American Studies* 48, no. 3 (Fall 2007): 29–48; and Esther Rothblum and Sondra Solovay, *The Fat Studies Reader* (New York: New York University Press, 2009).

8. In his article "Feeding Hard Bodies and Masculinities in Men's Fitness Magazines," Fabio Parasecoli shows the central role of food, since it is connected to body image and health, but also notes that the foods promoted in editorials and advertisements in these men's magazines are usually fast foods and ready-made foods. Moreover, "Potential readers are not supposed to have any connection with buying, storing, and cooking food, all activities apparently belonging to the feminine. Male subjects cannot perform activities related to the preparation of food without affecting their masculine traits" (28). Parasecoli finds that the recipes offered in these magazines usually do not require cooking beyond opening a can and warming the contents. The only time when it is appropriate for a man to cook is "when he wakes up after a night of sex, and he wants to fix breakfast for the naked woman dozing in his bed" (30).

9. See Charlotte Druckman, "Why Are There No Great Women Chefs?" *Gastronomica* 10, no. 1 (2010): 24–31; Rebecca Swenson, "Domestic Divo? Televised Treatments of Masculinity, Femininity and Food," *Critical Studies in Media Communication* 26, no. 1 (2009): 36–53; and Andrew Corcoran, "Taking a Big Bite Out of the Food Network: The Importance of Masculinity in Food Programming," *Food, Media, Culture* (2008), http://www.american.edu/cas/american-studies/food-media-culture/2008-index.cfm.

10. See for instance "Steak Sauté with Flaming Cognac and Cream Sauce," March 24, 2011, or "Slow Cooker Turkey Thighs with Beer and Onion," December 28, 2010, at DadCooksDinner.com. On CookingForDads.net, most of the recipes are meat-based. WhatsDadCooking.com creates its own "Dad's Rub" for barbecuing. For a detailed analysis of dad's cooking, see Katharina Vester, "'See Dad Cook': Fatherhood and Cooking Advice in the 21st Century," in Amanda Stone, ed., *The Contested and the Poetic: Gender and the Body* (Witney, England: Inter-Disciplinary Press, 2014).

11. See "About Us: History," RealMenCook.com/History.html.

12. See for instance Josée Johnston and Shyon Baumann, *Foodies: Democracy and Distinction in the Gourmet Foodscape* (New York: Routledge, 2010).

13. See for instance Lisa Heldke, *Exotic Appetites: Ruminations of a Food Adventurer* (New York: Routledge, 2003).

14. See for instance Emily Matchar, *Homeward Bound: Why Women Are Embracing the New Domesticity* (New York: Simon and Schuster, 2013).

15. See for instance this interview with Gabrielle Hamilton, in which she explains that she no longer identifies as gay, but calls herself "an honorary lesbian for life": Julie Belcobe, "Chef Talk: Gabrielle Hamilton," *Financial Times,* February 24, 2012.

16. "Keep On Trucking," August 18, 2013, season 17, episode 2 of the Food Network's *Chopped* program. See also Toni Newman, "Chef Chris Trapani, the First Transgender Chef to Appear on the Food Network, Discusses, Love, Transitioning and Food," *Huffington Post,* September 9, 2014, http://www.huffingtonpost.com /toni-newman/chef-chris-trapani-first-_b_5780350.html.

17. Marialisa Calta, "The Art of the Novel as Cookbook," *New York Times,* February 19, 1993, C1.

WORKS CITED

MAGAZINES AND NEWSPAPERS

American Cookery
The American Farmer
American Home
The American Mercury
American Quarterly Review
Better Homes & Gardens
Boys' Life
Collier's Weekly
Esquire
Forest and Stream
Good Housekeeping
Gourmet
Harper's Bazaar
Hours at Home
The Massachusetts Magazine
The New York Magazine
The New York Times
Niles' Weekly Register
The Pastime
Playboy
Popular Science Monthly
Putnam's Monthly Magazine
The Rotarian
USA Today
The Washington Post

Abdullah, Achmed. *For Men Only; a Cook Book*. New York: G. P. Putnam's Sons, 1937.

"About." *Baking Butches*. http://bakingbutches.tumblr.com/.

"About Us: History." *Real Men Cook*. http://www.realmencook.com/History.html.

Abraham, Roger. "Equal Opportunity Eating: A Structural Excursus on Things of the Mouth." In *Ethnic and Regional Foodways in the United States: The Performance of Group Identity*, 19–36. Edited by Linda Keller Brown and Kay Mussell. Knoxville: University of Tennessee Press, 1984.

Allison, Dorothy. "A Lesbian Appetite." In *Through the Kitchen Window: Women Explore the Intimate Meanings of Food and Cooking*, 276–95. Edited by Arlene Voski Avakian. Boston: Beacon Press, 1997. Originally published in Dorothy Allison, *Trash: Stories and Poems*, 151–62. Ann Arbor, MI: Firebrand Books, 1988.

[Alsop, Richard]. *The Universal Receipt Book*. New York: Van Winkle & Wiley, 1814.

"America's Weight Loss." Editorial. *Washington Post*, August 20, 2013, A14.

Anderson, Sherwood. *Perhaps Women*. New York: H. Liveright, 1931.

Appadurai, Arjun. "How to Make a National Cuisine: Cookbooks in Contemporary India." *Comparative Studies in Society and History* 30, no. 1 (January 1988): 3–24.

Armitage, Merle. *"Fit for a King"... the Merle Armitage Book of Food*. New York: Longmans, Green & Co., 1939.

Armstead, Jenice. *Lesbians Have to Eat, Too!*. CreateSpace Independent, 2011.

Arner, Robert D. "The Smooth and Emblematic Song: Joel Barlow's 'The Hasty Pudding.'" *Early American Literature* 7, no. 1 (Spring 1972): 76–91.

Avakian, Arlene Voski, ed. *Through the Kitchen Window: Women Explore the Intimate Meanings of Food and Cooking*. Boston: Beacon Press, 1997.

Ayres, Martha. "The Parable of the Lamb." In *Through the Kitchen Window: Women Explore the Intimate Meanings of Food and Cooking*, 155–61. Edited by Arlene Voski Avakian. Boston: Beacon Press, 1997.

"Bachelors Do Their Own Cooking." *Lawrence Daily Journal*, May 21, 1891, 1.

Balthrope, Robin. "Food as Representative of Ethnicity and Culture in George Tillman Jr.'s *Soul Food*, Maria Ripoll's *Tortilla Soup*, and Tim Reid's *Once Upon a Time When We Were Colored*," 101–16. In *Reel Food: Essays on Food and Film*. Edited by Anne Bower. New York: Routledge, 2004.

Barile, Mary. *Cookbooks Worth Collecting*. King of Prussia, PA: Wallace-Homestead Book Co., 1993.

Barlow, Joel. *Advice to the Privileged Orders in the Several States of Europe Resulting from the Necessity and Propriety of a General Revolution in the Principle of Government*. London: J. Johnson, 1792.

———. *The Hasty Pudding: A Poem, in Three Cantos: Written at Chambery, in Savoy, Jan. 1793*. Stockbridge, MA: Rosseter & Willard, 1797.

Barnes, Djuna. *Ladies Almanack: Showing Their Signs and Their Tides, Their Moons and Their Changes, the Seasons as It Is with Them, Their Eclipses and Equinoxes, as Well as a Full Record of Diurnal and Nocturnal Distempers.* Paris: Edward W. Titus, 1928.

———. *Nightwood.* London: Faber and Faber, 1936.

Batchelder, Ann. "Why Men Like to Eat Out." *Ladies' Home Journal* (March 1936): 36.

Beard, George Miller. *Eating and Drinking; a Popular Manual of Food and Diet in Health and Disease.* New York: G. P. Putnam & Sons, 1871.

Bederman, Gail. *Manliness and Civilization: A Cultural History of Gender and Race in the United States, 1880–1917.* Chicago: University of Chicago Press, 1995.

Beecher, Catherine Esther, and Harriet Beecher Stowe. *The American Woman's Home: Or, Principles of Domestic Science; Being a Guide to the Formation and Maintenance of Economical, Healthful, Beautiful, and Christian Homes.* New York: J. B. Ford and Company, 1869.

Beecher, Mrs. Henry Ward. "How to Prepare a Barbecue." *Harper's Bazaar* 14, no. 17 (April 23, 1881): 269.

Bégin, Camille. "'Partaking of Choice Poultry Cooked a la Southern Style': Taste and Race in the New Deal Sensory Economy." *Radical History Review* 110 (Spring 2011): 127–53.

Belasco, Warren J. *Appetite for Change: How the Counterculture Took on the Food Industry, 1966–1988.* New York: Pantheon Books, 1990.

Belcobe, Julie. "Chef Talk: Gabrielle Hamilton." *Financial Times,* February 24, 2012.

Bellerose, Sally. "Gravy." In *Through the Kitchen Window: Women Explore the Intimate Meanings of Food and Cooking,* 40–41. Edited by Arlene Voski Avakian. Boston: Beacon Press, 1997.

Benstock, Shari. *Women of the Left Bank: Paris 1900–1940.* Austin: University of Texas Press, 1986.

Bentley, Amy. *Eating for Victory: Food Rationing and the Politics of Domesticity.* Urbana: University of Illinois Press, 1998.

———. "Islands of Serenity: The Icon of the Ordered Meal in World War II." In *Food and Culture in the United States: A Reader,* 171–92. Edited by Carol Counihan. New York: Routledge, 2002.

Berglund, Jeff. "'The Secret's in the Sauce': Dismembering Normativity in *Fried Green Tomatoes.*" *Camera Obscura* 14, no. 3 (September 1999): 124–59.

Bernstein, Lenny. "Outside the Superstar Spotlight, Minorities Struggle with Obesity." *Washington Post,* September 15, 2009, HE03.

Berrett, Jesse. "Feeding the Organization Man: Diet and Masculinity in Postwar America." *Journal of Social History* 30, no. 4 (1997): 805–26.

Biester, Charlotte. "Milestones in American Cooking Literature." *Journal of the American Dietetic Association* 31, no. 12 (1955): 1214–17.

———. "The Story in the American Cookbook." *Journal of the American Dietetic Association* 29, no. 10 (1953): 988–92.

Biltekoff, Charlotte. *Eating Right in America: The Cultural Politics of Food and Health*. Durham, NC: Duke University Press, 2013.

———. "The Terror Within: Obesity in Post 9/11 U. S. Life." *American Studies* 48, no. 3 (Fall 2007): 29–48.

"Bisquit for Apple Jelly." Cartoon. *Gourmet* (February 1942): 66.

Blend, Benay. "'I Am an Act of Kneading': Food and the Making of Chicana Identity." In *Cooking Lessons: The Politics of Gender and Food*, 41–63. Edited by Sherrie A. Inness. Lanham, MD: Rowman and Littlefield, 2001.

Bleys, Rudi. *The Geography of Perversion: Male-to-Male Sexual Behaviour Outside the West and the Ethnographic Imagination, 1750–1918*. New York: New York University Press, 1995.

Blot, Pierre. "Female vs. Male Cooks." *The Galaxy. A Magazine of Entertaining Reading* 13 (May 1872): 720.

———. *Handbook of Practical Cookery for Ladies and Professional Cooks. Containing the Whole Science and Art of Preparing Human Food*. New York: D. Appleton and Co., 1868.

Boodman, Sandra. "Many Parents Can't See Child's Obesity." *Washington Post*, January 8, 2008, HE02.

Bordo, Susan. "Feminism, Foucault, and the Politics of the Body." In *Up Against Foucault: Explorations of Some Tensions Between Foucault and Feminism*, 179–202. Edited by Caroline Ramazanoglu. London: Routledge, 1993.

———. *Unbearable Weight: Feminism, Western Culture, and the Body*. Berkeley and Los Angeles: University of California Press, 1993.

Born, Wolfgang. *Still-Life Painting in America*. New York: Oxford University Press, 1947.

Bourdieu, Pierre. *Distinction: A Social Critique of the Judgment of Taste*. Cambridge, MA: Harvard University Press, 1979.

Bower, Anne L., ed. *Recipes for Reading: Community Cookbooks, Stories, Histories*. Amherst: University of Massachusetts Press, 1997.

Bowers, David. *Bake It Like a Man: A Real Man's Cookbook*. New York: Morrow, 1999.

Bowser, Pearl, and Joan Eckstein. *A Pinch of Soul: Fast and Fancy Soul Cookery for Today's Hostess*. New York: Avon Books, 1970.

Brachman, Wayne. *See Dad Cook: The Only Book a Guy Needs to Feed Family and Friends*. New York: Clarkson Potter, 2006.

Breger, Claudia. "Feminine Masculinities: Literary and Scientific Representations of 'Female Inversion' at the Turn of the 20th Century." *Journal of the History of Sexuality* 14, nos. 1–2 (2005): 76–106.

Breu, Christopher. "Going Blood-Simple in Poisonville: Hard-Boiled Masculinity in Dashiell Hammett's Red Harvest." *Men and Masculinities* 7, no. 1 (2004): 52–76.

———. *Hard-Boiled Masculinities*. Minneapolis: University of Minnesota Press, 2005.

Brillat-Savarin, Jean Anthelme. *The Physiology of Taste: Or Meditations on Transcendental Gastronomy*. Translated by M. F. K. Fisher. New York: Knopf Doubleday Publishing Group, 2009 [1825, trs. 1949].

Brody, Jane. "Many Fronts in the Obesity War." *New York Times,* May 21, 2013, 4.

Brown, Linda Keller, and Kay Mussell, eds. *Ethnic and Regional Foodways in the United States: The Performance of Group Identity.* Knoxville: University of Tennessee Press, 1984.

Brown, Sarah E. "About." *Queer Vegan Food.* http://queerveganfood.com/about/.

———. "Reflections on Being a Queer Food Blogger." *Queer Vegan Food.* October 14, 2012. http://queerveganfood.com/2012/10/14/reflections-on-being-a-queer-food-blogger/.

Brown, Will C. "Men, Meet the Kitchen! Women, Please Stay Out!" *American Home* (May 1933): 288–89, 311–12.

Browne, Belmore. "Ups and Downs of Cooking." In *The Boy Scouts Year Book,* 122–26. Edited by Franklin K. Mathiews. New York: D. Appleton Co., 1921.

Bryson, Norman. *Looking at the Overlooked: Four Essays on Still Life Painting.* Cambridge, MA: Harvard University Press, 1990.

Burdick, John. "Food, Eating and the Quest for the Authentic Exotic Other." American Studies Lecture Series, American University, Washington, DC, November 25, 2013.

Burke, Edmund. *Reflections on the Revolution in France.* London: Macmillan & Company, 1890 [1790].

Cain, James M. "Oh, les Crêpes Suzettes!" *Esquire* (February 1935): 33, 174.

———. *The Postman Always Rings Twice.* New York: A. A. Knopf, 1934.

———. *Three Novels.* New York: Knopf, 1969.

Campbell, Tunis G. *Hotel Keepers, Head Waiters, and Housekeepers' Guide.* Boston: Coolidge and Wiley, 1848.

Carniol, John J. "Pioneers of Gastronomy." *Gourmet* (February 1942): 20–21, 28.

Carter, Susannah. *The Frugal Housewife, or Complete Woman Cook.* London and Boston: Printed for F. Newbery, 1772.

Child, Lydia Maria. *The Frugal Housewife. Dedicated to Those Who Are Not Ashamed of Economy.* Boston: Marsh & Capen and Carter & Hendee, 1829.

———. *Hobomok, a Tale of Early Times.* Boston: Cummings, Hilliard & Co., 1824.

———. *Letters of Lydia Maria Child.* Boston: Houghton, Mifflin & Co., 1882.

Chudacoff, Howard P. *The Age of the Bachelor: Creating an American Subculture.* Princeton, NJ: Princeton University Press, 1999.

Cikovsky, Nicolai, Jr. "Democratic Illusions." In *Raphaelle Peale Still Lifes.* Edited by Nicolai Cikovsky Jr. Washington, DC: National Gallery of Art, 1988.

Clyatt, Steward H. *Campfire Cookery.* Cincinnati: W. B. Carpenter Co., 1921.

Coale, Anna Worthington. *Summer in the Girls' Camp.* New York: The Century Co., 1919.

"The Conversation: Epic Meal Time." ABC News segment. January 14, 2011. http://abcnews.go.com/Entertainment/conversation-epic-meal-time/story?id=12615307.

"Cooks and Cooks." *Harper's Bazaar* 26 (May 27, 1883): 418.

Corcoran, Andrew. "Taking a Big Bite Out of the Food Network: The Importance of Masculinity in Food Programming." *Food, Media, Culture* 1 (Fall 2008):

http://www.american.edu/cas/american-studies/food-media-culture/2008-index.cfm.

Counihan, Carol, ed. *Food and Culture in the United States: A Reader.* New York: Routledge, 2002.

Cowan, Ruth Schwartz. *More Work for Mother: The Ironies of Household Technology from the Open Hearth to the Microwave.* New York: Basic Books, 1983.

Coyle, L. Patrick. *Cooks' Books: An Affectionate Guide to the Literature of Food and Cooking.* New York: Facts on File Publications, 1985.

Curtin, Deane W. "Food/Body/Person." In *Cooking, Eating, Thinking: Transformative Philosophies of Food,* 3–22. Edited by Deane W. Curtin and Lisa M. Heldke. Bloomington: Indiana University Press, 1992.

D'Amore, Maura. "Suburban Men at the Table: Culinary Aesthetics in the Mid-Century Country Book." In *Culinary Aesthetics and Practices in Nineteenth-Century American Literature,* 21–34. Edited by Monika Elbert and Marie Drews. New York: Palgrave Macmillan, 2009.

Davidson, Cathy, and Jessamyn Hatcher. *No More Separate Spheres!.* Durham, NC: Duke University Press, 2002.

Davis, Phoebe Stein. "'Even Cake Gets to Have Another Meaning': History, Narrative, and 'Daily Living' in Gertrude Stein's World War II Writings." *MFS Modern Fiction Studies* 44, no. 3 (1998): 568–607.

Dean, Agnes L. "Approving the Pudding: A Husband Who Cooks." *American Cookery* 24, no. 8 (March 1920): 584–85.

Diat, Louis. "My Mother's Kitchen." *Gourmet* (January 1946): 10–11.

Dickens, Charles. *American Notes for General Circulation.* London: Chapman and Hall, 1842.

Diedrich, Maria. "'A Book in Translation About Eggs and Butter': Gertrude Stein's World War II." In *Women and War: The Changing Status of American Women from the 1930s to the 1950s,* 87–106. Edited by Maria Diedrich and Dorothea Fischer-Hornung. New York: Berg, 1990.

"The Diet of Brain-Workers." *Hours at Home: A Popular Monthly of Instruction and Recreation* (September 1869): 421–26.

Diner, Hasia R. *Hungering for America: Italian, Irish, and Jewish Foodways in the Age of Migration.* Cambridge, MA: Harvard University Press, 2001.

Doroshow, Ceyenne. *Cooking in Heels: A Memoir Cookbook.* Brooklyn: Red Umbrella Project, 2012.

Douglas, Ann. *The Feminization of American Culture.* New York: Farrar, Straus and Giroux, 1998.

Douglas, Mary, ed. *Food in the Social Order: Studies of Food and Festivities in Three American Communities.* New York: Russell Sage Foundation, 1984.

Druckman, Charlotte. "Why Are There No Great Women Chefs?" *Gastronomica* 10, no. 1 (2010): 24–31.

Duc, Aimée. *Sind es Frauen? Roman über das dritte Geschlecht.* Berlin: Eckstein, 1901.

Dunbar, Paul Laurence. *The Complete Poems of Paul Laurence Dunbar, with the Introduction to "Lyrics of Lowly Life."* New York: Dodd, Mead and Company, 1913.

DuSablon, Mary Anna. *America's Collectible Cookbooks.* Athens: Ohio University Press, 1994.

Eden, Trudy. *The Early American Table: Food and Society in the New World.* DeKalb: Northern Illinois University Press, 2008.

Ehrenreich, Barbara. *The Hearts of Men: American Dreams and the Flight from Commitment.* New York: Anchor Books, 1983.

Ehrhardt, Julia C. "Towards Queering Food Studies: Foodways, Heteronormativity, and Hungry Women in Chicana Lesbian Writing." *Food and Foodways* 14, no. 2 (July 2006): 91–109.

Ehrlich, Elizabeth. *Miriam's Kitchen: A Memoir.* New York: Viking, 1997.

Elias, Norbert. *The Civilizing Process: Sociogenetic and Psychogenetic Investigations.* Oxford: Blackwell Publishers, 2000 [1939].

Ellison, Ralph. *Invisible Man.* New York: Random House, 1952.

Endrijonas, Erika. "Processed Foods from Scratch: Cooking for a Family in the 1950s." In *Kitchen Culture in America: Popular Representations of Food, Gender, and Race,* 157–74. Edited by Sherrie Inness. Philadelphia: University of Pennsylvania Press, 2001.

Estes, Rufus. *Good Things to Eat, as Suggested by Rufus; a Collection of Practical Recipes for Preparing Meats, Game, Fowl, Fish, Puddings, Pastries, etc.* Chicago: The Author, 1911.

Farmer, Fannie Merritt. *The Boston Cooking-School Cook Book.* Boston: Little, Brown and Co., 1900.

"The Fat Trap." Editorial. *Washington Post,* March 4, 2014, B01.

Feuerbach, Ludwig. "Die Naturwissenschaft und die Revolution" (1850). In *Ludwig Feuerbach. Werke in sechs Bänden,* 243–65. Edited by E. Thies IV. Frankfurt: Suhrkamp, 1975–76.

Fino, Rocky. *Will Cook For Sex: A Guy's Guide to Cooking.* Las Vegas: Stephens Press LLC, 2010.

"First Date Couscous." Episode of *Cooking with Lesbians.* February 19, 2014. https://www.youtube.com/watch?v=4qqh5za2t3Q.

Fischer, Gayle. *Pantaloons and Power: A Nineteenth-Century Dress Reform in the United States.* Kent, OH: Kent State University Press, 2001.

Fisher, Carol. *The American Cookbook: A History.* Jefferson, NC: McFarland & Company, 2006.

Fisher, M. F. K. *How to Cook a Wolf.* New York: Duell, Sloan and Pearce, 1942.

Flagg, Fannie. *Fannie Flagg's Original Whistle Stop Café Cookbook.* New York: Ballantine Books, 1995.

———. *Fried Green Tomatoes at the Whistle-Stop Cafe.* New York: Random House, 1987.

Forth, Christopher E. *Masculinity in the Modern West: Gender, Civilization and the Body.* New York: Palgrave Macmillan, 2008.

Foucault, Michel. *Discipline and Punish: The Birth of the Prison*. Translated by Alan Sheridan. New York: Pantheon Books, 1977.

———. *The History of Sexuality*. Translated by Robert Hurley. New York: Pantheon Books, 1978.

———. "The Subject and Power." In *The Essential Foucault*, 126–44. Edited by Paul Rabinow and Nikolas Rose. New York: The New York Press, 1994.

Franklin, Benjamin. *Benjamin Franklin on the Art of Eating*. Princeton, NJ: American Philosophical Society, 1968.

———. *The Writings of Benjamin Franklin*. Vol. 4. New York: Macmillan, 1906.

Frederick, J. George. *Cooking as Men Like It*. New York: Business Bourse, 1930.

Fussell, Betty. *The Story of Corn*. New York: Alfred Knopf, 1992.

Gabaccia, Donna R. *We Are What We Eat: Ethnic Food and the Making of Americans*. Cambridge, MA: Harvard University Press, 1998.

GCE. "Dad's Rub." *What's Dad Cooking*. July 27, 2011. http://www.whatsdadcooking.com/2011/07/dads-rub.html.

Gerdts, William H. *Painters of the Humble Truth: Masterpieces of American Still Life, 1801–1939*. Columbia: Philbrook Art Center with University of Missouri Press, 1981.

Gilbert, Sandra M. *The Culinary Imagination: From Myth to Modernity*. New York: W. W. Norton & Company, 2014.

Gilbert, Sandra M., and Susan Gubar. *No Man's Land: The Place of the Woman Writer in the Twentieth Century*. New Haven, CT: Yale University Press, 1988.

Gilmore, Leigh. *Autobiographics: A Feminist Theory of Women's Self-Representation*. Ithaca, NY: Cornell University Press, 1994.

Glass, Montague. "Amateur Cooking for Husbands." *Good Housekeeping* (July 1931): 44–45, 207.

Glasse, Hannah. *The Art of Cookery Made Plain and Easy; Excelling Any Thing of the Kind Ever Yet Published . . . Also, the Order of a Bill of Fare for Each Month in the Manner the Dishes Are to Be Placed Upon the Table, in the Present Taste*. A new ed., with modern improvements. Alexandria, VA: Cottom and Stewart, 1805.

———. *The Art of Cookery, Made Plain and Easy; Which Far Exceeds Any Thing of the Kind Ever Yet Published*. 2nd ed. London: The Author, 1747.

Goldman, Anne E. *Take My Word: Autobiographical Innovations of Ethnic American Working Women*. Berkeley and Los Angeles: University of California Press, 1996.

"Goodbye Mammy, Hello Mom." Editorial. *Ebony* (March 1947): 36.

Goody, Jack. *Food and Love: A Cultural History of East and West*. London: Verso, 1998.

Gould, John Mead. *Hints for Camping and Walking. How to Camp Out*. New York: Scribner, Armstrong, & Company, 1877.

The Gourmet Cookbook. New York: Gourmet, 1950.

"Gourmet Is a Man's Magazine." *Gourmet* (October 1941): 35.

Graham, Steve H. *Eat What You Want and Die Like a Man: The World's Unhealthiest Cookbook*. New York: Citadel Press, 2008.

Graham, Sylvester. *A Treatise on Bread, and Bread-Making.* Boston: Light & Stearns, 1837.

Grege, Epicuri De. "Cookery." *The Emporium of Arts & Sciences* (April 1, 1814): 456.

Gregg, Hortense Gardner. *Camping for Girls.* Norway, ME: Advertiser Book Print, 1907.

Grieder, Theodore. "'The Hasty Pudding': A Study in American Neoclassicism." *Bulletin. British Association for American Studies* 11 (1965): 35–42.

Guendelman, Maya D., Sapna Cheryan, and Benoît Monin. "Fitting In But Getting Fat: Identity Threat and Dietary Choices among U.S. Immigrant Groups." *Psychological Science* 22, no. 7 (2011): 959–67.

Gunther, John. "Food Along the Danube: Fourth Station in Our Eating Tour and Here We Find That All Is Not Goulash in Hungary." *Esquire* (April 1935): 54–55, 126, 128.

———. "Life History of Spaghetti: Remarking That There Are Other Noble Foods in Italy—But Only as There May Be Other Duces, Too." *Esquire* (March 1935): 82–83, 94.

———. "Roast Beef of Old England: The British Have the Best French Restaurants, Native Mutton, and Foreign Delicacies." *Esquire* (May 1935): 52–53, 110, 113.

———. "Strong Stomach in Spain: Second of a Series of Articles on Gastronomy and Gluttony Abroad." *Esquire* (February 1935): 70, 111.

Guthrie, Jean. "Mere Men . . . But Can They Cook!" *Better Homes & Gardens* (June 1937): 70–71, 92–93.

Gygax, Franziska. *Gender and Genre in Gertrude Stein.* Westport, CT: Greenwood Press, 1998.

Haber, Barbara. *From Hardtack to Homefries: An Uncommon History of American Cooks and Meals.* New York: Free Press, 2002.

Hadas, Pamela. "Spreading the Difference: One Way to Read Gertrude Stein's Tender Buttons." *Twentieth Century Literature* 24, no. 1 (1978): 57–75.

Hale, Sarah Josepha Buell. *The Good Housekeeper.* Dover ed. Mineola, NY: Dover Publications, 1996 [1841].

Hall, Radclyffe. *The Well of Loneliness.* London: J. Cape, 1928.

Hallock, Charles. *Camp Life in Florida.* New York: Forest and Stream Publishing Co., 1876.

Hamilton, Gabrielle. *Blood, Bones & Butter: The Inadvertent Education of a Reluctant Chef.* New York: Random House, 2011.

Hammett, Dashiell. *The Maltese Falcon.* New York: Vintage Books, 1992 [1929].

———. *Red Harvest.* New York: Alfred A. Knopf, 1929.

Hardesty, Sue, Lee Lynch, and Nel Ward, eds. *The Butch Cookbook.* Newport, OR: Teal Ribbon Publications, 2008.

Harland, Marion. *Common Sense in the Household: A Manual of Practical Housewifery.* New York: C. Scribner & Co., 1872.

Harris, Jessica B. *High on the Hog: A Culinary Journey from Africa to America.* New York: Bloomsbury, 2011.

———. *Iron Pots and Wooden Spoons: Africa's Gifts to New World Cooking.* New York: Atheneum, 1989.

Hartsock, Nancy C. M. "Postmodernism and Political Change: Issues for Feminist Theories." In *Feminist Interpretations of Michel Foucault,* 39–55. Edited by Susan J. Hekman. University Park: Pennsylvania State University Press, 1996.

Harwood, Jim, and Ed Callahan. *Soul Food Cookbook.* San Francisco: Nitty Gritty Productions, 1969.

Hawthorne, Nathaniel. *The English Notebooks, 1853–1856: The Centenary Edition of the Works of Nathaniel Hawthorne.* Vol. 21. Edited by Thomas Woodson and Bill Ellis. Columbus: Ohio State University Press, 1997.

Heldke, Lisa M. *Exotic Appetites: Ruminations of a Food Adventurer.* New York: Routledge, 2003.

Hemingway, Ernest. "Camping Out." *Toronto Star,* June 26, 1920. grammar.about .com/od/classicessays/a/campinghemingway.htm.

———. *In Our Time.* New York: Scribner, 1925.

Henderson, Howard. *Practical Hints on Camping.* Chicago: Jansen, McClurg and Co., 1882.

Henderson, Mary Newton Foote. *Practical Cooking and Dinner Giving.* New York: Harper & Brothers, 1877.

Hess, John L., and Karen Hess. *The Taste of America.* Urbana: University of Illinois Press, 2000 [1977].

Hess, Karen. "Commentaries on Mary Randolph's *The Virginia House-wife.*" In Mary Randolph, *The Virginia House-wife.* ix–xlv. Columbia: University of South Carolina Press, 1984 [1824].

———. "Preface." In Amelia Simmons, *American Cookery.* 2nd ed. Bedford, MA: Applewood Books, 1996 [Albany: George R. & George Webster, 1796], ix–xv.

Hewitt, Nancy. "Taking the True Woman Hostage." *Journal of Women's History* 14, no. 1 (2002): 156–62.

Hirschfeld, Magnus. *Die Homosexualität des Mannes und des Weibes.* Berlin: L. Marcus, 1914.

Hogan, Lou Rand. *The Gay Cookbook.* New York: Bell Publishing Company Inc., 1965.

Hoganson, Kristin. *Consumers' Imperium: The Global Production of American Domesticity, 1865–1920.* Chapel Hill: University of North Carolina Press, 2007.

Holbrook, Stewart H. "Gastronomy in the Woods." *American Mercury* (July 1930): 338–41.

Hollows, Joanne. "The Bachelor Dinner: Masculinity, Class and Cooking in *Playboy,* 1953–1961." *Continuum: Journal of Media & Cultural Studies* 16, no. 2 (2002): 143–55.

Homespun, Priscilla. *The Universal Receipt Book; Being a Compendious Repository of Practical Information in Cookery, Preserving, Pickling, Distilling, and All the Branches of Domestic Economy. To Which Is Added, Some Advice to Farmers.* 2nd ed. Philadelphia: Isaac Riley, 1818.

hooks, bell. *Yearning: Race, Gender, and Cultural Politics.* Boston: South End Press, 1990.

Hoopes, Roy, and Lynne Barrett, eds. *James M. Cain Cookbook: Guide to Home Singing, Physical Fitness, and Animals, Especially Cats.* Pittsburgh: Carnegie-Mellon University Press, 1988.

Hough, Donald. "Come and Get Hit." *Esquire* (May 1937): 92, 130–32.

Hough, Emerson. *Out of Doors.* New York and London: D. Appleton and Company, 1915.

Hovey, Jaime. "Sapphic Primitivism in Gertrude Stein's Q. E. D." *MFS Modern Fiction Studies* 42, no. 3 (1996): 547–68.

Howard, Eric. "If I Had It My Way: When a Man Cooks." *Gourmet* (November 1941): 10–11, 46–47.

Howe, Stuart. "Dining Without Pain." *Esquire* (March 1934): 112.

Hunt, Frazier. "Give Me a Man Cook Every Time." *Better Homes & Gardens* (February 1935): 24–25, 58–60.

Inness, Sherrie. "Bachelor Bait: Men's Cookbooks and the Male Cooking Mystique." In *Dinner Roles: American Women and Culinary Cuisine,* 17–36. Edited by Sherrie Inness. Iowa City: University of Iowa Press, 2001.

———. *The Lesbian Menace: Ideology, Identity, and the Representation of Lesbian Life.* Amherst: University of Massachusetts Press, 1997.

———. *Secret Ingredients: Race, Gender, and Class at the Dinner Table.* New York: Palgrave Macmillan, 2006.

Inness, Sherrie, ed. *Dinner Roles: American Women and Culinary Culture.* Iowa City: University of Iowa Press, 2001.

———. *Kitchen Culture in America: Popular Representations of Food, Gender, and Race.* Philadelphia: University of Pennsylvania Press, 2001.

Isui, Kitty. "Thanksgiving Feast, Chinatown Style." In *Cookin' with Honey: What Literary Lesbians Eat,* 49–55. Edited by Amy Scholder. Ithaca, NY: Firebrand Books, 1996.

Jay, Karla. "The Outsider Among the Expatriates: Djuna Barnes' Satire on the Ladies of the *Almanack.*" In *Silence and Power: A Reevaluation of Djuna Barnes,* 184–206. Edited by Mary Lynn Broe. Carbondale, IL: SIU Press, 1991.

"Jeepers." Cartoon. *Gourmet* (February 1942): 66.

Jeffries, Bob. *Soul Food Cookbook.* Indianapolis: Bobbs-Merrill Co., 1970.

Joachim, David. *A Man, A Can, A Grill.* Emmaus, PA: Rodale Press, 2003.

———. *A Man, A Can, A Plan: 50 Great Guy Meals Even You Can Make.* Emmaus, PA: Rodale Press, 2002.

Johnston, Josée, and Shyon Baumann. *Foodies and Distinction in the Gourmet Foodscape.* New York: Routledge, 2010.

Jones, LeRoi [Amiri Baraka]. "Soul Food." In LeRoi Jones, *Home: Social Essays,* 101–3. New York: Morrow, 1966 [1962].

Jones, Maldwyn Allen. *American Immigration.* Chicago: University of Chicago Press, 1992.

Kaplan, Amy. *The Anarchy of Empire in the Making of U. S. Culture.* Cambridge, MA: Harvard University Press, 2002.

Karcher, Carolyn. *The First Woman in the Republic: A Cultural Biography of Lydia Maria Child.* Durham, NC: Duke University Press, 1994.

Katz, Jonathan. *Gay/Lesbian Almanac: A New Documentary in Which Is Contained, in Chronological Order, Evidence of the True and Fantastical History of Those Persons Now Called Lesbians and Gay Men.* New York: Harper & Row, 1983.

"Keep on Trucking." Episode of the Food Network TV show *Chopped.* August 18, 2013. Season 17, episode 2.

Kelly, Traci Marie. "'If I Were a Voodoo Priestess': Women's Culinary Autobiographies." In *Kitchen Culture in America: Popular Representations of Food, Gender, and Race,* 251–69. Edited by Sherrie A. Inness. Philadelphia: University of Pennsylvania Press, 2001.

Kent, Kathryn R. *Making Girls Into Women: American Women's Writing and the Rise of Lesbian Identity.* Durham, NC: Duke University Press, 2003.

Kerber, Linda. "Separate Spheres, Female Worlds, Woman's Place: The Rhetoric of Women's History." *Journal of American History* 75, no. 1 (June 1988): 9–31.

Kern-Foxworth, Marilyn. *Aunt Jemima, Uncle Ben, and Rastus.* New York: Praeger, 1994.

Kerr, Graham. "Bacon Fish Rolls." Episode of the TV show *The Galloping Gourmet.* Circa 1969–71. Accessible at https://www.youtube.com/watch?v=fffYQJGo-Cc.

———. *The Graham Kerr Cookbook.* Garden City, NY: Doubleday, 1969.

———. "Grillard & Grits." Episode of the TV show *The Galloping Gourmet.* Circa 1969–71. Accessible at https://www.youtube.com/watch?v=3GXLCVuIbp4.

———. "Jambalaya." Episode of the TV show *The Galloping Gourmet.* Circa 1969–71. Accessible at https://www.youtube.com/watch?v=qbjr_gIRyKI.

Kimball, Marie. *Thomas Jefferson's Cookbook.* Richmond, VA: Garrett and Massie, 1938.

Kimmel, Michael S. "Consuming Manhood: The Feminization of American Culture and the Recreation of the American Male Body, 1832–1920." *Michigan Quarterly Review* 33, no. 1 (Winter 1994): 7–36.

———. *Manhood in America.* New York: Free Press, 1986.

LaPrade, Malcolm. *That Man in the Kitchen: How to Teach a Woman to Cook.* Boston: Houghton Mifflin Company, 1946.

Leavitt, Sarah A. *From Catherine Beecher to Martha Stewart: A Cultural History of Domestic Advice.* Chapel Hill: University of North Carolina Press, 2002.

Lemay, J. A. Leo. "The Contexts and Themes of 'The Hasty-Pudding.'" *Early American Literature* 17, no. 1 (1982): 3–23.

Leonardi, Susan J. "Recipes for Reading: Pasta Salad, Lobster à la Riseholme, Key Lime Pie." In *Cooking by the Book: Food in Literature and Culture,* 126–37. Edited by Mary Anne Schofield. Bowling Green, KY: Bowling Green State University Popular Press, 1989.

"Lesbian Turkey Tacos." Episode of *Cooking with Lesbians.* August 6, 2014. https://www.youtube.com/watch?v=E0BH9s8lSh4.

Leslie, Eliza. *Directions for Cookery in Its Various Branches.* Philadelphia: E. L. Carey & Hart, 1840.

———. *Mrs. Washington Potts, and Mr. Smith, Tales.* Philadelphia: Lea and Blanchard, 1843.

———. *New Receipts for Cooking: Comprising All the New and Approved Methods for Preparing All Kinds of Soups, Fish, Oysters . . . with Lists of Articles in Season Suited to Go Together for Breakfasts, Dinners, and Suppers . . . and Much Useful and Valuable Information on All Subjects Whatever Connected with General Housewifery.* Philadelphia: T. B. Peterson, 1854.

———. *Seventy-Five Receipts for Pastry, Cakes, and Sweetmeats.* Boston: Munroe & Francis, 1828.

Levenstein, Harvey A. *Paradox of Plenty: A Social History of Eating in Modern America.* New York: Oxford University Press, 1993.

———. *Revolution at the Table: The Transformation of the American Diet.* New York: Oxford University Press, 1988.

Levine, Susan. "Study Finds Racial Divide in the District." *Washington Post,* November 6, 2007, B01.

Lévi-Strauss, Claude. *The Raw and the Cooked: Introduction to a Science of Mythology.* New York: Harper & Row, 1975.

Lincoln, Waldo. *American Cookery Books 1742–1860.* Worcester, MA: American Antiquarian Society, 1954.

Lindenfeld, Laura. "Women Who Eat Too Much: Femininity and Food in *Fried Green Tomatoes.*" In *From Betty Crocker to Feminist Food Studies: Critical Perspectives on Women and Food,* 221–45. Edited by Arlene Voski Avakian and Barbara Haber. Liverpool, England: Liverpool University Press, 2005.

Lindenmeyer, Antje. "'Lesbian Appetites': Food. Sexuality and Community in Feminist Autobiography." *Sexualities* 9, no. 4 (2006): 470–85.

Linzie, Anna. *The True Story of Alice B. Toklas: A Study of Three Autobiographies.* Iowa City: University of Iowa Press, 2006.

Loeb, Robert H., Jr. *Wolf in Chef's Clothing.* 4th ed. Chicago: Surrey Books, 2000 [1950].

Loftus, Brian. "Speaking Silence: The Strategies and Structures of Queer Autobiography." *College Literature* 24, no. 1 (February 1997): 28–44.

Long, Lucy M., ed. *Culinary Tourism.* Lexington: University Press of Kentucky, 2004.

Lorde, Audre. *Zami, a New Spelling of My Name.* Watertown, MA: Persephone Press, 1982.

Lubin, David. *Picturing a Nation: Art and Social Change in Nineteenth-Century America.* New Haven, CT: Yale University Press, 1994.

Lunt, Bob. *The Man Without a Mate Cookbook: The Successful Lifestyle Cookbook for the Unmarried Man.* Minneapolis: Garborg's Heart N Home, 1993.

"Lying Cheating Lasagna." Episode of *Cooking with Lesbians.* May 7, 2014. https://www.youtube.com/watch?v=gKnTK44FHm8.

Lynd, Robert Staughton. *Middletown in Transition: A Study in Cultural Conflicts.* New York: Harcourt, Brace and Company, 1937.

MacFadyen, Byron. "Breakfast Dishes Men Like." *Good Housekeeping* (February 1937): 82–3, 132.

———. "Dishes Fit for Gods—and Men!" *Good Housekeeping* (March 1933): 81, 112–14.

———. "Sweets to the Meat." *Good Housekeeping* (October 1935): 88–89, 112–13.

———. "When a Man Goes Culinary." *Good Housekeeping* (January 1930): 90–91, 104.

MacPherson, John. *The Mystery Chef's Own Cook Book*. Garden City, NY: Garden City Pub. Co., 1943.

Mac Sheridan, Carroll. *The Stag Cook Book: Written for Men by Men*. New York: George H. Doran Co., 1922.

Malcolm, Janet. "Gertrude Stein's War: The Years in Occupied France." *New Yorker* (June 2, 2003): 58–82.

Malone, Dorothy. *How Mama Could Cook!*. New York: A. A. Wyn Inc., 1946.

Manring, Maurice M. *Slave in a Box: The Strange Career of Aunt Jemima*. Richmond: University of Virginia Press, 1998.

Mario, Thomas. "Bachelor Dinners." *Playboy* (June 1956): 25.

———. "The Gourmet Gobbler." *Playboy* (November 1956): 178.

———. "The Holiday Dinner." *Playboy* (November 1956): 40.

———. "Playboy at the Salad Bowl." *Playboy* (July 1956): 32.

———. *Playboy's Gourmet*. HMH Publishing, 1971.

Markham, Gervase. *The English House-Wife*. London: Printed for H. Sawbridge, 1683.

The Marlboro Cook Like a Man Cookbook: The Last Male Art Form. Grill It. Smoke It. BBQ the Heck Out of It. Philip Morris USA, 2004.

Martin, Karin A. "Gender and Sexuality: Medical Opinion on Homosexuality, 1900–1950." *Gender and Society* 7, no. 2 (1993): 246–60.

Martinac, Paula. "Fast, Free Delivery." In *Through the Kitchen Window: Women Explore the Intimate Meanings of Food and Cooking*, 162–67. Edited by Arlene Voski Avakian. Boston: Beacon Press, 1997.

Matchar, Emily. *Homeward Bound: Why Women Are Embracing the New Domesticity*. New York: Simon and Schuster, 2013.

Matthews, Glenna. *Just a Housewife: The Rise and Fall of Domesticity in America, 1830–1963*. New York: Oxford University Press, 1987.

McFeely, Mary Drake. *Can She Bake a Cherry Pie? American Women and the Kitchen in the Twentieth Century*. Boston: University of Massachusetts Press, 2000.

McLaren, Margaret A. *Feminism, Foucault, and Embodied Subjectivity*. Albany: State University of New York Press, 2002.

McWilliams, James. *A Revolution in Eating: How the Quest for Food Shaped America*. New York: Columbia University Press, 2005.

McWilliams, Mark. *Food and the Novel in Nineteenth-Century America*. New York: Columbia University Press, 2012.

Mechling, Jay. *On My Honor: Boy Scouts and the Making of American Youth*. Chicago: University of Chicago Press, 2001.

Mencken, H.L. Review of Fannie Merritt Farmer's *The Boston Cooking-School Cookbook*. *American Mercury* 21, no. 4 (December 1930): 506–10.

Mennell, Stephen. *All Manners of Food: Eating and Taste in England and France from the Middle Ages to the Present*. Champaign: University of Illinois Press, 1996.

Miller, Warren H. *Camping Out*. New York: George H. Doran, 1918.

Mills, Marjorie. *Cooking on a Ration: Food Is Still Fun*. Boston: Houghton Mifflin Company, 1943.

Mintz, Sidney W. "Eating American." In *Food in the USA: A Reader*, 23–33. Edited by Carole Counihan. New York: Routledge, 2002.

———. *Sweetness and Power: The Place of Sugar in Modern History*. New York: Penguin Books, 1985.

Moore, Anne. "The Cook's Oracle: Cookbooks at the American Antiquarian Society." *Journal of Gastronomy* 5, no. 3 (Winter 1989–90): 19–31.

Morgan, Ffiona. *The Lesbian Erotic Cookbook: Cuisine Extraordinaire to Caress and Fondle the Palate*. Novato, CA: Daughters of the Moon, 1998.

Moyo, K. Kofi. *Real Men Cook: Rites, Rituals, and Recipes for Living*. New York: Fireside, 2005.

M'Quin, Abbé Ange Denis. *Tabella Cibaria, The Bill of Fare*. London: Sherwood, Neely, and Jones, 1820.

Murphy, Marguerite S. "'Familiar Strangers': The Household Words of Gertrude Stein's Tender Buttons." *Contemporary Literature* 32 (1991): 383–402.

Nemerov, Alexander. *The Body of Raphaelle Peale: Still Life and Selfhood, 1812–1824*. Berkeley and Los Angeles: University of California Press, 2001.

Neuhaus, Jessamyn. "Is Meatloaf for Men? Gender and Meatloaf Recipes, 1920–1960." In *Cooking Lessons: The Politics of Gender and Food*, 87–110. Edited by Sherrie A. Inness. Lanham, MD: Rowman and Littlefield, 2001.

———. *Manly Meals and Mom's Home Cooking: Cookbooks and Gender in Modern America*. Baltimore: Johns Hopkins University Press, 2003.

Newman, Toni. "Chef Chris Trapani, the First Transgender Chef to Appear on the Food Network, Discusses Love, Transitioning and Food." *Huffington Post*, September 9, 2014.

Noonan, Bode. *Red Beans and Rice: Recipes for Lesbian Health and Wisdom*. Trumansburg, NY: Crossing Press, 1986.

Nugent, Thomas. *The New Pocket Dictionary of the French and English Languages*. 12th ed. London: J. Mawman, 1808.

"Obesity in America: What's Driving the Epidemic?" *Harvard Health Publications*. *Harvard Men's Health Watch* (February 2012). http://www.health.harvard.edu/staying-healthy/obesity-in-america-whats-driving-the-epidemic.

O'Neill, Molly, ed. *American Food Writing: An Anthology with Classic Recipes*. New York: Library of America, 2007.

Opie, Frederick Douglass. *Hog and Hominy: Soul Food from Africa to America*. New York: Columbia University Press, 2010.

Osgerby, Bill. "A Pedigree of the Consuming Male: Masculinity, Consumption and the American 'Leisure Class.'" In *Masculinity and Men's Lifestyle Magazines*, 57–86. Edited by Bethan Benwell. Oxford: Blackwell Publishing, 2003.

———. *Playboys in Paradise: Masculinity, Youth and Leisure-Style in Modern America*. New York: Bloomsbury Academic, 2001.

Parasecoli, Fabio. "Feeding Hard Bodies: Food and Masculinities in Men's Fitness Magazines." *Food and Foodways* 13, no. 1 (2005): 135–58.

Park, Horace. *The Sportsman's Hand Book*. Cincinnati: Robert Clark & Co., 1886.

Parkhurst Ferguson, Priscilla. *Accounting for Taste: The Triumph of French Cuisine*. Chicago: University of Chicago Press, 2004.

Parloa, Maria. *Camp Cookery: How to Live in Camp*. Boston: Graves, Locke and Co., 1878.

———. *Miss Parloa's Kitchen Companion: A Guide for All Who Would Be Good Housekeepers*. Boston: Estes and Lauriat, 1887.

Peignot, G. "Of the Eatables and Wines." *American Quarterly Review* 2, no. 4 (December 1827): 426–27.

Peiss, Kathy. *Hope in a Jar: The Making of America's Beauty Culture,* Philadelphia: University of Pennsylvania Press, 2011.

Pemberton, Murdock. "If He Could Only Cook!" *Esquire* (April 1936): 54–55, 194–95.

Phillips, A. Lyman. *A Bachelor's Cupboard; Containing Crumbs Culled from the Cupboards of the Great Unwedded*. Boston: J. W. Luce & Company, 1906.

Pilcher, Jeffrey M. *Que Vivan los Tamales! Food and the Making of Mexican Identity*. Albuquerque: University of New Mexico Press, 1998.

Pitzulo, Carrie. *Bachelors and Bunnies: The Sexual Politics of Playboy*. Chicago: University of Chicago Press, 2011.

Playboy's Penthouse. TV series hosted by Hugh Hefner. Playboy Enterprises, 1959–60.

Plumley, Ladd. "Boys and Cookery." *American Cookery* (October 1917): 177–79.

Pohl, Frances. *Framing America: A Social History of American Art*. New York: Thames & Hudson, 2008.

Pollack, Stefanie. *The Cupcake Project: An Experimental Cupcake Blog*. cupcakeproject.com.

Pollock, Eleanor. "Men Are Dopes as Cooks." *Good Housekeeping* (February 1949): 32, 38, 118.

Prime-Stevenson, Edward. *The Intersexes: A History of Similisexualism as a Problem in Social Life*. 1908.

Probyn, Elspeth. *Carnal Appetites: FoodSexIdentities*. London: Routledge, 2000.

Quale, Eric. *Old Cook Books: An Illustrated History*. New York: E. P. Dutton, 1978.

Randolph, Mary. *The Virginia House-wife*. Columbia: University of South Carolina Press, 1984 [1824].

Ranhofer, Charles. *The Epicurean. A Complete Treatise of Analytical and Practical Studies on the Culinary Art, Including Table and Wine Service, How to Prepare and Cook Dishes . . . etc., and a Selection of Interesting Bills of Fare of Delmonico's from 1862 to 1894. Making a Franco-American Culinary Encyclopedia.* New York: C. Ranhofer, 1894.

Ray, Krishnendu. "Ethnic Succession and the New American Restaurant Cuisine." In *The Restaurants Book: Ethnographies of Where We Eat,* 97–114. Edited by David Beriss and David Sutton. Oxford: Berg, 2007.

———. "Exotic Restaurants and Expatriate Home Cooking: Indian Restaurants in Manhattan." In *The Globalization of Food,* 213–26. Edited by David Inglis and Debra Gimlin. Oxford: Berg, 2009.

———. "Nation and Cuisine: The Evidence from American Newspapers ca. 1830–2003." *Food & Foodways* 16, no. 4 (August 2008): 259–97.

Rayment, W. J. *The Real Man's Cookbook: How, When, What and Why to Cook.* Tucson, AZ: Hats Off Books, 2000.

Reade, Winwood. "Food in Central Africa." *Appletons' Journal: A Magazine of General Literature* (April 8, 1871): 412–13.

Rector, George. *Dine at Home with Rector: a Book on What Men Like, Why They Like It, and How to Cook It.* New York: E. P. Dutton & Co., 1937.

Ricci, David M. *Good Citizenship in America.* New York: Cambridge University Press, 2004.

Riesman, David. *The Lonely Crowd; a Study of the Changing American Character.* New Haven, CT: Yale University Press, 1950.

Roberts, Robert. *The House Servant's Directory, or a Monitor for Private Families: Comprising Hints on the Arrangement and Performance of Servants' Work.* New York: Charles S. Francis, 1827.

Rockler, Naomi R. "A Wall on the Lesbian Continuum: Polysemy and *Fried Green Tomatoes.*" *Women's Studies in Communication* 24, no. 1 (2001): 90–102.

Rodriguez, Jason. *Brew Science: Beer and Homebrewing Blog.* sciencebrewer.com.

Rombauer, Irma von Starkloff. *The Joy of Cooking.* St. Louis, MO: A. C. Clayton Co., 1931.

Roosevelt, Theodore. *American Big-Game Hunting.* New York: Forest and Stream Publishing Co., 1893.

———. *Hunting Trips of a Ranchman; Sketches of Sport on the Northern Cattle Plains.* New York and London: G. P. Putnam's Sons, 1885.

———. *The Rough Riders.* New York: C. Scribner's Sons, 1899.

———. "The Strenuous Life." In Theodore Roosevelt, *The Strenuous Life: Essays and Addresses,* 1–24. New York: The Century Co., 1900.

———. *The Wilderness Hunter.* New York: G. P. Putnam's Sons, 1909.

Root, Waverly, and Richard de Rochemont. *Eating in America.* New York: Ecco Press, 1981.

Rosario, Vernon. "Inversion's Histories / History's Inversions: Novelizing Fin-de-siècle Homosexuality." In *Science and Homosexualities,* 89–107. Edited by Vernon Rosario. New York: Routledge, 1997.

Rose, Kenneth. *Unspeakable Awfulness: America Through the Eyes of European Travelers, 1865–1900*. New York: Routledge, 2014.

Rothblum, Esther, and Sondra Solovay. *The Fat Studies Reader*. New York: New York University Press, 2009.

Rotskoff, Lori E. "Decorating the Dining Room: Still-Life Chromolithographs and Domestic Ideology in Nineteenth-Century America." *Journal of American Studies* 31, no. 1 (April 1997): 19–42.

Roulston, Marjorie Hillis. *Corned Beef and Caviar, for the Live-Aloner*. Indianapolis: The Bobbs-Merrill Company, 1937.

Rousseau, Signe. *Food and Social Media: You Are What You Tweet*. Lanham, MD: Rowman & Littlefield, 2012.

Salazar, Melissa L. "Public Schools, Private Foods: Mexicano Memories of Culture and Conflict in American School Cafeterias." *Food and Foodways* 15, no. 3–4 (2007): 153–81.

Sanderson, James M. *The Complete Cook*. Philadelphia: Lea and Blanchard, 1846.

Schisgal, Zachary. *A Man, A Can, A Tailgate Plan: 50 Easy Game-Time Recipes That Are Sure to Please*. Emmaus, PA: Rodale Books, 2006.

Schlesinger, Arthur M., Jr. "The Crisis of American Masculinity." *Esquire* (November 1958): 63–65. Reprinted in Arthur M. Schlesinger Jr., *The Politics of Hope and the Bitter Heritage: American Liberalism in the 1960s*, 292–303. Princeton, NJ: Princeton University Press, 2008.

Scholder, Amy, ed. *Cookin' with Honey: What Literary Lesbians Eat*. Ithaca, NY: Firebrand Books, 1996.

Schuman, Emily. *Cupcake and Cashmere*. cupcakesandcashmere.com.

Scobie, Stephen. "'I Is Another': Autobiography and the Appropriation of Voice." In *American Modernism Across the Arts*, 124–36. Edited by Jay Bochner and Justin D. Edwards. New York: Peter Lang, 1999.

Sedgwick, Eve Kosofsky. *Between Men: English Literature and Male Homosocial Desire*. New York: Columbia University Press, 1985.

Seldes, Gilbert. "Open Your Mouth and Shut Your Eyes." *North American Review* (April 1928): 428–34.

Shalhope, Robert E. "Republicanism and Early American Historiography." *William and Mary Quarterly* 29, no. 1 (1972): 334–56.

Shane, Ted. "Women Can't Cook." *Collier's* (March 18, 1939): 16, 73.

Shapiro, Laura. *Perfection Salad: Women and Cooking at the Turn of the Century*. New York: Farrar, Straus and Giroux, 1986.

———. *Something from the Oven: Reinventing Dinner in 1950s America*. New York: Viking, 2004.

Sherman, Sandra. *Invention of the Modern Cookbook*. Westport, CT: Greenwood Press, 2010.

Shortridge, Barbara G. "Ethnic Heritage Food." In *Culinary Tourism*, 268–96. Edited by Lucy M. Long. Lexington: University Press of Kentucky, 2004.

Siegel, Nancy. "Cooking Up American Politics." *Gastronomica* 8, no. 3 (Summer 2008): 53–61.

Silver, Charlotte. *Charlotte au Chocolat: Memories of a Restaurant Girlhood*. New York: Riverhead Books, 2012.

Simmons, Amelia. *American Cookery, or the Art of Dressing Viands, Fish, Poultry and Vegetables, and the Best Modes of Making Pastes, Puffs, Pies, Tarts, Puddings, Custards and Preserves, and all Kinds of Cakes, from the Imperial Plumb to Plain Cake. Adapted to This Country, and All Grades of Life.* Preface by Mary Tolford Wilson. 1st ed. facsimile: New York: Oxford University Press, 1958, reissued New York: Dover Publications, 1984 [Hartford: Hudson & Goodwin, 1796].

———. *American Cookery.* 2nd ed. facsimile: Preface by Karen Hess. Bedford, MA: Applewood Books, 1996 [Albany: George R. & George Webster, 1796].

Slotkin, Richard. *Gunfighter Nation: The Myth of the Frontier in Twentieth-Century America.* New York: Harper Perennial, 1993.

Smart-Grosvenor, Vertamae. *Vibration Cooking: Or, the Travel Notes of a Geechee Girl.* New York: Ballantine Books, 1986 [1970].

Smith, Andy. "In Praise of Maize: The Rise and Fall of Corny Poetry." In *Food in the Arts: Proceedings of the Oxford Symposium on Food and Cooking 1998.* Edited by Harlan Walker. Oxford: Oxford Symposium, 1999.

Sollors, Werner. *Beyond Ethnicity: Consent and Descent in American Culture.* Kindle ed. New York: Oxford University Press, 1986.

Sonneck, Oscar George Theodore. *Report on "The Star-Spangled Banner," "Hail Columbia," "America," and "Yankee Doodle."* Washington, DC: Government Printing Office, 1909. Reprint, New York: Dover Publications, 1972.

Soul Food. Directed by George Tillman. 20th Century Fox, 1997. DVD.

Squire, Marian. *The Stag at Ease: A Cookbook, Being the Culinary Preferences of a Number of Distinguished Male Citizens of the World.* Caldwell, ID: Caxton Printers, 1938.

Stavely, Keith, and Kathleen Fitzgerald. "This Beautiful Noble Eare: Corn." In *America's Founding Food: The Story of New England Cooking.* Edited by Keith Stavely and Kathleen Fitzgerald. Chapel Hill: University of North Carolina Press, 2004.

Steiman, Adina, and Paul Kita. *Guy Gourmet: Great Chefs' Best Meals for a Lean & Healthy Body.* Emmaus, PA: Rodale Books, 2013.

Stein, Gertrude. *The Autobiography of Alice B. Toklas.* London: John Lane, 1933.

———. *Everybody's Autobiography.* New York: Random House, 1937.

———. *Fernhurst, Q. E. D., and Other Early Writings.* New York: Liveright, 1971.

———. *Tender Buttons: Objects, Food, Rooms.* New York: C. Marie, 1914.

———. *Three Lives: Stories of the Good Anna, Melanctha, and the Gentle Lena.* New York: The Grafton Press, 1909.

Stein, Richard L. "Man's Place Is in the Kitchen." *Journal of Gastronomy* 65, no. 4 (1940): 245–47.

Stewart, Garrett. *Dear Reader: The Conscripted Audience in Nineteenth-Century British Fiction.* Baltimore: Johns Hopkins University Press, 1996.

"Still-Life: Raphaelle Peale, American, 1774–1825." National Gallery of Art website. http://www.nga.gov/feature/artnation/still_life/peale_4.shtm.

Stoddard, Charles Coleman. "When You Live in a Duffle-Bag: An Autumn Vacation in the Woods." *Popular Science Monthly* 95, no. 4 (October 1919): 87–89.

Storr, Annie V. F. "Raphaelle Peale's 'Strawberries, Nuts, &c': A Riddle of Enlightened Science." *Art Institute of Chicago Museum Studies* 21, no. 1 (1995): 24–34, 73–74.

Strasser, Susan. *Never Done: A History of American Housework.* New York: Pantheon, 1982.

Stratton, Barry. *The Hunter's Handbook Containing a Description of All Articles Required in Camp with Hints on Provisions and Stores and Receipts for Camp Cooking.* Boston: Lee and Shepard, 1885.

Strauss, David. *Setting the Table for Julia Child: Gourmet Dining in America, 1934–1961.* Baltimore: Johns Hopkins University Press, 2011.

"Swells Who Can Cook: Many Young Millionaires Are Expert Chefs." *Washington Post*, November 17, 1895, 20.

Swenson, Rebecca. "Domestic Divo? Televised Treatments of Masculinity, Femininity and Food." *Critical Studies in Media Communication* 26, no. 1 (2009): 36–53.

Telfer, Elizabeth. *Food for Thought: Philosophy and Food.* London: Routledge, 1996.

Theophano, Janet. *Eat My Words: Reading Women's Lives Through the Cookbooks They Wrote.* New York: Palgrave Macmillan, 2002.

Tipton, Edna Sibley. "When Men Entertain." *Better Homes and Gardens* (May 1931): 25, 116.

Todhunter, E. Neige. "Seven Centuries of Cookbooks." *Nutrition Today* 27, no. 1 (January–February 1992): 8–12.

Toklas, Alice B. *The Alice B. Toklas Cook Book.* New York: Harper, 1954.

———. *The Alice B. Toklas Cook Book.* Foreword by M. F. K. Fisher. New York: Harper & Row, 1984.

———. *What Is Remembered.* New York: Holt, Rinehart and Winston, 1963.

Tompkins, Kyla Wazana. *Racial Indigestion: Eating Bodies in the Nineteenth Century.* New York: New York University Press, 2012.

Tonkovich, Nicole. *Domesticity with a Difference: The Nonfiction of Catharine Beecher, Sarah J. Hale, Fanny Fern, and Margaret Fuller.* Jackson: University Press of Mississippi, 2010.

Tonsmeire, Michael. *The Mad Fermentationist: Beer, Bread, Cheese, Funk.* themadfermentationist.com.

Toombs, Alfred. "Man Over a Hot Stove." *Collier's* (August 27, 1949): 23–24, 43–44.

Trollope, Frances Milton. *Domestic Manners of the Americans.* New York: Penguin, 1997 [1832].

Truong, Monique. *The Book of Salt: A Novel.* Boston: Houghton Mifflin Harcourt, 2003.

"Tur-Bacon: Epic Thanksgiving." Episode of *Epic Meal Time.* November 23, 2010. https://www.youtube.com/watch?v=7Xc5wIpUenQ.

Twain, Mark. *The Adventures of Huckleberry Finn.* New York: Charles L. Webster and Co., 1885.

Veit, Helen Zoe. *Modern Food, Moral Food: Self-Control, Science, and the Rise of Modern Eating in the Early Twentieth Century.* Chapel Hill: University of North Carolina Press, 2013.

Verrill, A. Hyatt. *The Book of Camping.* New York: Alfred A. Knopf, 1917.

Vester, Katharina. "Queer Appetites, Butch Cooking: Recipes for Lesbian Subjectivities." In *Queers in American Popular Culture,* 11–21. Edited by Jim Elledge. Santa Barbara, CA: Praeger, 2010.

———. "Regime Change: Gender, Class, and the Invention of Dieting in Post-Bellum America." *Journal of Social History* 44, no. 1 (2010): 39–70.

———. "See Dad Cook! Fatherhood and Cooking Advice in the 21st Century." In *The Contested and the Poetic: Gender and the Body.* Edited by Amanda Stone. Witney, England: Interdisciplinary Press, 2014.

———. "Tender Mutton: Recipes, Sexual Identity and Spinster Resistance in Gertrude Stein." In *Another Language: Poetic Experiments in Britain and North America,* 289–300. Edited by Kornelia Freitag and Katharina Vester. Berlin: Lit Verlag, 2008.

Visser, Margaret. *Much Depends on Dinner.* New York: Grove Press, 1986.

Vrobel, Mike. "About." *Dad Cooks Dinner.* August 24, 2011. http://dadcooksdinner. com/mikevrobel/.

Walsh, Candace. *Licking the Spoon: A Memoir of Food, Family, and Identity.* Berkeley: Seal Press, 2012.

Warnes, Andrew. *Hunger Overcome? Food and Resistance in Twentieth-Century African American Literature.* Athens: University of Georgia Press, 2004.

Watson, Julia. "Unspeakable Differences: The Politics of Gender in Lesbian and Heterosexual Women's Autobiographies." In *De-Colonizing the Subject: The Politics of Gender in Women's Autobiography,* 139–68. Edited by Sidonie Smith and Julia Watson. Minneapolis: University of Minnesota Press, 1992.

Watts, Steven. *Mr. Playboy: Hugh Hefner and the American Dream.* Hoboken, NJ: Wiley, 2008.

Welch, Deshler. *The Bachelor and the Chafing Dish.* New York: F. T. Neely, 1896.

Welter, Barbara. "The Cult of True Womanhood: 1820–1860." *American Quarterly* 18, no. 2 (Summer 1966): 151–74.

"What's Cooking?" Cartoon. *Gourmet* (May 1942): 66.

Whyte, William Hollingsworth. *The Organization Man.* New York: Simon and Schuster, 1956.

Willan, Anne. *The Cookbook Library: Four Centuries of the Cooks, Writers, and Recipes That Made the Modern Cookbook.* Berkeley and Los Angeles: University of California Press, 2012.

Williams, Susan. *Savory Suppers and Fashionable Feasts: Dining in Victorian America.* Knoxville: University of Tennessee Press, 1996.

Williams-Forson, Psyche. *Building Houses Out of Chicken Legs: Black Women, Food and Power.* Chapel Hill: University of North Carolina Press, 2006.

Wilson, Mary Tolford. "The First American Cookbook." Preface to Amelia Simmons, *American Cookery.* 1st ed. facsimile: New York: Oxford University Press,

1958, reissued New York: Dover Publications, 1984 [Hartford: Hudson & Goodwin, 1796], vii–xxiv.

Wister, Owen. "The Evolution of the Cow-Puncher." *Harper's Magazine* 91 (September 1895): 602–17.

———. *Owen Wister's West: Selected Articles.* Albuquerque: University of New Mexico Press, 1987.

———. *The Virginian; a Horseman of the Plains.* New York: The Macmillan Company, 1902.

Witt, Doris. *Black Hunger: Soul Food and America.* Minneapolis: University of Minnesota Press, 2004.

———. "'My Kitchen Was the World': Vertamae Smart Grosvenor's Geechee Diaspora." In *Kitchen Culture in America: Popular Representations of Food, Gender, and Race,* 227–50. Edited by Sherrie A. Inness. Philadelphia: University of Pennsylvania Press, 2001.

Wolley, Hannah. *The Queen-Like Closet, or, Rich Cabinet: Stored with All Manner of Rare Receipts for Preserving, Candying & Cookery: Very Pleasant and Beneficial to All Ingenious Persons of the Female Sex.* London: Printed for R. Lowndes, 1670.

Wolverton, Terry. "Crumbs." In *Cookin' with Honey: What Literary Lesbians Eat,* 78–84. Edited by Amy Scholder. Ithaca, NY: Firebrand Books, 1996.

"The Word Feminism." *Two Lesbians Eating Out.* March 19, 2013. https://two lesbianseatingout.wordpress.com/2013/03/19/the-word-feminism/.

Yokota, Kariann Akemi. *Unbecoming British: How Revolutionary America Became a Postcolonial Nation.* Kindle ed. New York: Oxford University Press, 2011.

Young, Bob. *Jazz Cooks: Portraits and Recipes of the Greats.* New York: Stewart, Tabori & Chang, 1992.

Young, Hazel. *The Working Girl Must Eat.* Boston: Little, Brown and Company, 1938.

Young, Yolanda. "'Big is Beautiful': Not All Good News." *USA Today,* December 30, 2010, 11A.

Zafar, Rafia. "The Proof of the Pudding: Of Haggis, Hasty Pudding, and Transatlantic Influence." *Early American Literature* 31, no. 2 (1996): 133–49.

———. "The Signifying Dish: Autobiography and History in Two Black Women's Cookbooks." *Feminist Studies* 25, no. 11 (Summer 1999): 449–69.

INDEX